Gibril Fouad Haddad

SUNNA NOTES

Studies in Ḥadīth and Doctrine

Volume I: Ḥadīth History and Principles

with Musa Furber's Translation of

Ibn Ḥajar al-ʿAsqalānī's

NUKHBAT AL-FIKAR

SUNNA NOTES
Studies in Hadith and Doctrine
Volume I: Hadith History and Principles

Cover photo: Tomb of Imam Bukhari by Adeel Anwar
Reprint: Institute for Spiritual & Cultural Understanding, Fenton, MI (USA)
First edition: AQSA Publications, UK & WARDA Publications, Germany

Published in the US by Institute for Spiritual & Cultural Understanding
17195 Silver Parkway #401, Fenton, MI 48430 USA
Tel: (810) 593-1222
Email: info@sufilive.com
Web: http://www.sufilive.com
Purchase online at: http://www.isn1.net

ISBN: 978-1-938058-78-3

Cataloging-in-Publication Data

Haddad, Gibril Fouad, 1960-

Sunna Notes: Studies in Hadith and Doctrine. Volume I: Hadith History and Principles. With Ibn Hajar al-Asqalani's Nukhbat al-Fikar, translated by Musa Furber.
222 p. cm. Index.
1. Hadith -- History. 2. Hadith -- Interpretation. 3. Islam -- Doctrines. 4. Hadith -- Terminology. I. Author. II. Title.

To my beloved teacher
from a devoted son

مَنْ فَاتَهُ مِنْكَ وَصْلٌ حَظُّهُ النَّدَمُ   وَمَنْ تَكُنْ هَمَّهُ تَسْمُو بِهِ الْهِمَمُ

وَنَاظِمٌ فِي سِوَى مَعْنَاكَ حُقَّ لَهُ   يَقْتَصُّ فِي جَفْنِهِ بِالدَّمْعِ وَهُوَ دَمُ

CONTENTS

HADITH HISTORY AND PRINCIPLES

Abbreviations 8

Preface 9

Foreword to Volume One 11

The Story of Ḥadīth 15

Have You Ever Seen a *Faqīh*? 25

Superiority of *Fiqh* over Ḥadīth 36

Madhhāhib of the Imāms of Ḥadīth 48

Strictness and Laxity in Ḥadīth Criticism 53

Verifiable Transmission (*Isnād*) and the Sects 56

"Famous-Ḥadīth" and "Forgery" Compilations 63

The "Disclaimed" –*Munkar* – Ḥadīth 80

Use of Weak Ḥadīths in Islam 100

Weak Ḥadīths in *Ṣaḥīḥ al-Bukhārī*? 105

Lone-Narrator Reports 111

Ḥadīth Narration *ad Sensum vs. ad Litteram* 134

Ḥadīth Authentication by *Kashf* 141

Ibn Ḥajar al-ʿAsqalānī's *Nukhbat al-Fikar* 169

Index of Technical Terms in *Nukhbat al-Fikar* 193

Index of Qur'ānic Verses 195

Index of Narrations 197

Bibliography 205

ABBREVIATIONS

ʿAbd al-Razzāq = his *Muṣannaf*

Abū Dāwūd = his *Sunan*

Aḥmad = his *Musnad*

Al-Bazzār = his *Musnad*

Al-Bukhārī = his *Ṣaḥīḥ*

al-Dārimī = his *Musnad*, also known as the *Sunan*

Al-Ḥākim = his *Mustadrak ʿalā al-Ṣaḥīḥayn*

Al-Haythamī = his *Majmaʿ al-Zawāʾid*

Ibn Abī Shayba = his *Muṣannaf*

Ibn ʿAsākir = his *Tārīkh Dimashq*

Ibn Ḥibbān = his *Ṣaḥīḥ*

Ibn Mājah = his *Sunan*

Ibn Saʿd = his *Ṭabaqāt al-Kubrā*

Muslim = his *Ṣaḥīḥ*

Al-Nasāʾī = his minor *Sunan* known as *al-Mujtabā*

Al-Tirmidhī = his *Sunan*

الحمد لله رب العالمين والصلاة والسلام على سيد الاولين و الاخرين
و على آله وصحبه والتابعين لهم الى يوم الدين

Editor's Preface

Endless Praise belongs to Allah Almighty, our Generous Creator, the Munificient Lord of all Dominions. His blessings and His peace be upon the Best of His creation, our Master on the path towards His Divine Presence and well-accepted Intercessor on the Judgment Day – Sayyidinā Muḥammad – and upon his Family, Companions, and whoever follows in his noble footsteps until the Last Day.

Allah the All-Wise and Possessor of absolute Knowledge says in the Holy Qur'ān, {*Of knowledge it is only a little that is communicated to you, (O men!)*} (17:85) and {*We raise to degrees (of wisdom) whom We please: but over every possessor of knowledge is one who kows more.*} (12:76).

From the limitless Oceans of His Knowledge He sent His Revelation and His Wisdom through the most beloved one in His Divine Presence, to let mankind know the purpose of their existence and the ways to happiness and salvation. He says, {*It is He Who has sent amongst the unlettered an apostle from among themselves, to rehearse to them His Signs, to sanctify them, and to instruct them in Scripture and Wisdom,– although they had been, before, in manifest error*} (62:2). The Wisdom mentioned in these Holy Words of Revelation is, as the commentators say, the noble Sunna of Allah's Most Beloved Messenger – may Allah bless him eternally and grant him peace.

Which task could be deserving of higher reward than the sincere attempt to preserve and defend this dearest heritage of mankind against the onslaughts of all the protagonists and propagandists of the "second Jāhiliyya" we are without a doubt witnessing in our times, skillfully being sold to the bewildered public with a flood of well-funded advertising as the most develeoped, highest and best form of civilisation ever?

To rid Islam of this indispensable element, the Prophetic Sunna, would be shayṭān's superbest triumph; and he never tires of looking for new means and methods to undermine and destroy the Sunna – even in the guise of those who claim to purify and establish it "as it should be" according to their personal whims and mad ideas.

We thank Allah the Bountiful that he has granted us the priviledge to meet and know one of those rare people who devote their life to the search for, verification and preservation of the knowledge of the noble Sunna, treading the classical way through studies with authorised *Mashāyikh*, obtaining their precious *Ijāzas* and making this valuable knowledge available to those who are in dire need of ammunition against all the ruthless attackers on their faith.

We speak of Shaykh Gibril Fouad Haddad, who ever since we met him has never ceased to amaze us with his high energy, collecting and presenting priceless gems from the Knowledge Oceans of Allah's Beloved ﷺ. May Allah reward him and benefit the *Umma* with his efforts!

We feel pleased and honoured to support his work by publishing this collection of essays, which we intend to be only the first of a series of *SUNNA NOTES* by Shaykh Gibril.

And from Allah is all success!

Abd al-Hafidh Wentzel
Sāliḥīyya, Damascus,
Friday, 16 Muḥarram 1426

بسم الله الرحمن الرحيم

و به نستعين

الحمد لله والصلاة والسلام على سيّدنا رسول الله وآله وصحبه ومن والاه

Foreword
To Volume One

Glory and praise all belong to Allah Most High Who said, {*Whatsoever the Messenger gives you, take it, and whatsoever he forbids, abstain*} (59:7)! Blessings and peace on our liege-lord Muḥammad and upon his House and all his Companions, Leader of the first and the last, who said: "Allah brighten the face of His servant that hears my saying, records it, remembers it, and transmits it just as he heard it! It may be one will carry wisdom without understanding it; and it may be one will carry wisdom to one that understands it better than he."[1]

عَنْ أَنَسِ بْنِ مَالِكٍ رَضِيَ اللهُ عَنْهُ قَالَ: قَالَ رَسُولُ اللهِ صَلَّى اللهُ عَلَيْهِ وَآلِهِ وَصَحْبِهِ وَسَلَّمَ: نَضَّرَ اللهُ عَبْدًا سَمِعَ مَقَالَتِي فَوَعَاهَا ثُمَّ بَلَّغَهَا عَنِّي، فَرُبَّ حَامِلِ فِقْهٍ غَيْرِ فَقِيهٍ، وَرُبَّ حَامِلِ فِقْهٍ إِلَى مَنْ هُوَ أَفْقَهُ مِنْهُ. الحديث رواه الترمذي، وأبو داود، وابن ماجه، وهذا لفظه، وأحمد. وهو متواتر. وعند الترمذي عن عبد الله بن مسعود مرفوعاً: فَوَعَاهَا وَحَفِظَهَا وَبَلَّغَهَا. وفي مسند الشافعي: سَمِعَ مَقَالَتِي فَحَفِظَهَا وَوَعَاهَا، فَأَدَّاهَا كَمَا سَمِعَهَا.

[1] A mass-transmitted (*mutawātir*) ḥadīth beginning with the words *naḍḍara Allahu imri'an* (May Allah brighten the face = grant prosperity and felicity), narrated from nineteen Companions cf. al-Kattānī, *Naẓm al-Mutanāthir*. See note 47

It pleased our bountiful Creator to make knowledge of Ḥadīth and its ancillary sciences the exclusive characteristic of Muslim civilization. Alone among the nations that walked the face of the earth, this *Umma* received and kept this Divine trust together with the Last Testament – the Qur'ān – to pass it on to subsequent generations unchanged with an ever-refined array of disciplines for verification and authentication.

Among those disciplines, Ḥadīth methodology and criticism ensured that nothing alien crept into the pure Prophetic Sunna as conveyed by the upright (*'adl*) and precise (*ḍābiṭ*) transmitters known as the "trustworthy" (*thiqa*, pl. *thiqāt*) under the strict perusal of their peers and subsequent experts. When Ibn al-Mubārak was asked about the forged ḥadīths he replied, "The giant scholars (*al-jahābidha*) dispose of them!" Then he recited, {*Lo! We, even We, have revealed the Reminder, and lo! We verily are its Guardian*} (15:9).[2] Thus he reiterated in the pithiest way that the Prophetic Sunna and authentic Ḥadīth are part and parcel of the Final Revelation – which no Muslim denies! – and that the Lawgiver preserves His *Dhikr* through the surest human means imaginable.

To that end, the Friends of Allah Most High and caliphal inheritors of the Prophet ﷺ known as the *Ḥuffāẓ* spared no effort. Those were the Repellers of False Imputations to the Prophet, the Preservers, Custodians, Protectors, Caretakers, Trustees, and Storehouses of the Faith envied by the erudite Caliph Abū Ja'far al-Manṣūr who described them as "the stained-clothed, scaly-footed, long-haired rovers of faraway lands."[3] With their photographic memories, inkwells in hand, wearing out – like Dulaf ibn Jahdar – up to seventy book-satchels, obsessed with detail, these

[2] Narrated by al-Khaṭīb in *al-Kifāya* (p. 80=p. 37).

[3] Narrated by al-Sam'ānī in *Adab al-Imlā' wal-Istimlā'* (p. 19) and al-Suyūṭī, chapter on al-Manṣūr in his *Tārīkh al-Khulafā'* cf. Abū Ghudda, *Maṣnū'* (p. 187).

hawk-eyed jewellers tracked the Prophetic narrative and its reporters to the ends of the earth, oblivious of food and sleep, laughing at wealth and the world, selling the shirt on their back and eating grass if necessary as did Muḥammad ibn Ismāʿīl al-Bukhārī, losing their eyesight through candle-lit night work as happened to his tireless student Abū ʿĪsā al-Tirmidhī, laughing at wealth and the world, moving their libraries on camel-back through three continents like Abū Ṭāhir al-Silāfī, sifting the sound from the unsound, the fair from the weak, the Prophetic from the non-Prophetic, the broken-chained, and the fabricated ḥadīths, living only for the three words "*Qāla Rasūl Allah* ﷺ." May Allah be well-pleased with all of them!

The present work is a tribute to those prestigious Predecessors. It is intended as a presentation of their thought on some of the core issues and principles of the Sunna. The first article, "The Story of Ḥadīth," is a brief description of what we mean by that term and the genesis of its genres in response to a layperson's question. The next two articles address the epistemic relationship of learning, understanding, and practicing in the view of the early Ulema of Ḥadīth and *Fiqh*: "Have You Ever Seen a *Faqīh*?" and "The Superiority of *Fiqh* over Ḥadīth." The fourth article, "*Madhāhib* of the Imāms of Ḥadīth," summarizes what we know of the schools of Law the compilers of the *Musnad*, two *Ṣaḥīḥs*, and *Sunan* followed. The fifth article, "Strictness and Laxity in Ḥadīth Criticism," diagnoses the two extremes that distinguish the derogators and the unscrupulous from the careful ḥadīth critic. The sixth article, "*Isnād* and the Sects," takes a glimpse at the lose/lose scenario of ill-prepared tradition-minded Muslims facing Western-minded Muslims and their agendas.

The remaining articles bring the English-speaking reader the most thorough documentation to date on seven seldom-addressed topics in ḥadīth science:

"Famous-Ḥadīth and Forgery Compilations" is a brief descriptive history of these two genres. "The Disclaimed (*Munkar*) Ḥadīth" is a comprehensive study of a sub-category of the weak ḥadīth that is notoriously misunderstood. "Use of Weak Ḥadīths in Islam" puts to rest once and for all – *in shā' Allah!* – the programmed confusion between weak and forged. "Weak Ḥadīths in al-Bukhārī?" recapitulates the views of the Masters on the unparalleled integrity of the principal motherbook of Islam after the Holy Qur'ān. "Lone-Narrator Reports (*Āḥād*)" recapitulates their proofs on the probative parameters of non-mass-transmitted narrations between the two extremes of neo-Ẓāhirīs and neo-Mu'tazilīs. "Narration *ad Sensum vs. ad Litteram*" chronicles the two fashions of narrating that were equally accepted among the Predecessors: literally or to the general meaning. "Ḥadīth Authentication by *Kashf*" links the practice of the *Ṣaḥīḥ* and *Sunan* compilers and the proofs of spiritual disclosure (*kashf*) in the Qur'ān and Sunna – routinely misrepresented as the exclusive province of the Sufis – to the delicate issue of verification.

The book ends with its musk-seal, a full original translation of Ibn Ḥajar's complete primer on ḥadīth science, *Nukhbat al-Fikar*, by my esteemed colleague Shaykh Musa Furber. May Allah reward him, our tireless editor, Shaykh Abd al-Hafidh Wentzel, and all our blessed teachers. *Āmīn*.

May Allah bless this humble endeavor, redress its mistakes, and accept it among the ornaments in illustration of the Crown Jewel of His creation ﷺ and the good pleasure of His friends.

Gibril Fouad Haddad
Mount Qasyūn, Damascus
in the white nights of mid-Muḥarram 1426
corresponding to February 2005.

The Story of Ḥadīth

Someone asked, "Could you tell me where ḥadīths come from and how they were compiled?"

Ḥadīths come from the Bringer of the Qur'ān ﷺ and they were heard, learnt, practiced, narrated, preserved, and compiled according to his instructions and in obedience to Its commands.

When the best generation of humankind ever to walk the earth realized that the Lord of the Heaven was addressing them directly with His timeless Speech in the language which they had mastered better than any human nation ever mastered a language, they realized that not only had Allah Almighty deputized the worthiest of them as the carrier of the final Message to humanity, but He had also made belief in that most honorable, most distinguished, and most accomplished Messenger – our liege-lord Muḥammad ﷺ – an integral condition of belief in Allah Himself by saying repeatedly "Believe in Allah **and** the Messenger."

They also heard Allah again and again command them to "obey Allah **and** the Messenger." They also realized that Allah Almighty stressed to them that that Messenger was their paramount model of behavior and of belief in Allah and the Last Day. They also heard and understood it meant they had to follow him and love him before they could claim to follow and love Allah.

They further understood the required levels of following the Prophet ﷺ properly and truly on which one's actual belief in Allah Most High depended: {*But nay, by your Lord! they will not believe (in truth) until they make you judge of what is in dispute between them*}. (4:65) But to make the Prophet ﷺ judge is not enough, this must be done without any mental reservation toward the Prophet ﷺ and his decision: {*and find within themselves no dislike of that which you decide*} (*ibid.*).

Even this unalloyed acceptance of the Prophet's judgment is not enough, there must be full embrace of the heart, mind and soul for the Prophet ﷺ: {*and submit with full submission*} (*ibid.*)!

They also noticed that Allah had made such love and following of His Prophet ﷺ the easiest and most natural thing in the world for people of sound hearts, because that blessed man encompassed all the human qualities imaginable. So they understood it all the more when Allah Himself stressed that whatever magnificent human character there could exist, the Prophet possessed it, and more. Hence, by listening to the majestic Qur'ān and taking to heart its message, the Companions realized that its study and practice necessitated the absolute study, understanding, and imitation of the Prophet ﷺ himself. Allah Most High further reassured them that that same Prophet ﷺ did not speak out of whim. Accordingly those most pragmatic and wisest of people – whom Allah Himself chose as the friends and companions of His dearest Beloved – set to the task of obeying, following, imitating, and loving the Prophet Muḥammad ﷺ as no other leader and savior was ever faithfully obeyed, followed, imitated, and loved before. They became absorbed into his paradigm yet with their eyes wide open and in a systematic manner like the dedicated and uncompromising hunters of blessings that they were.

So they learned from the Prophet ﷺ and they worshipped with the Prophet ﷺ. They lived with the Prophet ﷺ and for the Prophet ﷺ. They moved with the Prophet ﷺ and they rested with the Prophet ﷺ. They sought to look through his eyes, hear with his hearing, fight when he fought, make peace when he made peace, taste what he tasted, love what he loved, and hate what he hated. They wished to think his thoughts. They longed to visit him again, gaze at him again, be addressed by him again. They found they could not exhaust nor begin to describe the endearment of his voice, his touch, his scent, his gaze, his gait, his energy, his repose, his bravery, his intelligence, his eloquence, his generosity, his gentleness, his humbleness, his majesty. His comfort and safety, or rather the comfort and safety of his very foot they would ransom with their lives and that of their own parents. They lived to act as his human shields from spears and arrows or spend the last of their honor in defense of the first of his. When he spoke they were attentive and when he was silent they observed him with baited breath. Their hearts kept custody over their senses in his presence so that they understood, they obeyed, they memorized, and they taught one another in turn with full discipline. They knew Allah had changed them forever at his hands, turning the humblest of them into a reformer for humanity!

The Prophet ﷺ encouraged them and said, "**Bright does Allah make the face of his servant that records and conveys what he hears from me**." And he said, "Narrate from me and let those that are present teach those that are absent." And he pointed to his noble mouth and said "Nothing but truth issues from this." And he formed them under his kind gaze, asking Allah Most High to give this one a flawless memory, that one an encyclopedic pen, the third one superlative understanding, the fourth one faith to lead all others, the fifth one the wisest judgment. His wife 'A'isha ؓ became in ten ineffable years the most knowledgeable woman of humankind.

Allah then turned them, at His Prophet's ﷺ hands, into the paragon teachers of the next layer and so forth: "From every succeeding generation its upright folk shall carry this knowledge in turn...." and "This knowledge is Religion, so watch from whom you take it...."

When He took back His Beloved ﷺ, Allah did not leave us but in the best hands!

> *"We are blessed, Muslim kind, for we enjoy*
> *of Divine support an indestructible Pillar!"*
> (al-Būṣīrī, *Burda*)

The Companions ؓ knew better than anyone he was a human being and they saw in the Prophet ﷺ, also better than anyone, a living Qur'ān brimming infinitely with all sorts of qualities that spelled perfection. Those sincere and pure Arab-tongued men and women vied in poetic expressions because prose was too poor to describe the rising sun of Hāshim that he was, the full moon in its beauty, goodness itself, and the nearest thing to eternal beauty they felt they could experience here and now: their forerunner to Paradise, the Mercy to the worlds! No wonder they recorded faithfully, in addition to his teaching of the Creator's Names and Attributes and the purpose of our creation, also: his Prophetic dispensation, "the Wisdom" which Allah mentions in so many verses and which refers to what we call the Sunna of the Prophet ﷺ. It includes not only the do's and don'ts of the Religion that elucidate and illustrate the Qur'ānic rulings but also his historical battles, treaties, polity, travels, marriages etc. which we call the *Sīra*; his states, character, moral and psychological traits, and physical features which form the genre we call the *Shamā'il*; and his exclusive special and specific characteristics which we call the *Khaṣā'iṣ*.

This Prophetic Wisdom of the Sunna comes to us, textwise, in the form of transmitted sayings which in Arabic are called *ḥadīth*, plural: *aḥādīth*. This is the "genesis of the ḥadīths" the question asked about.

Most importantly to us, this Sunna and its practicing servants among the Friends of Allah represent the Prophet ﷺ among us – a living body of Prophetic knowledge and practice of which this *Umma* shall never be bankrupt, without which there is no Qur'ān, and of which the Qur'ān is never divorced nor orphaned until they both return back to the Prophet ﷺ at his *Kawthar*-Pond in Paradise!

Our forefathers and mothers carried that huge responsibility and trust. They collectively and individually transmitted, as faithfully and to the nearest detail possible, the totality of the information Allah wanted the last, mercied community of mankind to receive and preserve about His final elect representative. They did so for the guidance and happiness of humanity here and hereafter just as they faithfully transmitted His Book. No one could have done their job better because it was Allah Himself Who chose them. He was and is well-pleased with them and they are well-pleased with Him, He loves them and they love Him; see for yourself what He says of {*The First and Foremost of the Muhājirūn and the Anṣār*}(9:100)!

Allah Most High also says: {*Muḥammad is the Messenger of Allah and those with him are hard against the disbelievers and merciful among themselves. You (O Muḥammad) see them bowing and falling prostrate (in worship), seeking bounty from Allah and (His) acceptance. The mark of them is on their foreheads from the traces of prostration. Such is their likeness in the Torah; and their likeness in the Gospel like as sown corn that sends forth its shoot and strengthens it and rises firm upon its stalk, delighting the sowers that He may enrage the disbelievers with (the sight of) them*} (48:29). Imām Mālik said: "Whoever harbors spite toward any of the Companions of the Prophet ﷺ, this verse has hit him!" May it never hit you, dear reader, nor me!

Allah Most High chose them and they are all upright. He made them the keenest of people in memory, the most precise in language, the most familiar with the Prophet's ﷺ gracious person, and the most masterful of the Revelation he had brought, both its recited aspect (the Qur'ān) and its non-recited aspect (the Sunna) in its language, meanings, and subtle explanations and applications.

Their successors faithfully followed in their steps and so did the latter's successors. Then came the age of compilation and the magnificient manuals they named with various names according to their arrangement such as:

- The *Jāmi*ʿ-type compilations, *i.e.* encyclopedias arranged by topical sub-divisions. *E.g.* by Maʿmar ibn Rāshid, Sufyān al-Thawrī, al-Bukhārī, Muslim, al-Tirmidhī....
- The *Muwaṭṭa'*, *Muṣannaf*, and *Āthār*-type topical compilations that focus on legal rulings and include non-Prophetic *fatwās*, *e.g.* by Mālik, ʿAbd al-Razzāq, and Abū Ḥanīfa.
- The *Sunan*-type topical compilations: like the previous type but consisting only of Prophetic reports *e.g.* the *Sunan* of Abū Dāwūd, al-Nasā'ī, al-Tirmidhī, Ibn Mājah, al-Dārimī.
- The *Musnad*-type compilations arranged by Companion-narrators *e.g.* by the heroic Imām Aḥmad and Isḥāq ibn Rāhūyah.
- The countless *Juz'*-type compilations *i.e.* "Monographs" on a single topic or from a single narrator and so forth.
- The *Muʿjam*-type compilations *i.e.* alphabetical *Musnads* of Companions or other authorities narrating back to the latter *e.g.* the works of al-Ṭabarānī.

Among the extant manuscripts of the numerous ḥadīth collections compiled in the first Hijrī century are

- 'Abd Allah ibn 'Amr ibn al-'Āṣ' (d. 63) *al-Ṣaḥifāt al-Ṣādiqa*, originally containing about 1,000 ḥadīths of which 500 reached us, copied down by 'Abd Allah directly from the Prophet ﷺ and transmittedby to us his great-grandson 'Amr ibn Shu'ayb (d. 118);
- Hammām ibn Munabbih's (d. 101 or 131) *al-Ṣaḥifa al-Ṣaḥīḥa* which has reached us complete in two manuscripts containing 138 ḥadīths narrated by Hammām from Abū Hurayra (d. 60) from the Prophet ﷺ;
- and, from the second Hijri century, the massive, partly-recovered *Muṣannaf* of the Yemenite ḥadīth Master 'Abd al-Razzāq ibn Hammām ibn Nāfi' al-Ṣan'ānī (d. 211), which includes the compendium of his teacher Ma'mar ibn Rāshid al-Azdī (d. 151 or 154) – both principal sources of the Two Arch-Imāms al-Bukhārī and Muslim in their *Ṣaḥīḥs* – and is, with its over 21,000 narrations, the largest authentic early source of ḥadīth extant.

The earliest *Sīras* or Prophetic biographies are

- the lost folios of Abān (d. 105), the son of 'Uthmān ibn 'Affān (d. 35), from whom Muḥammad ibn Isḥāq ibn Yasār al-Muṭṭalibī (80-150/152) narrated;
- the accomplished works of 'Urwa (d. c.92-95) – the son of al-Zubayr ibn al-'Awwām and Asmā' and nephew of 'Ā'isha the learned daughters of Abū Bakr the Truthful – which 'Urwa ordered burnt, after a lifetime of teaching from them, during the sack of Madina by the armies of Syro-Palestine under Yazīd ibn Mu'āwiya in 63;

- the most reliable Muḥammad ibn Shihāb al-Zuhrī's (d. 120) *Sīra*, from which Ibn Isḥāq borrowed much;
- ʿĀṣim ibn ʿUmar ibn Qatāda ibn al-Nuʿmān al-Anṣārī's (d. 120 or 129) *Maghāzī* and *Manāqib al-Ṣaḥāba*, another principal *thiqa* source for Ibn Isḥāq and al-Wāqidī;
- ʿAbd Allah ibn Abī Bakr ibn Muḥammad ibn ʿAmr ibn Ḥazm al-Anṣārī's (d. 135) tome, another main source for Ibn Isḥāq, al-Wāqidī, Ibn Saʿd, and al-Ṭabarī;
- the most reliable, partly preserved *Sīra* of the Madinan Mūsa ibn ʿUqba al-Asadī (d. 141), praised by Imām Mālik and used by Ibn Saʿd and al-Ṭabarī;
- Muḥammad ibn Isḥāq's *Sīra*, praised by Imām al-Shāfiʿī, the oldest extant;
- Ibn ʿĀ'idh al-Azdī's (d. 191) *Maghāzī*; and Sayf ibn ʿUmar al-Tamīmī's (d. 200) *al-Ridda wal-Futūḥ* and *al-Jamāl* as per Ibn Ḥajar in *Tahdhīb al-Tahdhīb*.
- A junior contemporary of Ibn Isḥāq, the erudite Muḥammad ibn ʿUmar ibn Wāqid al-Aslamī al-Wāqidī (d. 207) compiled the *Maghāzī* and *Futuḥ al-Shām* among others. He is the principal source of Imām al-Ṭabarī (d. 310) in the latter's *Tārīkh* and his student and scribe Muḥammad ibn Saʿd (d. 230) relied heavily on him in his *Ṭabaqāt*.

The early and late masters devised finely-tuned scientific gauntlets for the verification of ḥadīth authenticity. The ḥadīths of the Two *Ṣaḥīḥs* – by the Arch-Masters al-Bukhārī (194-256) and Muslim (204-261) – and the *Muwaṭṭa'* of Imām Mālik (93-179) are rigorously sound and need no further authentication.

Next in reliability come the *Sunan* of the major Masters al-Tirmidhī (c.210-279), Abū Dāwūd (202-275), al-Nasā'ī (215-303), al-Dārimī (181-250), and Ibn Mājah (209-273) as well as the *Musnad* of Imām Aḥmad ibn Ḥanbal (164-241).

Next come the lesser collections of *ṣaḥīḥ* narrations such as – in descending order of strength – the *Ṣaḥīḥ* of Ibn Khuzayma (223-311), three quarters of which are lost; that of his student Ibn Ḥibbān (d. 354); al-Ḍiyā' al-Maqdisī's (567-643) *al-Aḥādīth al-Jyād al-Mukhtāra*; Ibn al-Sakan's (294-353) *al-Sunan al-Ṣiḥāḥ*; Ibn al-Jārūd's (d. 307) *al-Muntaqā min al-Sunan al-Musnada*; Abū ʿAwāna's (d. 316) *Musnad*; al-Ḥākim's (321-405) *Mustadrak*.

Next come – in chronological order – the compilations of Abū Dāwūd al-Ṭayālisī (d. 204), Ibn Abī Shayba (d. 235), Ibn Abī ʿĀsim (d. 287), al-Ḥārith ibn Abī Usāma (d. 282), al-Bazzār (215-292), Abū Yaʿlā (210-307), al-Ṭaḥāwī (229-321), the Narrator of the World al-Ṭabarānī (260-360), al-Dāraquṭnī (306-385), Abū Nuʿaym (336-430), al-Bayhaqī (384-458), al-Khaṭīb al-Baghdādī (392-463), al-Baghawī (d. 516), Ibn ʿAsākir (499-571), and others including the *Sīra* sources already mentioned.

Forgeries were identified and tagged in the two or three dozen compilations in the sub-genre devoted to their diagnosis. It is impermissible to use or narrate them as Prophetic reports. Preventive knowledge of the forgeries is an indispensable part of ḥadīth science. The guideline in this is the verdict of the authorities.

The Prophet ﷺ said time and again: "**Avoid relating my words except what you know for sure. Whoever lies about me willfully, let him take from now his seat in the Fire!**"

This terrible threat addresses not only willful liars but also those well-intentioned Muslims who, in the course of *da'wa* or otherwise, are habitually lax in attributing to the Prophet ﷺ untraceable or unverified matters. Let not their good intentions become their own specious law over and above the emphatic command of the Lawgiver! We belong to Allah and to Him do we return.

This is in short the story of the Prophetic Ḥadīth, its origins and why and how it was compiled. Allah revive our hearts for its sake with His ancient blessing, as He blessed those who preserved it and kept it alive for us.

Allah bless our Prophet and his Family and Companions, and may Allah be well-pleased with all of the sincere scholars and students of Ḥadīth to the Day of Judgment!

Have you ever seen a *Faqīh*? Reason and Knowledge in Islam

1. Reason

Allah Most High praised reason in many verses of His Book:

{*He gives wisdom unto whom He will, and he unto whom wisdom is given, he truly has received abundant good. But none remember except people of understanding*} (2:269)

{*Those who are of sound instruction say: We believe therein; the whole is from our Lord; but only people of understanding really heed*} (3:7)

{*Those are signs for people who have sense*} (2:164, 3:190, 13:4, 30:24, 45:5)

{*Have you then no sense?*} (2:44, 6:32, 37:138)

{*Lo! herein indeed are portents for people who have sense*} (16:12)

{*And verily of that We have left a clear sign for people who have sense*} (29:35)

{*These similitudes We coin for Man but none grasps their meaning save the wise*} (29:43)

{*Thus We display the revelations for people who have sense*} (30:28)

{*And verily We gave Luqmān wisdom*} (31:12)

{*That people of understanding may reflect*} (38:29)

{*Lo! herein verily is a reminder for people of understanding*} (39:21, 40:54)

{*Perhaps you may understand*} (40:67)

{*Lo! therein verily is a reminder for him who has a heart, or gives ear with full intelligence*} (50:37)

{*We have made clear Our revelations for you that perhaps you may understand*} (57:17)

{*Deaf, dumb, blind, therefore they [the disbelievers] have no sense*} (2:171)

{*Among them some look at you. But can you guide the blind even if they see not?*} (10:43)
{*Is he who knows that what is revealed unto you from your Lord is the truth like him who is blind? But only people of understanding heed*} (13:19)
{*The blind man is not equal with the seer; Nor is darkness equal with light; Nor is the shadow equal with the sun's full heat; Nor are the living equal with the dead. Lo! Allah makes whom He will to hear. You cannot reach those who are in the graves*} (35:19-22)
{*Are those who know equal with those who know not? But only people of understanding will pay heed*} (39:9)
{*Deem you most of them hear or understand? They are as cattle or farther astray*} (25:44)
{*But most of them have no sense*} (5:103, 29:63)
{*But most of them know not*} (6:37, 31:25).

It is related that the Prophet ﷺ asked about a man who was being eulogized by the Companions for his great piety and religion: "How intelligent is he?" (*kayfa ʿaqluhu?*) They replied: "Not much, Messenger of Allāh" (*Laysa bi shay'*). The Prophet ﷺ said: "Your friend does not reach the level that you think." Another narration states that the Prophet ﷺ said: "Do not hasten to commend him" (*arjūh*).[4]

The Prophet ﷺ also said: "Lo! Verily, there is in the body a small piece of flesh; if it is good the whole body is good and if it is corrupted the whole body is corrupted; lo! it is the heart."[5]

[4] Narrated from Abū al-Dardā' by al-Ṭabarānī, *Musnad al-Shāmiyyīn* (2:87), al-Bayhaqī, *Shuʿab al-Īmān* (3-4:157), al-Ḥakīm al-Tirmidhī, *Nawādir al-Uṣūl* (p. 405-406), Ibn ʿAdī, *al-Kāmil fil-Ḍuʿafā'* (6:384). Ibn Ḥajar and others said that the Prophetic narrations on the merit of reason are all weak. However, there are numerous narrations to that effect from the Companions and *Salaf. E.g.* al-Muḥāsibī's *Māhiyyat al-ʿAql wa-Faḍluh*, Ibn Abī al-Dunyā's *Kitāb al-ʿAql wa-Faḍlih*, al-Ḥakīm al-Tirmidhī's chapter on the merit of the mind in *Nawādir al-Uṣūl* (p. 405-406), and the similar chapter at the beginning of *Iḥyā ʿUlum al-Dīn*.

Al-Nawawī said: "This ḥadīth was used as proof that the seat of the intellect is the heart (*al-ʿaql fīl-qalb*) and not the head. There is a well-known difference of opinion concerning this. The position of our [*Shāfiʿī*] scholars and the overwhelming majority of the scholars of *kalām* is that it is the heart, while Abū Ḥanīfa said it is the brain, and it might also be said to be the head. The philosophers are said to hold the first position, the physicians the second. Al-Māzarī said: "Those who hold that it is in the heart adduced as proof the saying of Allah {*Have they not travelled in the land, and have they hearts wherewith to feel and ears wherewith to hear? For indeed it is not the eyes that grow blind, but it is the hearts, which are within the bosoms, that grow blind*} (22:46) and {*Lo! therein verily is a reminder for him who has a heart, or gives ear with full intelligence*} (50:37)."[6]

The Prophet ﷺ said, pointing to the heart: "Fear of Allah is right here" (*al-taqwā hāhunā*).[7]

Another narration states: "Verily, Allah looks not at your bodies nor at your faces but He looks at your hearts."[8]

[5] Narrated from al-Nuʿmān ibn Bashir in the Six Books. It is ḥadīth 6 of Imām al-Nawawī's "*Forty*": "Verily, the lawful is manifest and the forbidden is manifest, but between them there are dubious matters which many people do not know. Therefore, whoever bewares of dubious matters has made himself exempt [of guilt] for the sake of his religion and his honor, and whoever falls into dubious matters, falls into the forbidden. It is as with the shepherd that grazes his herd around guarded grounds: he greatly risks grazing it inside it. Lo! Every king possesses guarded grounds. Lo! Verily, Allah's guarded grounds are His prohibitions. Lo! Verily, there is in the body a small piece of flesh; if it is good the whole body is good and if it is corrupted the whole body is corrupted; lo! It is the heart."

[6] Al-Nawawī, *Sharḥ Ṣaḥīḥ Muslim* (1972 ed. 11:29).

[7] Narrated from Abū Hurayra by Muslim, and in various wordings from Abū Hurayra, Anas, and others by al-Tirmidhī (*ḥasan gharīb*), Aḥmad, al-Ṭabarānī, Abū Yaʿlā, and Abū Nuʿaym. Also narrated from Wābiṣa ibn Maʿbad al-Asadī by Aḥmad with the wording: "Righteousness (*al-birr*) is whatever your chest becomes dilated in doing, while iniquity (*al-ithm*) is whatever your chest becomes constricted in doing, regardless of what people recommend."

Imām al-Nawawī stated that these two narrations were also used as proof that the seat of the intellect is the heart and Ibn Ḥajar similarly adduced all the above texts as evidence of the same.[9]

ʿAlī ibn Abī Ṭālib ﷺ said at the battle of Ṣiffīn: "The seat of the intellect is the heart (*al-ʿaqlu fil-qalb*), that of mercy is the liver, that of sympathy is the spleen, and that of breath is the lung."[10]

Imām al-Shāfiʿī defined the intellect as experience (*al-ʿaql al-tajriba*)[11] while Imām Aḥmad defined it as "One of the necessary types of knowledge that characterize animate beings endowed with speech. Its seat is the heart."[12]

Al-Ḥārith al-Muḥāsibī said: "Intellect is the light of instinct together with trials, and it increases and becomes stronger through knowledge and good character."[13]

Another authoritative definition was given by Shaykh al-Islām Zakariyyā al-Anṣārī: "Lexically it means 'prevention' (*al-manʿ*), as it prevents its possessor from straying from the correct path. By convention it denotes instinct (*gharīza*) through which one is prepared to comprehend the theoretical sciences. It is also said to be a light cast into the heart."[14]

Shaykh Tāj al-Dīn ibn ʿAṭā' Allah al-Sakandarī related in *Laṭā'if al-Minan* from Shaykh Abū al-ʿAbbās al-Mursī that the latter said: "One time I recited {*By the fig and the olive*} (95:1) until I arrived at His saying {*Surely We created man of the best stature Then We*

[8] Narrated from Abū Hurayra by Muslim and Ibn Mājah.

[9] Respectively in *Sharḥ Ṣaḥīḥ Muslim* (16:122) and *Fatḥ al-Bārī* (1959 ed. 1:129).

[10] Narrated from ʿIyāḍ ibn Khalifa by al-Bukhārī in *al-Adab al-Mufrad* (p. 192) with a fair chain because of Muḥammad ibn Muslim al-Ṭā'ifī, and al-Bayhaqī in *Shuʿab al-Īmān* (3-4:161).

[11] Narrated by Ibn ʿAbd al-Barr in *al-Intiqā'* (p. 138).

[12] Aḥmad ibn Ḥanbal in Ibn Abī Yaʿlā's *Ṭabaqāt al-Ḥanābila* (2:281).

[13] Narrated by al-Mālīnī in *al-Arbaʿīn* (p. 146) and Ibn al-Subkī in *Ṭabaqāt al-Shāfiʿiyya al-Kubrā* (2:281). See also al-Muḥāsibī's *Māhiyyat al- ʿAql*, in print.

[14] Zakariyyā al-Anṣārī, *al-Ḥudūd al-Anīqa* (p. 67).

reduced him to the lowest of the low} (95:4-5). I reflected upon the meaning of these verses, and Allah inspired to me that their meaning is *{Surely We created man of the best stature}* in soul and intellect (*rūḥan wa-ʿaqlan*), *{Then We reduced him to the lowest of the low}* in ego and lust (*nafsan wa-hawā*)."[15] Ibn al-Jawzī said: "If you see one lacking in his reason at the onset of the matter then do not hope for any good for him. However, if he is reasonable enough – although his lusts may overcome him – then keep hope."[16]

2. Knowledge and the Knowledgeable

Among the sayings of ʿAlī ibn Abī Ṭālib ؓ on this topic, narrated by Abū Nuʿaym with his chains:

– From Abū Araka: "I have seen a remnant of the Companions of the Messenger of Allah ﷺ. I see no one that resembles them. By Allah! They used to rise in the morning disheveled, dust-covered, pale, with something between their eyes like a goat's knee, having spent the night chanting the Book of Allah, turning and returning from their feet to their foreheads. When Allah was mentioned they swayed the way trees sway on a windy day, then their eyes poured out tears until – by Allah! – they soaked their clothes. By Allah! Folks today are asleep and heedless."[17]

– From al-Ḥasan ibn ʿAlī: "Blessed is the servant that cries constantly to Allah, who has known people [for what they are] while they have not known him, and Allah has marked him with His contentment. These are the true beacons of guidance. Allah repels from them every dissension and He shall enter them into His own mercy. They are not the wasteful talebearers[18] nor the ill-mannered self-displayers."[19]

---

[15] In al-Suyūṭī, *Asrār Tartīb al-Qurʾān* (p. 153).
[16] In *Ṣayd al-Khāṭir* (p. 324).
[17] Abū Nuʿaym, *Ḥilya* (1985 ed. 1:76, 10:388).

- From ʿĀṣim ibn Ḍamura:"The true, the real *faqīh* is he who does not push people to despair from the mercy of Allah, nor lulls them into a false sense of safety from His Punishment, nor gives them licenses to disobey Allah, nor leaves the Qur'ān for something else. There is no good in worship devoid of knowledge, nor in knowledge devoid of understanding, nor in inattentive recitation."
- From ʿAmr ibn Murra: "Be wellsprings of the Science and beacons in the night, wearing old clothes but possessing new hearts for which you shall be known in the heaven and remembered on the earth."
- "Thus does Knowledge die: when those who possess it die. By Allah, I do swear it! The earth will never be empty of those who establish the proofs of Allah so that His proofs and signs never cease. They are the fewest in number, but the greatest in rank before Allah. Through them Allah preserves His proofs until they bequeath it to those like them (before passing on) and plant it firmly in their hearts. By them knowledge has taken by assault the reality of things, so that they found easy what those given to comfort found hard, and found intimacy in what the ignorant found desolate. They accompanied the world with bodies whose spirits were attached to the highest regard. Ah, ah! How one yearns to see them!"[20]

Al-Ḥasan al-Baṣrī said:

"**Have you ever seen a *faqīh*?** The *faqīh* is he who has renounced the world, longs for the hereafter, possesses insight in his Religion, and worships his Lord without cease."[21]

[18] Those who fanned dissension between ʿAlī and the other Companions.
[19] The *Khawārij.*
[20] Ibn al-Jawzī, *Ṣifat al-Ṣafwa* 2(4):10 (§570) and 1(2):203 (§254); Abū Nuʿaym, *Ḥilyat al-Awliyā'* (6:155).

Ibn Mufliḥ al-Ḥanbalī mentions that al-Ḥasan al-Baṣrī categorized the act of "kissing the hand of the *'Ālim*" as "obedience to Allah".[22]

Sahl ibn ʿAbd Allah al-Tustarī:

Al-Barbahārī said he heard Sahl say: "Allah ﷻ created the world and placed in it those who are ignorant and those who have knowledge. The best knowledge is that which one acts upon. For knowledge is all a proof [against oneself] except what is put into practice. But what is put into practice is all wind except what is sound and correct! As for what is sound and correct: I do not declare with certainty any act to be so, except what Allah wills."[23]

Imām al-Awzāʿī:

Baqiyya ibn al-Walīd said that al-Awzāʿī said: "Baqiyya! Do not mention any of your Prophet's ﷺ Companions except kindly. Baqiyya! Knowledge (*al-ʿilm*) is whatever came to us from the Companions of Muḥammad ﷺ. Whatever did not come to us from them, is not knowledge."[24]

Imām Mālik:

From Ibn al-Qāsim: "I heard Zayd ibn Aslam say: {*And unto each of them We gave judgment* (*ḥukm*) *and knowledge*} (21:79) that wisdom (*al-ḥikma*) is intellect (*al-ʿaql*). What comes to my heart is that wisdom is superlative understanding (*al-fiqh*) in the Religion of Allah. What clearly shows this is that you may see someone quite reasonable and clear-sighted in worldly matters, and

[21] As cited by al-ʿAynī in *'Umdat al-Qārī*, Book of *'Ilm*, in his commentary on the ḥadīth: "He for whom Allah desires immense good, He grants him understanding in the Religion" cf. Ibn al-Jawzī, *Manāqib al-Ḥasan al-Baṣrī.*

[22] Ibn Mufliḥ, *al-Ādāb al-Sharʿiyya* (2:271).

[23] In Ibn Abī Yaʿlā, *Ṭabaqāt al-Ḥanābila* (2:18).

[24] In al-Dhahabī, *Siyar* (1997 ed. 7:95), Ibn Ḥajar, *Fatḥ al-Bārī* (1959 ed. 13:291).

someone else weak in worldly matters but knowledgeable and judicious in the matter of his Religion. Allah gave him this but deprived the former of it. This wisdom, therefore, is superlative understanding in the Religion of Allah (*al-fiqhu fī dīnillāh*)."[25]

Related to Mālik's words are the Prophet's ﷺ ḥadīths:

"O Allah! Do not make any loss of ours be in our Religion, nor make the world our greatest concern, nor make it the sum total of our knowledge!"[26]

"Most of the people of Paradise are the naïve (*al-bulh*)."[27]

"Forbidden to the Fire is every gentle, lenient, easy-going one who is near to the people."[28]

"Paradise says: None enters me except the weak and wretched among the people and their simple-minded (*ghirratuhum*)."[29]

[25] Cf. al-Ṭabarī, *Tafsīr* (verse 21:79) and al-Mahdawī, *Taḥṣīl* cf. Ḥamīd Laḥmar in *al-Imām Mālik Mufassiran* (p. 279).

[26] Narrated from Ibn ʿUmar by al-Tirmidhī (*ḥasan gharīb*) and al-Ḥākim(1:528 *ṣaḥīḥ*, al-Dhahabī concurring).

[27] Narrated from Anas by al-Bazzār (§1983) who graded it weak and al-Quḍāʿī in *Musnad al-Shihāb* (2:110 §989-990) while al-Qurṭubī declared it *ṣaḥīḥ* in his *Tafsīr* (verses 26:83-89) and *Tadhkira* (2:228); this was questioned by al-ʿIrāqī in *al-Mughnī 'an Ḥaml al-Asfār*, who quoted Ibn ʿAdī's rejection of the ḥadīth in *al-Kāmil* (3:313 §773): "disclaimed as narrated through this chain" (*hādha al-ḥadīth bi-hādha al-isnād munkarun*). The best grading for the chain of Anas' narration is that of "soft" (*layyin*) in al-Fattanī's *Tadhkirat al-Mawḍūʿāt* (p. 29) and al-ʿAjlūnī, *Kashf al-Khafā'* (1:164, 1:286) because of Salama ibn Rawḥ. See also al-Mizzī, *Tahdhīb* (26:113 §5465), al-Suyūṭī, *al-Durar al-Muntathira* (p. 93 §68), al-Sakhāwī, *al-Maqāṣid al-Ḥasana* (p. 74), al-Zarkashī, *al-Tadhkira* (p. 170). Also with a weak chain from Jābir by Ibn ʿAdī (1:191 §31), Ibn al-Jawzī, *al- 'Ilal al-Mutanāhiya* (2:934-935 §1558-1559), and Ibn Ḥajar, *Lisān al-Mīzān* (1:240 §755).

[28] Narrated from [1] Ibn Masʿūd by Aḥmad, Ibn Ḥibbān(2:215-216), al-Ṭabarānī in *al-Kabīr* (10:231 §10562), and al-Bayhaqī, *Shuʿab* (7:535 §11251); [2] Jābir by Abū Yaʿlā (3:379 §1853), al-Ṭabarānī, *al-Awsaṭ* (1:256 §837) and *al-Ṣaghīr* (1:72 §89), al-Bayhaqī, *Shuʿab* (6:272 §8126); [3] Abū Hurayra by al-Ṭabarānī, *al-Awsaṭ* (6:38 §5725), Abū Nuʿaym, *Ḥilya* (2:356), al-Bayhaqī, *Shuʿab* (6:271 §8124).

"The believer is guileless and noble (*al-mu'minu ghirrun karīm*) while the wicked man is perfidious and miserly (*wal-fājiru khib-bun la'īm*)."[30]

"The believer is easy and lenient (*hayyinun layyinun*) to the point you will think him a fool (*aḥmaq*) in his leniency."[31]

The *ghirr* and *bulh* are those who were ignorant of evil ways in the world but knowledgeable in their Religion,[32] or those whose hearts were guileless towards people,[33] or those who lacked skill in worldly ways,[34] or those like old women, Bedouins, and their like, who remained staunch in their Religion.[35] Ibn al-Athīr cites some of these narrations under the entries *b-l-h* and *gh-r-r* in *al-Nihāya* as well as Muḥammad ibn Abī Bakr al-Rāzī in *Mukhtār al-Siḥāḥ*.

From Ibn Wahb: "In the verse {*and he shall instruct them in the Book and in wisdom*} (2:129, 62:2), 'wisdom' is the Sunna. In the verses {*And We gave him wisdom when a child*} (19:12), {He *said: I have come unto you with wisdom*} (43:63), {*And He will teach him the Scripture and wisdom*} (3:48), {*And bear in mind that which is recited in your houses of the revelations of Allah and wisdom*}

[29] Narrated from Abū Hurayra by Muslim and Aḥmad.

[30] Narrated from Abū Hurayra by al-Tirmidhī (*gharīb*), Abū Dāwūd, Aḥmad, al-Ḥākim (1:43), and 'Abd al-Razzāq, a fair narration as indicated by al-Dhahabī in his *Talkhīṣ* and stated by Ibn Ḥajar in *al-Ajwiba 'alā al-Qazwīnī* [with al-Qārī's *Mirqāt* 1994 ed. 1:546-549].

[31] Narrated from Abū Hurayra by al-Bayhaqī in the *Shu'ab* (6:272 §8127) cf. al-Qārī, *al-Mirqāt* (1994 ed. 8:813). Al-Bayhaqī said it is *mursal ṣaḥīḥ*.

[32] As explained by Abū 'Uthmān al-Maghribī and al-Awzā'ī in *Kashf al-Khafā'* and *Siyar A'lām al-Nubalā'* (1997 ed. 7:92), also al-Munāwī, *Fayḍ al-Qadīr* (2:79).

[33] As stated by Ibn Qutayba, *Ta'wīl Mukhtalif al-Ḥadīth* (1995 ed. p. 270= p. 297).

[34] Cf. al-Nawawī, *Sharḥ Ṣaḥīḥ Muslim* and al-Suyūṭī, *al-Dībāj* (6:191 §2847).

[35] As stated by al-Qārī in *al-Asrār al-Marfū'a* (p. 125-127 §53). The "*Salafī*" editor of the latter, M.L. al-Ṣabbāgh, rejected the ḥadīth as *munkar* and exclaimed: "Islam was never for one day a Religion that supports naïveness or the simple-minded!" This is refuted by the narrations of Muslim and the *Sunan* cited above.

(33:34), 'wisdom' is obedience of Allah, observance of Him, superlative understanding in the Religion, and deeds in conformity with it."

Ibn Wahb also said: "I also heard Mālik say: 'Wisdom and knowledge are a light by which Allah guides whomever He pleases; it does not consist in knowing many things.'"[36]

Another version states: "Knowledge does not consist in narrating much. Knowledge is but a light which Allah places in the heart."[37] This is similar to the statements of Ibrāhīm al-Khawwāṣ: "Knowledge does not consist in narrating much. Only he is learned who follows up on knowledge and puts it into practice, obeying the *Sunan*, even if he knows little";[38] and ʿAbd Allah ibn ʿUtba: "Knowledge does not consist in narrating much. Knowledge is fear of Allah (*al-khashya*)."[39]

Imam al-Shāfiʿī:

"Knowledge is what contains the words: 'Narrated to us.' All else is satanic whisperings."[40]

"Knowledge is not what one has memorized. Knowledge is what benefits."[41]

"You [the Scholars of ḥadīth] are the pharmacists but we [the Jurists] are the physicians."[42]

[36] In al-Khaṭīb, *al-Jāmiʿ li-Akhlāq al-Rāwī* (2:174 §1526), Abū Nuʿaym, *Ḥilya* (1985 ed. 6:319), Ibn ʿAbd al-Barr, *Jāmiʿ Bayān al- ʿIlm* (1:83-84), al-Qāḍī ʿIyāḍ, *Tartīb al-Madārik* (2:62), al-Shāṭibī, *al-Muwāfaqāt* (4:97-98), al-Ghazzālī, *Iḥyā'* (1:27), and al-Dhahabī, *Siyar* (*Risāla* ed. 8:107).
[37] Cited by Ibn al-Jawzī, *Ṣifat al-Ṣafwa* (2:179) and Ibn Kathīr in his *Tafsīr* (3:555)
[38] Narrated by al-Bayhaqī in *Shuʿab al-Īmān* (2:294 §1823).
[39] Narrated by Ibn Abī ʿĀṣim in *al-Zuhd* (p. 158), Aḥmad in *al-Waraʿ* (p. 80), and Abū Nuʿaym in the *Ḥilya* (1985 ed. 1:131).
[40] Al-Shāfiʿī, *Dīwān* per al-Qārī in his introduction to *Sharḥ al-Fiqh al-Akbar*.
[41] Narrated from al-Khallāl by al-Bayhaqī in *Manāqib al-Shāfiʿī* (2:149).
[42] Cited from al-Rabīʿ by al-Dhahabī in the *Siyar* (*Risāla* ed. 10:23).

Ibn Ḥibbān al-Bustī:

Among Ibn Ḥibbān's notable remarks in his *Ṣaḥīḥ* is his definition of knowledge to mean "knowledge of the Sunna" in the Prophet's ﷺ ḥadīth: "Time shall grow short and knowledge decrease,"[43] in view of the increase of every other type of knowledge in modern times.

Imām Ibn ʿAṭā' Allah al-Sakandarī:

"The Knowledge that benefits is that whose rays expand in the breast and whose veil is lifted in the heart."[44]

Al-Dhahabī:

"[Knowledge (*al-ʿilm*) is] not the profusion of narration but a light which Allah casts into the heart. Its condition is followership (*ittibāʿ*) and the flight away from egotism (*hawā*) and innovation."[45]

The blessings and peace of Allah on the Prophet, his Family, and his Companions!

[43] Narrated from Abū Hurayra by al-Bukhārī, Muslim, Abū Dāwūd, and Ibn Mājah: "Time shall grow short, knowledge decrease, dissensions appear, avarice confront the people, and massacres abound." He was asked: "Messenger of Allah, what is the latter?" He replied: "Killing, killing!" See the discussion of this ḥadīth in al-ʿIrāqī's *Ṭarḥ al-Tathrīb* (4:26-29).
[44] Ibn ʿAṭā' Allah, *Ḥikam* (§213).
[45] *Siyar* (10:642).

The Superiority of *Fiqh* over Ḥadīth

Allah Most High said, {*He gives wisdom to whomever He will, and whoever receives wisdom receives immense good*} (2:269).

The Holy Prophet ﷺ said, "He for whom Allah desires immense good, He grants him superlative understanding in the Religion (*yufaqqihhu/yufqihhu fil-dīn*). I only distribute and it is Allah Who gives. That group shall remain in charge of the Order of Allah, unharmed by those who oppose them, until the coming of the Order of Allah."[46]

"It may be that one carries understanding without being a person of understanding; it may be that one carries understanding to someone who possesses more understanding than he."[47]

[46] Narrated from Mu'āwiya by al-Bukhārī and Muslim, cf. note 118.

[47] A mass-transmitted (*mutawātir*) ḥadīth narrated from nineteen Companions: (1) Zayd ibn Thābit by al-Tirmidhī (*ḥasan* in the printed eds.), Abū Dāwūd, Ibn Mājah, Aḥmad, al-Dārimī, al-Shāfi'ī in his *Risāla* (§1102), al-Ṭabarānī in *al-Kabīr* (§4891-4892, §4925, §4994), Ibn 'Abd al-Barr in *Jāmi' Bayān al- 'Ilm* (1:175 §184), al-Rāmahurmuzī in *al-Muḥaddith al-Fāṣil* (p. 64), Ibn Abī 'Āṣim in *al-Sunna* (p. 45 §94), al-Khaṭīb in *Sharaf Aṣḥāb al-Ḥadīth* (p. 24) and *al-Faqīh wal-Mutafaqqih* (2:71), al-Ṭaḥāwī in *Sharḥ Mushkil al-Āthār* (2:232=4:282 §1600), and Ibn Ḥibbān (1:270 §67, 2:454 §680), all with sound chains as stated by al-Arna'ūṭ and others; (2) Jubayr ibn Muṭ'im by Ibn Mājah, Aḥmad, al-Dārimī, al-Ṭabarānī in *al-Kabīr* (§1541-1544), Abū Ya'lā in his *Musnad* (1:347 §7413), al-Ḥākim (1:87= 1990 ed. 1:162), al-Quḍā'ī in *Musnad al-Shihāb* (§1421), al-Ṭahāwī in *Sharḥ Mushkil al-Āthār* (2:232= 4:282 §1601), al-Khaṭīb in *Sharaf Aṣḥāb al-Ḥadīth* (p. 18), and Ibn 'Abd al-Barr in *Jāmi' Bayān al- 'Ilm* (1:184-187 §195-197), all with weak chains because of Muḥammad ibn Isḥāq who is a concealer in his narrative chains (*mudallis*), cf. al-Haythamī (1:139); (3) Anas by Ibn Mājah, Aḥmad, al-Ṭabarānī in *al-Awsaṭ*, and Ibn 'Abd al-Barr in *Jāmi' Bayān al- 'Ilm* (1:187-189 §198-199) with weak chains – as stated by al-Haythamī (1:138-139) – the collected force of which raise the ḥadīth to the grade of fair; (4) Abū Sa'īd al-Khudrī by al-Bazzār with a chain of trustworthy narrators except for Sa'īd ibn Bāzigh who may be unknown as stated by al-Haythamī (1:137); (5) Abū al-Dardā' by al-Dārimī and al-Ṭabarānī in *al-Kabīr* with a very weak chain because of 'Abd al-Raḥmān ibn Zayd ("ibn Zubayd al-Yāmī" in al-Dārimī) as stated by al-Haythamī (1:137); (6) 'Umayr ibn Qatāda al-Laythī by al-Ṭabarānī in *al-Kabīr* with a chain containing one narrator

Imām al-Shāfi'ī apparently took from Imām Abū Ḥanīfa his famous statement, "You [the Scholars of ḥadīth] are the pharmacists but we [the Jurists] are the physicians."[48] This is also reported from al-A'mash and Abū Sulaymān Ibn Zubar[49] and was probably proverbial. Mullā 'Alī al-Qārī commented: "The early scholars said: 'The ḥadīth scholar without knowledge of *fiqh* is like a seller of drugs who is no physician': he has them but he does not know what to do with them; 'and the *fiqh* scholar without knowledge of ḥadīth is like a physician without drugs': he knows what constitutes a remedy, but does not have it available."[50]

whose state is unsure as mentioned by al-Haythamī (1:138); (7) al-Nu'mān ibn Bashīr by al-Ṭabarānī in *al-Kabīr* with a very weak chain because of 'Īsā al-Khabbāṭ and by al-Ḥākim (1:88=1990 ed. 1:164) with a sound chain as confirmed by al-Dhahabī and as indicated by al-Haythamī (1:138); (8) Jābir and (9) Sa'd ibn Abī Waqqāṣ by al-Ṭabarānī, *al-Awsaṭ* with weak chains as stated by al-Haythamī (1:138-139); (10) Ibn Mas'ūd by al-Tirmidhī with two chains (*ḥasan ṣaḥīḥ*), Ibn Mājah, Aḥmad, Abū Ya'lā in his *Musnad* (§5126, §5296), al-Shāfi'ī in his (1:14), al-Baghawī, *Sharḥ al-Sunna* (1:233-234), al-Khaṭīb, *al-Kifāya* (p. 29, p. 173) and *Sharaf Aṣḥāb al-Ḥadīth* (p. 18-19, p. 26), al-Bayhaqī, *Ma'rifat al-Sunan* (1:15-16, 1:43), *Dalā'il al-Nubuwwa* (6:540), Abū Nu'aym, *Tārīkh Aṣbahān* (2:90), *al-Ḥilya* (7:331) where he graded it *ṣaḥīḥ*, al-Ḥākim, *Ma'rifat Anwā' 'Ulūm al-Ḥadīth* (p. 322), Ibn 'Abd al-Barr, *Jāmi' Bayān al-'Ilm* (1:178-182 §188-191), Ibn Ḥibbān (1:268 §66, 1271-272 §68-69) with three fair chains according to al-Arna'ūṭ, one of them with the wording "Allah have mercy on someone who hears a ḥadīth from me then conveys it." Kattānī in *Naẓm al-Mutanāthir* adds the following Companion-narrators of this ḥadīth: (11) Bashīr ibn al-Nu'mān; (12) Mu'ādh ibn Jabal; (13) Abū Qirfāṣa; (14) Rabī'a ibn 'Uthmān al-Taymī; (15) Ibn 'Umar; (16) Zayd ibn Khālid al-Juhanī; (17) 'Ā'isha; (18) Abū Hurayra; and (19) Shayba ibn 'Uthmān. Al-Tirmidhī's version does not mention the last sentence while al-Shāfi'ī's adds "and guard them from delusion." This is also the first narration in al-Ājurrī's book *al-Sharī'a* and others. On the variant wordings of this important ḥadīth also see 'Abd al-Fattāḥ's *al-Rasūl al-Mu'allim* (p. 55-56).

[48] See note 42.

[49] Narrated by Ibn Ḥibbān in *al-Thiqāt* (8:467-468), al-Khaṭīb in *Naṣīḥat Ahl al-Ḥadīth* (p. 45) cf. al-Zayla'ī, *Naṣb al-Rāya* (introduction), al-Dhahabī, *Tadhkirat al-Ḥuffāẓ* (3:997) and *Siyar* (*Risāla* ed. 16:441), and al-Ṣāliḥī, *'Uqūd al-Jumān* (p. 322).

Imām Aḥmad is related by his students Abū Ṭālib and Ḥumayd ibn Zanjūyah to say: "I never saw anyone adhere more to ḥadīth than al-Shāfiʿī. No one preceded him in writing down ḥadīth in a book." The meaning of this is that al-Shāfiʿī possessed the intelligence of ḥadīth after which Aḥmad sought, as evidenced by the latter's statement: "How rare is *fiqh* among those who know ḥadīth!"[51] This is a reference to the ḥadīth: "It may be one carries understanding (*fiqh*) – meaning: memorizes the proof-texts of *fiqh* – without being a person of understanding (*faqīh*)."[52] The *Salaf* and *Khalaf* elucidated this rule in many famous statements showing that, for all the exalted status of the *Muḥaddith*, yet the *Faqīh* excels him.

Ḥadīth Misguides Those Devoid of *Fiqh*

Cautioning against the danger of misusing ḥadīth to the point of committing sin, Imām Aḥmad narrated from Muḥammad ibn ibn Yaḥyā al-Qaṭṭān (d. 233) that the latter said: "If one were to follow every *rukhṣa* that is in the ḥadīth, he would become a transgressor (*fāsiq*)."[53]

Ibn Abī Zayd al-Mālikī reports Sufyān ibn ʿUyayna as saying: "Ḥadīth is a pitfall (*maḍilla*) except for the *fuqahā'*," and Mālik's companion ʿAbd Allah ibn Wahb very frequently said: "Ḥadīth is a pitfall except for the Ulema. Every memorizer of ḥadīth that does not have an Imām in *fiqh* is misguided (*ḍāll*), and if Allah had not rescued us with Mālik and al-Layth [ibn Saʿd], we would have been misguided."[54] Ibn Abī Zayd comments: "He [Sufyān]

[50] Al-Qārī, *Muʿtaqad Abī Ḥanīfata al-Imām fī Abaway al-Rasūl* ﷺ (p. 42).
[51] Narrated by Abū Yaʿlā in *Ṭabaqāt al-Ḥanābila* (1:329) cf. Abū Ghudda's introduction to Muḥammad's *Muwaṭṭa'* and his essay *al-Isnād min al-Dīn* (p. 68).
[52] See note 47.
[53] Aḥmad, *al-ʿIlal* (1:219).
[54] Ibn Abī Ḥātim in the introduction of *al-Jarḥ wal-Taʿdīl* (p. 22-23); Ibn Abī Zayd, *al-Jāmiʿ fil-Sunan* (p. 118-119); Ibn ʿAbd al-Barr, *al-Intiqā' fī Faḍā'il al-*

means that other than the jurists might take something in its external meaning when, in fact, it is interpreted in the light of another ḥadīth or some evidence which remains hidden to him; or it may in fact consist in discarded evidence due to some other [abrogating] evidence. None can meet the responsibility of knowing this except those who deepened their learning and obtained *fiqh*." Imām al-Haytamī said something similar.[55]

Ibn Wahb is also reported to say: "I met three hundred and sixty learned people of knowledge but without Mālik and al-Layth I would have strayed."[56] Another versions states: "Were it not for Mālik ibn Anas and al-Layth ibn Sa'd I would have perished; I used to think everything that is [authentically] related from the Prophet ﷺ must be put into practice."[57]

Another version has: "I gathered a lot of ḥadīths and they drove me to confusion. I would consult Mālik and al-Layth and they would say to me, 'take this and leave this.' "[58] Ibn Wahb had compiled 120,000 narrations according to Aḥmad ibn Ṣāliḥ.[59]

Hence, Ibn 'Uqda replied to a man who had asked him about a certain narration: "Keep such ḥadīths to a minimum for, truly, they are unsuitable except for those who know their interpretation. Yaḥyā ibn Sulayman narrated from Ibn Wahb that he heard Mālik say: 'Many of these ḥadīths are [a cause for] misguidance; some ḥadīths were narrated by me and I wish that for

A'immat al-Thalāthat al-Fuqahā' (p. 60-61); See Shaykh 'Abd al-Fattāḥ Abū Ghudda's comments on this statement in his notes on al Lacknawī's *al-Raf' wal-Takmīl* (2nd ed. p. 368-369, 3rd ed. p. 90-91).

[55] In *al-Fatāwā al-Ḥadīthiyya* (p. 283).

[56] Narrated by Ibn Ḥibbān in the introduction to *al-Majrūḥīn* (1:42). He then narrates from Ibn Wahb a similar statement where he adds the names of 'Amr ibn al-Ḥārith and Ibn Mājishūn.

[57] Narrated by Ibn 'Asākir al-Bayhaqī cf. Ibn Rajab, *Sharḥ al-'Ilal* (1:413) and 'Awwāma, *Athar al-Ḥadīth al-Sharīf fī Ikhtilāf al-A'immat al-Fuqahā'* (p. 76).

[58] Narrated by Qāḍī 'Iyāḍ in *Tartīb al-Madārik* (2:427).

[59] In Ibn al-Subkī, *Ṭabaqāt al-Shāfi'iyya al-Kubrā* (2:128).

each of them I had been flogged with a stick twice. I certainly no longer narrate them!'"[60] By his phrase, "Many of these ḥadīths are misguidance," Mālik means their adducing them in the wrong place and meaning, because **the Sunna is wisdom and wisdom is to place each thing in its right context.**[61] An example of this is al-Shāfiʿī's report that Mālik regretted including in the *Muwaṭṭa'* the ḥadīth of the Pond in which the Prophet ﷺ is told, "You do not know what they did after you"[62] because of the inevitable abuse at the hands of Shīʿīs (or shīʿified Sunnis such as the Ghumārī school and others in our time).

Ibn al-Mubārak said: "If Allah had not rescued me with Abū Ḥanīfa and Sufyān [al-Thawrī] I would have been like the rest of the common people." Al-Dhahabī relates it as: "I would have been an innovator."[63]

The *Imāms* of Ḥadīth Defer to the *Imāms* of *Fiqh*

Imām Aḥmad's teacher, Yaḥyā ibn Saʿīd al-Qaṭṭān (d. 198), despite his foremost status as the Master of ḥadīth Masters and expert in narrator-recommendation and discreditation (*al-jarḥ wal-taʿdīl*), would not venture to extract legal rulings from the evidence but followed in this the *fiqh* of Abū Ḥanīfa as he explicitly declared: "We do not belie Allah. We never heard better than the juridical opinion (*ra'ī*) of Abū Ḥanīfa and we followed most of his positions."[64] Similarly, Muḥammad ibn ʿAbd Allah ibn ʿAbd al-Ḥakam said: "If it were not for al-Shāfiʿī I would not have known how to reply to anyone. Because of him I know what I know."[65]

[60] Narrated by al-Khaṭīb, *al-Faqīh wal-Mutafaqqih* (2:80).
[61] Shaykh Ismāʿīl al-Anṣārī as quoted by ʿAwwāma, *Athar* (p. 77).
[62] As related by Ibn Shākir al-Qaṭṭān (d. 407) in his *Manāqib al-Shāfiʿī* from Ibn ʿAbd al-Aʿlā, cf. al-Zarqānī, *Sharḥ al-Muwaṭṭa'* (1:98).
[63] Ibn Ḥajar, *Tahdhīb* (10:449-452 §817) and al-Dhahabī's *Manāqib Abī Ḥanīfa.*
[64] Al-Dhahabī, *Tadhkirat al-Ḥuffāẓ* (1:307) and Ibn Ḥajar, *Tahdhīb* (10:450).
[65] Ibn ʿAbd al-Barr, *al-Intiqā' fī Faḍā'il al-A'immat al-Thalāthat al-Fuqahā'* (p. 124).

As for Muḥammad ibn Yaḥyā al-Dhuhlī (d. 258) of Khurāsān, whom Abū Zurʿa ranked above Imām Muslim and who is considered an *Amīr al-Mu'minīn fil-Ḥadīth,*[66] he never considered himself a non-*muqallid* but said: "I have made Aḥmad ibn Ḥanbal an *Imām* in all that stands between me and my Lord."[67] Misʿar ibn Kidām said the same with regard to Imām Abū Ḥanīfa.[68]

Knowledge Is not Memorization but a Light

Fiqh is the context of many statements of the *Imāms* on knowledge consisting in wisdom, benefit, deeds, and light rather than learning and memorization as we already mentioned. Mālik said: "Wisdom and knowledge are a light by which Allah guides whomever He pleases; it does not consist in knowing many things."[69] Al-Shāfiʿī: "Knowledge is what benefits. Knowledge is not what one has memorized."[70] Al-Dhahabī: "[Knowledge (*al-ʿilm*) is] not the profusion of narration, but a light which Allah casts into the heart. Its condition is followership (*ittibāʿ*) and the flight away from egotism (*hawā*) and innovation."[71]

Al-Khaṭīb in his brief *Iqtiḍā' al-ʿIlm al-ʿAmal* ("Learning Necessitates Deeds") narrates many statements to this effect from Ibn Masʿūd, Abū Hurayra, Abū al-Dardā', Abū Qilāba, al-Zuhrī, al-Tustarī, Ibn ʿUyayna, and others of the *Salaf*. This Islamic

[66] "Commander of the Believers in the Science of Ḥadīth," the topmost title for a ḥadīth Master, given only to thirty people in Islam such as Imām Sufyān al-Thawrī, Imām Mālik, the Two Shaykhs – al-Bukhārī and Muslim – and al-Dāraquṭnī. Cf. Abū Ghudda, *Umarā al-Mu'minīn fil-Ḥadīth.*

[67] Narrated by al-Dhahabī in the *Siyar* (10:205).

[68] Cf. Ibn Abī al-Wafā, last page of the Karachi edition of *al-Jawāhir al-Muḍiyya fī Tabaqāt al-Ḥanafiyya.*

[69] In Ibn ʿAbd al-Barr, *Jāmiʿ Bayān al-ʿIlm* (1:83-84), al-Qāḍī ʿIyāḍ, *Tartīb al-Madārik* (2:62), al-Shāṭibī, *al-Muwāfaqāt* (4:97-98).

[70] See note 43.

[71] *Siyar Aʿlām al-Nubalā'* (10:642).

understanding of knowledge elucidates al-Ḥasan al-Baṣrī's report that the Prophet ﷺ said: "The energy of the Ulema is care and help while the energy of fools is to quote" (*himmat al-'ulamā' al-ri'āya wa-himmat al-sufahā' al-riwāya*)[72] and the statement of the 'Abbāsī Caliph 'Abd Allah ibn al-Mu'tazz (249-296): "The learning of the hypocrite consists in his discourse while the learning of the Believer consists in his deed."[73]

The Ḥadīth of the Jurists is Preferable to That of the Non-Jurists

Wakī' ibn al-Jarrāḥ preferred long-chained narrations through the *fuqahā'* to short-chained ones through non-*fuqahā'* and said: "The ḥadīth current among the jurists is better than the one current among ḥadīth scholars."[74] This is a foundational rule in the *Ḥanafī* School which, like Yaḥyā al-Qaṭṭān, Wakī' followed.[75]

Al-A'mash also said: "The ḥadīth that jurists circulate among themselves is better than that which ḥadīth narrators circulate among themselves."[76] Ibn Rajab said Abū Dāwūd in his *Sunan* was more concerned with the *fiqh* of the ḥadīth than with its chains of transmission.[77] This is also the case with al-Bukhārī's *Ṣaḥīḥ* while Muslim, Ibn Mājah, and al-Nasā'ī focussed on the benefits of its transmission chains and text variants – Muslim being the most thorough and reliable in these regards. Al-Tirmidhī gave equal weight to the *fiqh* of the ḥadīth and the study of its transmission although Abū Dāwūd is somewhat stricter in ḥadīth authentication while al-Nasā'ī surpasses them both.[78]

[72] Narrated *mursal* from al-Ḥasan by Ibn 'Asākir and al-Khaṭīb, *al-Jāmi' li Akhlāq al-Rāwī* (1983 ed. 1:88 §27) cf. *al-Jāmi' al-Ṣaghīr* (§9598) and *Kanz* (§29337).
[73] Narrated by al-Khaṭīb in *Iqtiḍā' al- 'Ilm al- 'Amal* (p. 38).
[74] Cited by al-Dhahabī in the *Siyar* (al-Arna'ūṭ ed. 9:158, 12:328-329).
[75] Cf. al-Dhahabī, *Tadhkira* (1:307) and Ibn Ḥajar, *Tahdhīb* (11:126-127).
[76] In al-Sakhāwī, *al-Jawāhir wal-Durar* (p. 21).
[77] Ibn Rajab, *Sharḥ 'Ilal al-Tirmidhī* (1:411).

Knowing the Ḥadīth is Different From Practicing It

Sufyān al-Thawrī used to say to the ḥadīth scholars: "Come forward, O weak ones!"[79] He also said: "If ḥadīth were a good thing it would have vanished just as all goodness has vanished," and "Pursuing the study of ḥadīth is not part of the preparation for death, but a disease that preoccupies people." Al-Dhahabī commented: "He said this verbatim. He is right in what he said because pursuing the study of ḥadīth is other than the ḥadīth itself."[80]

Understanding the Ḥadīth is Superior to Knowing It

Isḥāq ibn Rāhūyah said: "I would sit in Iraq with Aḥmad ibn Ḥanbal, Yaḥyā ibn Ma'īn, and our companions, rehearsing the narrations from one, two, three routes of transmission... But when I said: What is its intent? What is its explanation? What is its *fiqh*? they would all remain mute except Aḥmad ibn Ḥanbal."[81]

Sufyān al-Thawrī said: "The explanation (*tafsīr*) of the ḥadīth is better than the ḥadīth."[82] Another wording has: "The explanation of the ḥadīth is better than its audition."[83]

Abū 'Alī al-Naysābūrī said: "We consider understanding superior to memorization."[84]

Ibn Mahdī regretted not having written, after every ḥadīth he had recorded, its explanation.[85]

[78] Cf. al-Kawtharī's notes on al-Ḥāzimī's *Shurūṭ al-A'immat al-Khamsa* (p. 72-73).
[79] Cited from Zayd ibn Abī al-Zarqā' by al-Dhahabī, *Siyar* (al-Arna'ūṭ ed. 7:275).
[80] In al-Sakhāwī, *al-Jawāhir wal-Durar* (p. 20-23).
[81] Narrated by Ibn Abī Ḥātim in the introduction to *al-Jarḥ wal-Ta'dīl* (p. 293), Ibn al-Jawzī, *Manāqib Aḥmad* (p. 63), and al-Dhahabī, *Tārīkh al-Islām* (ch. on Aḥmad).
[82] Narrated by al-Harawī al-Anṣārī in *Dhamm al-Kalām* (4:139 §907).
[83] In Ibn 'Abd al-Barr, *Jāmi' Bayān al-'Ilm* (2:175).
[84] In al-Dhahabī , *Tadhkirat al-Ḥuffāẓ* (2:776).
[85] In Ibn Rajab, *Sharḥ 'Ilal al-Tirmidhī* (1:41).

The perspicuity and *fiqh* of Abū Thawr among the ḥadīth Masters is famous. A woman stood by a gathering of scholars of ḥadīth comprising Yaḥyā ibn Maʿīn, Abū Khaythama, Khalaf ibn Sālim, and others. She heard them saying: "The Prophet ﷺ said," and "So-and-so narrated," and "No one other than So-and-so narrated," etc. She asked them: "Can a woman in her menses wash the dead?" for that was her occupation. No one in the entire gathering could answer her and they began to look at each other. Abū Thawr arrived and they referred her to him. She asked him the same question and he said: "Yes, she can wash the dead, as per the ḥadīth of al-Qāsim ibn Muḥammad from ʿĀʾisha: 'Your menses are not in your hand,'[86] and her narration that she would scrub the Prophet's ﷺ hair at a time she was menstruating.[87] If the head of the living can be washed [by a woman in her menses], then a fortiori the dead!" Hearing this, the ḥadīth scholars said: "Right! So-and-so narrated it, and So-and-so told us, and we know it from such-and-such a chain," and they plunged back into the narrations and chains of transmission. The woman said: "Where were you all until now?"[88]

Ibn ʿAbd al-Barr cites Imām Aḥmad as saying: "From where does Yaḥyā ibn Maʿīn know al-Shāfiʿī? He does not know al-Shāfiʿī nor has any idea what al-Shāfiʿī says!"[89] Similarly Ibn Rāhūyah, one of the major ḥadīth Masters, conceded defeat before al-Shāfiʿī's *fiqh* although himself reputed for *fiqh*.[90]

[86] In Muslim and the Four *Sunan*.

[87] In al-Bukhārī and Muslim.

[88] Ibn al-Subkī, *Ṭabaqāt al-Shāfiʿiyya*, al-Sakhāwī, introduction to *al-Jawāhir wal-Durar*, al-Haytamī, *Fatāwā Ḥadīthiyya* (p. 283) cf. Aḥmad's report in Ibn Rajab, *Dhayl Ṭabaqāt al-Ḥanābila* (1:131); al-ʿUlaymī, *al-Manhaj al-Aḥmad* (2:208).

[89] Ibn ʿAbd al-Barr, *Jāmiʿ Bayān al-ʿIlm* (2:160).

[90] Isḥāq ibn Ibrāhīm ibn Makhlad, known as Isḥāq ibn Rāhūyah or Rāhawayh, Abū Yaʿqūb al-Tamīmī al-Marwazī al-Hanẓalī (d. 238). Abū Qudāma considered him greater than Imām Aḥmad in memorization of ḥadīth, a remarkable assess-

Most Ḥadīth Scholars Do Not Possess Intelligence of the Ḥadīth

ʿAbd al-Razzāq al-Ṣanʿānī, Sufyān al-Thawrī's contemporary, was the teacher of the pillars of ḥadīth memorization in their time – Aḥmad, Ibn Rāhūyah, Ibn Maʿīn, and Muḥammad ibn Yaḥyā al-Dhuhlī. Yet when Muḥammad ibn Yazīd al-Mustamlī asked Aḥmad: "Did he [ʿAbd al-Razzāq] possess *fiqh*?" Aḥmad replied: **"How rare is *fiqh* among those who know ḥadīth!"**[91]

Anas ibn Sīrīn said: "I came to Kūfa and found in it 4,000 persons pursuing ḥadīth and 400 persons who had obtained *fiqh*."[92]

Sufyān al-Thawrī: "Knowledge in our view is only the dispensation of a trustworthy learned person. As for strictness, anyone can be strict!"[93]

Ḥujjat al-Islām Imām al-Ghazzālī in *al-Mustaṣfā* and Imām Ibn Qudāma in *Rawḍat al-Nāẓir* both said that an *ʿĀlim* may be an Imām in a particular science and an uneducated common person in another.

Ibn ʿAbd al-Salām said: "Most ḥadīth scholars are ignorant in *fiqh*."[94] A majority of 90% according to Anas ibn Sīrīn – among the *Salaf*!

ment considering Aḥmad's knowledge of 700,000 to a million narrations according to his son ʿAbd Allah's and Abū Zurʿa al-Rāzī's estimations. He once said of himself: "I never wrote anything except I memorized it, and I can now see before me more than 70,000 ḥadīths in my book"; "I know the place of 100,000 ḥadīths as if I were looking at them, and I memorize 70,000 of them by heart – all sound (*ṣaḥīḥ*) – and 4,000 falsified ones." [Narrated by al-Khaṭīb in *al-Jāmiʿ li-Akhlāq al-Rāwī* (2:380-381 §1832-1833).] He did not reach the same stature in *fiqh*. Al-Bayhaqī and others narrate that he unsuccessfully debated al-Shāfiʿī on a legal question, as a result of which the latter disapproved of his title as the "jurisprudent of Khurāsān."

[91] See note 51.

[92] Narrated by al-Rāmahurmuzī in *al-Muḥaddith al-Fāṣil* (p. 560).

[93] Narrated by Ibn ʿAbd al-Barr in *Bayān Faḍl al-ʿIlm* (1:784 §1467).

[94] Ibn ʿAbd al-Salām, *al-Fatāwā al-Mawṣiliyya* (p. 132-134).

Al-Dhahabī said: "The majority of the ḥadīth scholars have no understanding, no diligence in the actual knowledge of ḥadīth, and no fear of Allah regarding it."[95] All of the authorities al-Dhahabī listed as "those who are imitated in Islam" are Jurisprudents and not merely ḥadīth masters.[96]

Al-Sakhāwī in his biography of Ibn Ḥajar entitled *al-Jawāhir wal-Durar fi Tarjamat Shaykh al-Islām Ibn Ḥajar* states that al-Fāriqī said: "One who knows chains of ḥadīth but not the legal rulings derived from them cannot be counted among the Scholars of the Law." Al-Fāriqī's student Ibn Abī ʿAṣrūn (d. 585) also followed this view in his book *al-Intiṣār*.[97]

Not Every Sound Hadīth Forms Evidence

Ibrāhīm al-Nakhaʿī said: "I hear a ḥadīth then I look to see what part of it applies. I apply it and leave the rest."[98] Muḥammad ʿAwwāma said: "Meaning, what is recognized by the authorities is retained while anything odd (*gharīb*), anomalous (*shādhdh*), or disclaimed (*munkar*) is put aside."

Yazīd ibn Abī Ḥabīb said: "When you hear a ḥadīth, proclaim it; if it is recognized, [keep it,] otherwise, leave it."[99]

Ibn Abī Laylā said: "A man does not understand ḥadīth until he knows what to take from it and what to leave."[100]

ʿAbd al-Raḥmān ibn Mahdī, the Commander of the believers in ḥadīth, said: "It is impermissible for someone to be an Imām [i.e. to be imitated] until he knows what is sound and what is un-

[95] In al-Sakhāwī, *al-Jawāhir wal-Durar* (p. 18).
[96] See al-Dhahabī, *Siyar* (Fikr ed. 7:410).
[97] Al-Sakhāwī, *al-Jawāhir wal-Durar* (p. 20-23).
[98] Narrated from Ibn Abī Khaythama by Abū Nuʿaym in the *Ḥilya* (4:225) and Ibn Rajab in *Sharḥ ʿIlal al-Tirmidhī* (1:413).
[99] In Ibn Rajab, *Sharḥ ʿIlal al-Tirmidhī* (1:413).
[100] In Ibn ʿAbd al-Barr, *Jāmiʿ Bayān al-ʿIlm* (2:130).

sound and until he does not take everything [sound] as evidence, and until he knows the correct way to infer knowledge [in the Religion]."[101]

Al-Shāfiʿī narrated that Mālik ibn Anas was told: "Ibn ʿUyayna narrates from al-Zuhrī things you do not have!" He replied: "Why, should I narrate every single ḥadīth I heard? Only if I wanted to misguide people!"[102]

Shaykh ʿAbd al-Fattāh. Abū Ghudda mentioned some of the above examples and commented: "If the likes of Yaḥyā al-Qaṭṭān, Wakīʿ ibn al-Jarrāḥ, ʿAbd al-Razzāq, Yaḥyā ibn Maʿīn, and those who compare with them, did not dare enter into *ijtihād* and *fiqh*, then how rash are the claimants to *ijtihād* in our time! On top of it, they call the *Salaf* ignorant without the least shame nor modesty! Allah is our refuge from failure."[103]

The blessings and peace of Allah on the Prophet, his Family, and his Companions!

[101] Narrated by Abū Nuʿaym in the *Ḥilya* (9:3).
[102] Narrated by al-Khaṭīb in *al-Jāmiʿ li Akhlāq al-Rāwī* (2:109).
[103] Abū Ghudda, *al-Isnād min al-Dīn* (p. 68). He means by his remarks al-Albānī and the like such as modernists who apply the term "medieval" to early Islam. Abū Ghudda's student, Muḥammad ʿAwwāma, listed several examples of this rule of the *Salaf* in his *Athar al-Ḥadīth al-Sharīf fī Ikhtilāf al-A'immat al-Fuqahā'* ("The Effect the Noble Ḥadīth Had on the Differences of the Imāms of Jurisprudence").

Madhāhib of the Imāms of Ḥadīth

Aḥmad, al-Bukhārī, Muslim, al-Tirmidhī, Abū Dāwūd, al-Nasā'ī, Ibn Mājah, al-Dārimī

Imām Aḥmad ibn Ḥanbal (164-241) began as a Shāfiʿī like Dāwūd al-Ẓāhirī (d. 275), al-Ṭabarī (224-310), al-Ṭaḥāwī (229-321), and Ibn Ḥazm (384-465), and is one of the transmitters of Imām al-Shāfiʿī's (150-204) 'Old School' (*al-Madhhab al-Qadīm*), to the point that Ibn Khuzayma (223-311) rebuked someone who had brought up the Ḥanbalī School with the words: "Is Aḥmad ibn Ḥanbal anything but one of al-Shāfiʿī's pupils?" However, Aḥmad moved away from his teacher and favored a more textualist approach that crystallized into an independent school first codified by Abū Bakr al-Khallāl (230?-311) into a massive, forty-volume collection titled *al-Jāmiʿ li- 'Ulūm Aḥmad ibn Ḥanbal.*

Ṣiddīq Ḥasan Khān al-Qinnawjī included Imām al-Bukhārī (194-256) and Imām Muslim (204-261) among the Shāfiʿīs in *Abjad al- 'Ulūm*, *al-Ḥiṭṭa fī Dhikr al-Ṣiḥāḥ al-Sitta*, and *Itḥāf al-Nubalā' al-Muttaqīn* while Ibn Abī Yaʿlā included them among the Ḥanbalīs in his *Ṭabaqāt al-Ḥanābila*. Ibn al-Subkī included al-Bukhārī among the Shāfiʿīs in his *Ṭabaqāt al-Shāfiʿiyya al-Kubrā*. Imām al-Kawtharī counted the young al-Bukhārī among the Ḥanafīs due to his remark that in his beginnings he "memorized the compilations of Ibn al-Mubārak (118-181) and Wakīʿ ibn al-Jarrāḥ (d. 196)," meaning the *fiqh* of Imāms Abū Ḥanīfa (80-150) and Sufyān al-Thawrī (97-161). The Bukhārī of the *Ṣaḥīḥ* undoubtedly leans to the Shāfiʿī School as per *Fatḥ al-Bārī* and others; and by his recurring phrase "Some people say" (*qāla baʿḍ al-nās*) he means to refute the positions of Abū Ḥanīfa, however, he also contravenes al-Shāfiʿī in much.[104]

[104] Cf. al-Ghunaymī's *Kashf al-Iltibās 'ammā Awrada al-Imām al-Bukhārī 'alā Baʿḍ al-Nās* and Shāh Walī Allāh's *al-Inṣāf*.

In reality, al-Bukhārī is a *Mujtahid Muṭlaq* (qualified to extract rulings from proofs independently) with his own *madhhab* which did not survive him as he was uninterested in other than his *Ṣaḥīḥ* for a school, and the *Ṣaḥīḥ* is truly a complex and concise *fiqh* manual.

Imām Muslim was al-Bukhārī's close student but differed with him in some matters of ḥadīth methodology and narrator-criticism. He leans to the Shāfiʿī School to the point that Shāh Walī Allāh in *al-Inṣāf fī Bayān Sabab al-Ikhtilāf* considers him a dedicated Shāfiʿī; but he was at the very least a *Mujtahid Murajjiḥ* or *Muntasib* (qualified to verify rulings within a *madhhab*), someone with full knowledge of *Ijmāʿ* and *Khilāf*, competent to evaluate all the pre-existing juridical conclusions of the Schools of the Companions and *Tābiʿīn* and choose the most correct in his view. Yet, unlike his teacher, he was more interested in the transmission chains of the ḥadīth than in its jurisprudence. Only al-Bukhārī arranged his *Ṣaḥīḥ* according to jurisprudential subheadings while Muslim's *Ṣaḥīḥ* was devoid of subheadings until Imām al-Nawawī added them three and a half centuries later.

In *kalām* theology the Two Shaykhs are proto-Ashʿarīs and derive their positions principally from Ibn Kullāb and al-Karābīsī.[105]

Imām al-Tirmidhī (c.210-279) was also al-Bukhārī's faithful student and a *Mujtahid Murajjiḥ* and comparatist of the first rank whose method and school, like al-Bukhārī's, are developed in his book – the *Sunan* – not only in the chapter-titles like his teacher, but in the bodies of the chapters themselves and in far more explicit terms than al-Bukhārī. Hence, al-Tirmidhī frequently mentions the various positions of the Imāms of *fiqh* such as al-Awzāʿī (88-158), Sufyān al-Thawrī, Aḥmad, or Isḥāq ibn Rāhūyah (d. 238) (although he never mentions al-Bukhārī in relation to

[105] Cf. Ibn Ḥajar, *Fatḥ al-Bārī* (1:243).

fiqh but only ḥadīth rulings), leaning so thoroughly to that of al-Shāfiʿī that Shaykh Muḥammad Anwar Shāh al-Kashmīrī considers him a Shāfiʿī in his *Fayḍ al-Bārī Sharḥ Ṣaḥīḥ al-Bukhārī* and *al-ʿArf al-Shadhī* while Shāh Walī Allāh in *al-Inṣāf* deems him closer to Aḥmad and Isḥāq. Al-Tirmidhī leans least to the *fiqh* of the Kufans which includes Wakīʿ ibn al-Jarrāḥ, al-Thawrī, Ḥammād ibn Abī Sulaymān, and Abū Ḥanīfa, whom he mentions three times in the *Sunan* and once in the *ʿIlal* and with whom he differs sharply. He also discussed narrator-criticism, paid close attention to the chains of transmission as Muslim had done, and graded the hadīths in very reliable fashion. In this double respect he brought together the method of the two *Ṣaḥīḥs* in ideal fashion and also kept to the highest standard of authenticity among the books of *Sunan* with the possible exception of al-Nasāʾī although some rank Abū Dāwūd higher than both.[106]

Imām Abū Dāwūd (202-275) focussed on jurisprudence even more than any of the above-named and shows more respect than any of them to Imām Abū Ḥanīfa as a *Faqīh* but he does not show full-fledged independent *ijtihād* in the *Sunan*. He was a student of Imām Aḥmad, narrates *masāʾil* from him, and his *riwāya* from Imām Aḥmad comes up frequently in the books of the Ḥanbalīs. Hence Ibn Abī Yaʿlā includes him in *Ṭabaqāt al-Ḥanābila* and al-Shīrāzī counts him among the Ḥanbalīs in his *Ṭabaqāt al-Fuqahāʾ* (the only author of the *Ṣaḥīḥayn* and *Sunan* mentioned therein) as do Anwar Shāh in *al-ʿArf al-Shadhī* and Shāh Walī Allāh. Nevertheless, Abū Dāwūd was explicit in his *Risāla ilā Ahli Makka* that his *Sunan* is a compilation of jurisprudential proofs aiming at comprehensiveness (*istiqṣāʾ*) with especial care for three schools of law in particular: al-Thawrī, Mālik, and al-Shāfiʿī's. Ibn al-Subkī included him among the

[106] Cf. Nūr al-Dīn ʿItr's *al-Imām al-Tirmidhī wal-Muwāzanatu Bayna Jāmiʿihi wa-Bayn al-Ṣaḥīḥayn*.

Shāfiʿīs in his *Ṭabaqāt al-Shāfiʿiyya al-Kubrā* but mentions that Abū Dāwūd was a close student of Imām Aḥmad. The *Risāla* also shows Abū Dāwūd's well-honed criterion for authencity whereby anything he narrates uncritically in the *Sunan* can be relied upon as authentic with few exceptions.

Imām al-Nasā'ī (215-303) was a dedicated Shāfiʿī according to Ibn al-Subkī in his *Ṭabaqāt al-Shāfiʿiyya al-Kubrā* and Shāh Walī Allāh in *al-Inṣāf* but – curiously – a Ḥanbalī according to Anwar Shāh in the *'Arf*. Both al-Dhahabī and Taqī al-Dīn al-Subkī considered him stronger in memorization than Imām Muslim. His standard of authenticity in his minor book of *Sunan* rivals or even gets stricter than that of the two Shaykhs to the point that some named it a *Ṣaḥīḥ* and put it first in order of reliability after the two *Ṣaḥīḥs*, although he did include some unknown and weak narrators and disclaimed narrations.[107] Ṣiddīq Ḥasan Khān al-Qinnawjī includes both him and Abū Dāwūd among the Shāfiʿīs in *Abjad al- 'Ulūm*.

Imām Ibn Mājah (209-273) was the student of Ibn Abī Shayba and focussed on *fiqh* like him and the rest of the *Sunan* with an eye for concision but he included forgeries and fell short of their reliability to the point that al-ʿAlā'ī, Ibn Ḥajar and others considered al-Dārimī's *Musnad* a better sixth for the two *Ṣaḥīḥs* and *Sunan*. Anwar Shāh al-Kashmīrī says in *Fayḍ al-Bārī* that his School is not known then he suggests he might be a Shāfiʿī in his *'Arf al-Shadhī* but Shāh Walī Allāh in the *Inṣāf* considers him a *Mujtahid*.

Imām al-Dārimī (181-250) was the peerless rival of al-Bukhārī in memorization and piety, teacher to all of the above except Aḥmad. At the news of his death al-Bukhārī hung his head and wept. He was a *Mujtahid* as per al-Dhahabī in his *Tārīkh* and

[107] Cf. al-Suyūṭī, beginning of *Zahr al-Ribā 'alā al-Mujtabā* and Ibn Kathīr in his *Ikhtiṣār 'Ulūm al-Ḥadīth*.

Shāh Walī Allāh in the *Inṣāf.* Ibn Abī Ya'lā included him in *Ṭabaqāt al-Ḥanābila* but al-Dārimī shows in his *Sunan* – also known as his *Musnad* – that he takes positions in dissent of the schools of Imām Aḥmad and Imām Mālik. Allah have mercy on all of them!

Strictness and Laxity in Ḥadīth Criticism

Mullā ʿAlī al-Qārī – Allah have mercy on him! – showed in his "Major Dictionary of Ḥadīth Forgeries" known under the two titles of *al-Mawḍūʿāt al-Kubrā* and *al-Asrār al-Marfūʿa fīl-Akhbār al-Mawḍūʿa* that many of the reports supposed by some of the authorities to be false are not forgeries at all. This is an important corrective for today's semi-educated censors that condemn many true reports as false on the false assumption that "stricter is better." They forgot that as long as the proof of forgery is unestablished beyond reasonable doubt and short of compelling assumption regarding a weak report, it becomes a lie to cry forgery and bar people from the benefit of belief in it. This holds true even if its chain of transmission falls short of the rank of "sound" (*ṣaḥīḥ*). Godfearing precaution toward the Prophet ﷺ goes both ways: not only with respect to steering clear from attributing to him what he never said or did, but also with respect to steering clear from belying what he might have said or done.

Allah Most High said, {*For the best provision is godfearing. So fear you Me, men possessed of minds!*} (2:197); and the Messenger of Allah ﷺ said in one of the wordings of the most famous mass-transmitted (*mutawātir*) ḥadīth, "Whoever attributes a lie to me or rejects something I have ordered, let him take possession of a house in Gehenna." When the *Muḥaddith* of Irāq Sirāj al-Dīn ʿUmar ibn ʿAlī al-Qazwīnī (d. 750) declared eighteen of the ḥadīths of al-Tibrīzī's *Mishkāt al-Maṣābīḥ* forged, the peerless *Ḥāfiẓ* Ibn Ḥajar al-ʿAsqalānī replied with his *Ajwiba ʿalā Risālat al-Qazwīnī*, in which he graded five to seven of the eighteen supposed forgeries "weak" (*ḍaʿīf*), nine to eleven of them "fair" (*ḥasan*), two "sound" (*ṣaḥīḥ*), and none of them forged! This anecdote is a shining illustration of the difference between half-baked ḥadīth science and the real thing.

Yet, al-Qazwīnī was a qualified *Muḥaddith*. What excuse can pseudo-scholars give? The reader may have seen them at work. They make speeches and publish censorious articles, webpages, and books on "ḥadīth forgeries" and "innovations" that resemble fiction more than *'ilm*. Nor do their manners and ethics resemble those of Muslims, let alone the small pupils of the Ulema. Rather, they are unscrupulous, unwelcome proselytes working under the glossy cover of moneyed propaganda. They clang ever so loud in ostentatious defense of the Sunna from deviation when they themselves are of dubious doctrine and unqualified even to be students of this noble art. Worst of all, they have no qualms about trying to alter the Prophetic legacy of ḥadīth and persuade the *Umma* that the Prophet ﷺ said and did other than what 1,400 years of Scholarship of the Sunna have led you to believe.

As incompetent strictness is rejected, so is ignorant laxity which consists in attributing anything and everything to the Prophet ﷺ, his Companions, the Imāms of the Law, those of the Prophetic Household, or the rest of the *Awliyā'* without any standard of honesty and accuracy in reporting.

Among the worst offenders are those that sit to preach without having paid their learning dues at the feet of the Ulema because they cannot wait for others to sit at their own feet. What matters for them is to appear to quote from authority so as to assume authority and reap its benefits. Unscrupulosity or misconceived piety among the followers of such admonishers has them drink up what they hear unconditionally as spiritual directives (*irshād*) even if it should be baseless, foolish, incoherent, even irreligious. Ignorance has reached the point where one that rightly sues for authenticity is branded as a fastidious ignoramus by the ignoramus who has no idea whether a report is in the *Ṣaḥīḥ* or in *Kalīla wa-Dimna* nor cares to check!

The above-mentioned types stand at odds with the Sunna from two opposite extremes and can be called the Laxists and the Strictists:

1. The Laxists have no idea who spoke what but insist on attributing it without the least scruple of authenticity, in the manner of story-tellers, even after it is made clear to them that they perpetuate untruths or have no proof for their discourse other than self-perpetuating tradition or unverified hearsay. As Ibn al-Mubārak ﷺ said in Muslim's *Muqaddima*, "The chain of transmission is part and parcel of the Religion, and were it not for the chain of transmission, anyone could say anything." Examples of this type are the anthropomorphists, the modernists ("progressives", feminists, secularists), some of the Sufis, and most of the general public known as the *ʿawāmm* including preachers that are neither full-fledged *ʿawāmm* nor Ulema.
2. The Strictists think it a light matter to cry lies at some of what the Messenger of Allah ﷺ might have said, pretexting forgery in blind mimicry of what they think is strictness even after they have been shown that their proofs of forgery are themselves sickly and controverted to begin with. Examples of this type are the Wahhābīs and "Salafīs" and those leaning to them.

Among the latter type are those that routinely cry forgery at the ḥadīth "My Companions are like the stars," claiming that it is "*ḍaʿīf* or *mawḍūʿ* as stated by Aḥmad ibn Ḥanbal, Ibn ʿAbd al-Barr, al-Bazzār and many others"[108] – as if *ḍaʿīf* and *mawḍūʿ* were synonyms, if only those references were not a half-lie in the first place! In reality, this ḥadīth is not forged but admissible as shown in a forthcoming volume – and from Allah comes all success.

108 www.usc.edu/dept/MSA/fundamentals/hadithsunnah/scienceofhadith/aape.html, (§15), and www.allaahuakbar.netahaadeethweak_fabricated_and_baatil_ahaadeeth.htm – an incoherent *"Salafi"* website – (both as of April, 2004) and the thoroughly irresponsible booklet titled *100 Fabricated Hadith* by an Abdullah Faisal.

Verifiable Transmission (*Isnād*) and the Sects

The Commander of the Believers, our liege-lord ʿUmar ibn al-Khaṭṭāb ﷺ was careful to prevent the dissemination of unverified knowledge – chainless knowledge – that was to proliferate after his time. He said: " Whoever finds a book containing knowledge that he did not hear from a person of learning, let him dip it in water until its ink is diluted."[109]

This hyperbolic ruling stresses the rigorous normative method in the conveyance of knowledge in Islam – encapsulated in Ibn al-Mubārak's axiom on *isnād* – and underlines, in passing, that such conveyance is personal and both oral and written because the pedigrees of books are their unbroken chains of transmission back to their authors.

Western-Minded Anti-Traditionists and Purists

In complete contrast, today, many purportedly educated Muslims – both purists and anti-traditionists – revere bookish knowledge and non-Muslim institutions of learning over and even at the exclusion of Islamic ones. They accredit Western titles and disciplines above the Islamic offices of learning and *mashyakhas*. They speak, write, read, study, teach, debate after the fashion of non-Muslims just as they may also eat, dress, marry, divorce, and die as Westerners, without a second thought other than implicit or expressed hostility at the heritage of the forerunners in the Religion of Truth (although purists have managed to trumpet the art of lip service to "The *Salaf*" into a full-fledged ideology).[110] Their approach to learning in our time is to orphan themselves of the

[109] Narrated by al-Khaṭīb, *al-Kifāya* (p. 352), al-Sakhāwī, *Fatḥ al-Mughīth* (2:153).
[110] "Qur'ān-only," feminists, Mawdūdists, and other "downgraded" neo-Muʿtazilites such as the Californian Khālid Abū al-Faḍl and, at opposite extremes, the Quṭbian Ḥizb al-Taḥrīr, Muhājirūn, Ikhwānīs, and other Islamists. They are all one in their modernist reformism and fluid reinterpretations of the Qur'ān and Sunna.

principles of the learned Muslims of previous generations – their spiritual foreparents as Imām al-Nawawī defined one's Muslim teachers in *al-Taqrīb wal-Taysīr li-Ma'rifati Sunan al-Bashīr al-Nadhīr* ﷺ. They still have *isnād* – not so much to the people of the Prophetic Way and the Muslim Congregation as to the culture of the non-Muslim world and the ideas of professors, journalists, activists, news analysts, social scientists, and, at the other end of the spectrum, Marxist-Leninists, Arab revolutionaries, nationalists, and anarchists born-again as purists. Such are the manufactured imāms that have infiltrated the ranks of Muslim leadership and pose as the very Ulema they and their followers desert and belie. The Seal and Last of all Prophets ﷺ said: "There will be, towards the end of time, Anti-Christs and arch-liars who shall discord among you."[111] A commentator of *Mishkāt al-Maṣābīḥ* said: "The Prophet ﷺ meant those that will say to the people, 'We are scholars and *shaykhs* and are calling you to the Religion' whereas, in fact, they are liars and deceivers."[112] In another ḥadīth, Ḥudhayfa ﷺ asked about the trials of the ends of time:

> "I said, 'Is there, after this good, any evil, O Messenger of Allah?' He said, 'Yes, the evil of those who call others while standing at the gates of the Fire.' I said, 'Messenger of Allah! Describe them for us.' He said, 'They are people of our complexion saying the same exhortations we do and speaking our languages.' I said, 'What are your orders for me concerning them in case this happens in my lifetime?' He said, Stick to the Congregation of the Muslims.' I said, 'What if there is no Congregation?' He said, 'Isolate yourself from those sects even if you must chew on a tree-trunk [for food], until death comes to you while you are in that state!'"[113]

[111] Narrated from Abū Hurayra by Muslim and Aḥmad.
[112] As cited in the introduction of *Misbāḥ al-Anām* by al-Ḥabīb 'Alawī ibn Aḥmad al-Ḥaddād.

Ill-Prepared Tradition-Minded Muslims

Some tradition-minded Muslims rush to the opposite extreme and emphasize supererogatory works and garb, forgetting that a servant must approach his Lord with obligatory works first – including the pursuit of necessary knowledge and truthful *naṣīḥa* to king and country. Their solution to what they rightly view as a corrupt form of Muslim consciousness is to promote a few ostensible facets of tradition out of many but they neglect the intellectual formation that underlies it. The reason for such neglect is either that their defense of tradition is not genuine or that they come to such defense unequipped.

As Imām Sufyān al-Thawrī ﵀ said, "The chain of transmission (*al-isnād*) is the weapon of the believer. Whoever has no weapon, how can he fight?"[114] So they leave the long-term formative work to others but aspire to claim its fame and receive credit for it anyway. They might even oppose those that are better prepared when they should aid them or learn from them. "There is no rarer *zuhd* than the renouncing of leadership!" (Sufyān again) All of the above shares the trappings of sectarianism and deviation.[115]

The Resulting Salad

In such a context thrive the modern types of false teaching, this one in the name of tradition, that one in the name of reform, the third one in the name of purism. The Law-bending Sufis and perennialists invoke tradition (or claim to). The tie-clad *Muʿtazilīs*

[113] Narrated from Ḥudhayfa ibn al-Yamān by al-Bukhārī and Muslim.

[114] Cf. Ibn Rajab, *Sharḥ ʿIlal al-Tirmidhī* (ʿItr ed. 1:56-62).

[115] As do the pseudo-Sufi *mudhabdhabūn* who are alternately traditional and anti-traditional depending on convenience but positively adore the West and bow to the darkest sides of its ethos, such as the Scottish Hitler-eulogizing ex-actor who calls himself "Shaykh Dr. ʿAbd al-Qādir al-Murābiṭ" cf. http://mac.abc.se/home/onesr/ez/dc/sdph_e.html. (as of March, 2005)

and other hybrid or anti-traditional havana-puffing *dā ʿīs* that curse the *Awliyā* and worship Mammon, invoke reform on the theme of a return to caliphate, or to the gold dinar, or on keeping a kennel at home and praying behind one's wife.[116] The less nescient but hypocritical, corrupt-to-the-bone purists invoke "The *Salaf*" to justify the self-immolating murder of civilians. Such types have now replaced the *murabbī* in the education of the character and the *ʿālim* in the education of the mind – to Allah we belong and to Him we return!

But if "Every Community has its Zoroastrians, every Community has its Jews, and every Community has its Christians,"[117] it remains also true that "There shall not cease to be a group in my Community who shall always overcome and stand for truth until the end of time."[118]

The Prophet ﷺ declared that victorious group invulnerable to the wrong of their enemies when he said, in another narration: "That group shall remain in charge of the Command of Allah, unharmed by those that oppose them, until the coming of the Command of Allah!"[119] In the chapter of his *Ṣaḥīḥ* in which he cites this ḥadīth, Imām al-Bukhārī states: "These are the People of Knowledge" in the sense, of course, of traditional Sunni knowledge of the Companion-*fiqh*-based Schools of Law and not the

[116] Cf. Teresa Watanabe's 2002 New York Times article on Khalid Aboul Fadl and http://www.livingislam.org/o/ftnw_e.html. Self-named "Progressives" also promote sexual permissiveness, usurious banking laws in the name of free trade, making teetotalism optional, and other endeavors to Judeo-Christianize Islam.

[117] Narrated from Sahl ibn Saʿd al-Saʿidī by al-Ṭabarānī in *al-Awsaṭ* (9:93 §9223).

[118] A mass-transmitted ḥadīth cf. al-Kattānī in *Naẓm al-Mutanāthir* (p. 141).

[119] From Muʿāwiya in al-Bukhārī and Muslim as well as from Abū Hurayra and Ibn ʿAbbās: "He for whom Allah desires great good, He grants him (superlative) understanding in the Religion (*yufaqqihhu/yufqihhu fīl-dīn*). I only distribute and it is Allah Who gives. That group shall remain in charge of the Order of Allah, unharmed by those who oppose them, until the coming of the Order of Allah." The scholars have explained that the first command in the ḥadīth is Law and Religion, while the second is the Day of Resurrection and Judgment.

orphaned, newfangled knowledge of the sects. The Prophet ﷺ also said, in praise of the latter-day generations (*al-Khalaf*):

"From every succeeding generation its upright folk shall carry this knowledge in turn. They shall repeal from it the distortions of the extremists (*taḥrīf al-ghālīn*), the misinterpretations of the ignorant (*ta'wīl al-jāhilīn*), and the pretenses of the liars (*intiḥāl al-mubṭilīn*)."

This is an authentic narration graded *ḥasan gharīb ṣaḥīḥ* by al-ʿAlāʾī in *Bughyat al-Multamis* and *ṣaḥīḥ* according to Aḥmad, Ibn ʿAbd al-Barr (per Ibn Kathīr and al-Ṣanʿānī), and Ibn al-Wazīr but *ḍaʿīf muʿḍal* according to others.[120] Narrated:

1– from Abū Hurayra ؓ by al-Ṭabarānī with two chains, one of which is fair, and by al-Khaṭīb in *Sharaf Aṣḥāb al-Ḥadīth* and *al-Jāmiʿ* with a very weak chain because of Maslama ibn ʿAlī;[121]
2– from Abū Umāma ؓ by al-ʿUqaylī with a weak chain;[122]
3– from Usāma ibn Zayd ؓ by al-Khaṭīb;[123]
4– from Abū Hurayra and ʿAbd Allah ibn ʿUmar ؓ by al-Bazzār, Tammām al-Rāzī, Ibn ʿAbd al-Barr, and al-ʿUqaylī (the latter two stating "ibn ʿAmr") with very weak chains because of ʿUmar ibn Khālid who is discarded as a narrator (*matrūk*) as indicated by al-Haythamī;[124]

---

[120] Al-ʿAlāʾī, *Bughyat al-Multamis* (p. 34-35), Ibn Kathīr, *Bidāya* (1993 Turāth ed. 10:371), al-Ṣanʿānī, *Thamarāt al-Naẓar* (p. 144), Ibn al-Wazīr, *ʿAwāṣim* (1:312), Ibn al-Mulaqqin, *Muqniʿ* (1:246), ʿAbd al-Ḥaqq al-Ishbīlī, *al-Aḥkām al-Wusṭā* (1:121), Ibn Kathīr, *Ikhtiṣār ʿUlūm al-Ḥadīth*, al-ʿIrāqī, *Taqyīd* (p. 116), and al-Bulqīnī, *Maḥāsin al-Iṣṭilāḥ* (p. 219).
[121] Al-Ṭabarānī, *Musnad al-Shāmiyyīn* (1:344) and al-Khaṭīb, *Sharaf Aṣḥāb al-Ḥadīth* (p. 28 §52) and *al-Jāmiʿ* (1991 ed. 1:193 §137=1983 ed. 1:128).
[122] Al-ʿUqaylī, *Ḍuʿafāʾ* (1:9).
[123] Al-Khaṭīb, *Sharaf Aṣḥāb al-Ḥadīth* (p. 28 §53).
[124] Ibn Ḥajar, *Mukhtaṣar Musnad al-Bazzār* (1:122 §86), Tammām al-Rāzī, *Fawāʾid* (1:350), Ibn ʿAbd al-Barr, *Tamhīd* (1:59), al-ʿUqaylī, *Ḍuʿafāʾ* (1:10), al-Haythamī (1:140).

5- from ʿAbd Allah ibn Masʿūd ﷺ – the first sentence only, and with "inherit" instead of "carry" – by al-Khaṭīb;[125]

6-9- From a number of other Companions – Abū al-Dardā', ʿAlī ibn Abī Ṭālib, Jābir ibn Samura, and Muʿādh ibn Jabal ﷺ – through weak chains as stated by Abū Nuʿaym followed by al-ʿIrāqī and al-Qārī.[126]

10- *mursal* from the Tābiʿī Abū ʿAbd al-Raḥmān Ibrāhīm ibn ʿAbd al-Raḥmān al-ʿUdhrī by al-Bayhaqī, Ibn ʿAbd al-Barr, Ibn Abī Ḥātim, Ibn Ḥibbān, and al-Khaṭīb. The latter narrates that Imām Aḥmad declared it sound (*ṣaḥīḥ*), a grading faulted by Yaḥyā ibn Saʿīd al-Qaṭṭān as cited by Ibn ʿAdī from al-Khallāl's *'Ilal*. Ibn ʿAdī then cites a chain of trustworthy narrators for it. Al-Dhahabī in the *Mīzān* states that Muʿān ibn Rifāʿa (who reports from al-ʿUdhrī) is not reliable (Ibn Ḥajar grades him *layyin*) but in *al-Mughnī* states that Ibn al-Madīnī declared him trustworthy as did Aḥmad, as also reported by al-Khaṭīb. Al-ʿIrāqī said: "This narration is missing al least two narrators (*muʿḍal*) or missing the Companion-link (*mursal*). And this Ibrāhīm, who related it without naming the Companion, is not known to relate any narration other than this."[127]

In view of al-Ṭabarānī's fair chain, Ibn ʿAdī's chain of reliable transmitters, Aḥmad and Ibn ʿAbd al-Barr's grading of *ṣaḥīḥ*, al-ʿAlā'ī's similar grading, the number of Companions related to narrate it, and the widespread acceptance of this narration among the Masters, the correct grading appears is that of "sound" (*ṣaḥīḥ*) and Allah knows best.[128]

[125] In *Sharaf Aṣḥāb al-Ḥadīth* (p. 28 §54).

[126] Al-Qārī, *Mirqāt* (1994 ed. 1:509 §248), al-Arna'ūṭ, notes on al-Ṭaḥāwī's *Sharḥ Mushkil al-Āthār* (10:18 §3884).

[127] Al-Bayhaqī, *al-Sunan al-Kubrā* (10:209 §20685-20686) and *Shuʿab al-Īmān* (10:209), Ibn ʿAbd al-Barr, *Tamhīd* (1:59), Ibn Abī Ḥātim, *al-Jarḥ wal-Taʿdīl* (2:17), Ibn Ḥibbān, *Thiqāt* (4:10), al-Khaṭīb, *Sharaf Aṣḥāb al-Ḥadīth* (p. 28-29 §52-56), Ibn ʿAdī, *Kāmil* (1:153), al-Dhahabī, *Mīzān* (1:45 §137), *Mughnī* (2:308 §6309), Ibn Ḥajar, *Taqrīb* (§6747), al-ʿIrāqī, *Taqyīd* (p. 116) and *Tabṣira* (1:298).

Imām Jamāl al-Dīn al-Ḥubayshī (712-782) said: "This narration is a proof that the Ulema of *Ahl al-Sunna* are all upright and there is no higher honor than the recommendation of the Prophet ﷺ himself!"[129]

May Allah Most High continue to raise their honor here and hereafter and bring the scheming of their detractors to nothing!

[128] Cf. also al-Harawī's *Dhamm al-Kalām* (3:294-330), *al-Bidāya* (Turāth ed. 6:287= al-Maʿārif ed. 6:258), *al-Iṣāba* (1:225), *Tadrīb al-Rāwī* (1997 ed. 2:356-357= 2:302-303) and *Kashf al-Khafā'* (§143). This is the very first ḥadīth the writer heard the late Shaykh Abd al-Qādir al-Arna'ūṭ narrate, in his study in Damascus.
[129] Al-Ḥubayshī, *Nashr Ṭay al-Taʿrīf fī Faḍl Ḥamalat al-ʿIlm al-Sharīf* (p. 40)

"Famous Ḥadīth" and "Forgery" Compilations and Mullā ʿAlī al-Qārī's Use of Them

Ḥadīth literature often treats the "forgery" genre as a subset of the "famous ḥadith" genre because forgeries are often famous sayings and vice-versa. The following is a mostly chronological, mostly descriptive list of extant works in each of these two genres followed by remarks on the critical ranking of Ibn al-Jawzī's *Mawḍūʿāt* and a brief study of al-Qārī's *al-Asrār al-Marfūʿa* – two of the most important works in the forgery genre.

Chronology of extant works in the "famous ḥadīth" genre

- Abū al-Faraj Ibn al-Jawzī (d. 597) describes his *ʿIlal al-Mutanāhiya fīl-Aḥādīth al-Wāhiya* ("The Excessive Defects in the Flimsy Reports") as a compilation of "very weak ḥadīths which some might deem not so weak and include among the fair narrations and some might deem too weak and include among the forgeries." He himself did include many of these narrations in his *Mawḍūʿāt* and vice-versa. Al-Dhahabī summarized it.
- Ibn al-Jawzī's descendent Shams al-Dīn Ibn Qayyim al-Jawziyya's (d. 751) *al-Manār al-Munīf fīl-Ṣaḥīḥ wal-Ḍaʿīf* ("The Radiant Beacon on the Sound and Weak Ḥadīth"), in which he followed many of the exaggerations of his teacher Aḥmad ibn Taymiyya (d. 728) in claiming as forged many ḥadīths that are merely weak or even established as authentic,[130] as did Marʿī

[130] Such as his disputing in *Minhāj al-Sunna* the authenticity of a mass-transmitted report from twenty-five Companions, "Anyone whose patron (*mawlā*) I am, ʿAlī is his patron"! He goes on to declare "categorically false" the addition: "O Allah! Be the patron of whoever takes him as a patron, and the enemy of whoever takes him as an enemy." However, it is also *ṣaḥīḥ*: narrated from ʿAlī and Zayd ibn Arqam by al-Ṭaḥāwī in *Mushkil al-Āthār* (5:18 §1765 *ṣaḥīḥ* per Shaykh Shuʿayb al-Arnaʾūṭ), al-Nasāʾī in his *Khaṣāʾiṣ ʿAlī* (§79) and *Faḍāʾil al-Ṣaḥāba* (§45), al-

ibn Yūsuf al-Karmī in his slim *al-Fawā'id al-Mawḍū'a fīl-Aḥādīth al-Mawḍū'a*. Al-Qārī epitomized the *Manār* at the end of the *Asrār*.

- Ibn Ḥajar's "Master, leader, teacher, benefactor, and almus pater (*mukharrijunā*)" Imam Zayn al-Dīn 'Abd al-Raḥīm ibn al-Ḥusayn al-Kurdī al-'Irāqī al-Irbilī thumma al-Miṣrī al-Shāfi'ī al-Atharī (725-806) in *al-Bā'ith 'alā al-Khalāṣ min Ḥawādith al-Quṣṣāṣ* excoriates the misuse of ḥadīth by semi-educated shaykhs and imāms and critiques the same-themed *al-Quṣṣāṣ wal-Mudhakkirīn* by Ibn al-Jawzī and *Aḥādīth al-Quṣṣāṣ* by Aḥmad ibn Taymiyya. Al-Suyūṭī recapitulates those works in *Taḥdhīr al-Khawāṣṣ min Akādhīb al-Quṣṣāṣ*.
- Al-Zarkashī's (745-794) *al-Tadhkira fīl-Aḥādīth al-Mushtahara* ("Memorial of the Famous Ḥadīths"), critiqued and expanded by
- al-Suyūṭī (d. 911) in *al-Durar al-Manthūra fīl-Aḥādīth al-Mashhūra* ("The Scattered Pearls Concerning the Famous Ḥadīths"), also titled *al-Durar al-Muntathira fīl-Aḥādīth al-Mushtaharā*; he was outdone by his great contemporary and rival
- al-Sakhāwī (d. 902) with his most influential, meticulous, and comprehensive *al-Maqāṣid al-Ḥasana fīl-Aḥādīth al-Mushtahara* ("The Excellent Objectives Concerning the Famous Ḥadīths"), al-Qārī's principal source although he also cites the previous two frequently. Al-Sakhāwī may have built on
- *al-La'ālī' al-Manthūra fīl-Aḥādīth al-Mashhūra mimmā Alifahu al-Ṭab' wa-Laysa lahu Aṣlun fīl-Shar'* by his teacher the peerless arch-Master Ibn Ḥajar al-'Asqalānī (d. 852).

Ḥākim (3:109) who declared it sound, and al-Ṭabarānī (§4969); Zayd or Abū Sarīḥa by al-Tirmidhī (*ḥasan gharīb*); and Abū al-Ṭufayl by Aḥmad in his *Musnad* (al-Arna'ūṭ ed. 2:262-263 §950-952 *ṣaḥīḥ lighayrih*), al-Bazzār (§2541), al-Nasā'ī in *al-Sunan al-Kubrā* (5:132-134), *Khaṣā'iṣ 'Alī* (p. 107-108), and *Musnad 'Alī* as well as al-Ḥākim (3:371). On Ibn Taymiyya's exaggerations see Ibn Ḥajar, *Lisān al-Mīzān* (6:319) and *Durar* (2:71), al-Lacknawī, *Raf'* (p. 330), *al-Ajwibat al-'Ashara* (p. 174-176), *Tuḥfat al-Kamala* in the *Raf'* (p. 198-199 n.), and al-Kawtharī's still-manuscript *al-Ta'aqqub al-Ḥathīth limā Yanfīhi Ibnu Taymiyyata min al-Ḥadīth*.

- The *Maqāṣid* was abridged by [1] al-Suyūṭī's student the erudite Mālikī Shādhilī *Faqīh* of Egypt Abū al-Ḥasan ʿAlī ibn Muḥammad al-Minnawfī (857-939) in *al-Wasā'il al-Sunniyya min al-Maqāṣid al-Sakhāwiyya wal-Jāmiʿ wal-Zawā'id al-Asyūṭiyya*, apparently also known as *al-Durrat al-Lāmiʿa fī Bayān Kathīr min al-Aḥādīth al-Shā'iʿa*.[131] Al-Qārī often refers to his work under the cryptic title of *al-Mukhtaṣar*.
- [2] al-Sakhāwī's student Ibn al-Daybaʿ (866-944) in *Tamyīz al-Ṭayyib min al-Khabīth fīmā Yadūru ʿalā Alsinat al-Nās min al-Ḥadīth* ("Distinguishing the Good from the Wicked among the Ḥadīths that are Circulating among the People");
- [3] al-Shaʿrānī (d. 973) in *al-Badr al-Munīr fī Gharīb Aḥādīth al-Bashīr al-Nadhīr* ﷺ in which he added selections from al-Suyūṭī's *Jāmiʿ al-Kabīr*, his *Jāmiʿ al-Ṣaghīr*, and its *Zawā'id* totalling 2,300 ḥadīths;
- [4] al-Zarqānī (1055-1122) - named by Abū Ghudda "the Seal of the Scholars of ḥadīth"[132] - in his *Mukhtaṣar al-Maqāṣid* ("Abridgment of the 'Excellent Intentions'").
- The Shāfiʿī Sharīf *Musnid* of Damascus Najm al-Dīn Muḥammad ibn Muḥammad al-Ghazzī al-ʿĀmirī (d. 984) in *Itqān Mā Yaḥsun min Bayān al-Akhbār al-Dā'irati ʿalāl-Alsun* gathered together al-Zarkashī's *Tadhkira*, al-Suyūṭī's *Durar*, and the *Maqāṣid* with some additions.
- ʿIzz al-Dīn Muḥammad ibn Aḥmad al-Khalīlī (d. 1057) authored *Kashf al-Iltibās fīmā Khafya ʿalā Kathīr min al-Nās*. This title may have inspired
- the Sufi Damascene Seal of the Imāms of Ḥadīth Abū al-Fidā' Ismāʿīl ibn Muḥammad al-Jarrāḥī al-ʿAjlūnī (1087-1162) with *Kashf al-Khafā wa-Muzīl al-Albās ʿammā Ishtahara min al-*

[131] This is not by Aḥmad ibn Muḥammad al-Minnawfī as erroneously thought by Muḥammad Bashīr Ẓāfir in *Taḥdhīr al-Muslimīn min al-Aḥādīth al-Mawḍūʿa*.
[132] In Abū Ghudda's marginalia on al-Qārī's *Maṣnūʿ* (p. 87).

Aḥādīth 'alā Alsinat al-Nās ("The Removal of Secrecy and Doubts Regarding the Famous Ḥadīths People Often Say"), a work second to fame only to the *Maqāṣid* in which he abridged the latter and added notes from various other works.

- The Yemenī qāḍī Ibn Jār Allah al-Ṣaʿdī (d. 1181) in *al-Nawāfiḥ al-'Aṭira fil-Aḥādīth al-Mushtahara* gathered together al-Suyūṭī's *Durar*, Ibn al-Daybaʿ and al-Zarqānī's abridgments, and his own many additions.
- *Asnā al-Maṭālib fī Aḥādītha Mukhtalifati al-Marātib* by Muḥammad ibn Darwīsh al-Ḥūt al-Bayrūtī.

Chronology of extant works devoted to forgery classification

- *Tadhkirat al-Ḥuffāẓ*, also known as *Tadhkirat al-Mawḍūʿāt*, by the Malāmatī ascetic and pious examplar of the traveling scholars, the *Ḥāfiẓ* Abū al-Faḍl Muḥammad ibn Ṭāhir ibn ʿAlī al-Maqdisī al-Qaysarānī al-Atharī al-Ẓāhirī al-Ṣūfī known as Ibn Ṭāhir (448-507). Apparently the earliest systematic digest of forgeries, it is unreliably severe due to its uncritical imitation of Ibn Ḥibbān's rulings in his *Ḍuʿafā'* and other overly stringent sources.[133]
- *Al-Abāṭīl wal-Manākīr wal-Ṣiḥāḥ wal-Mashāhīr* by al-Ḥusayn ibn Ibrāhīm al-Jawzaqānī or Jawraqānī (d. 543). Al-Dhahabī says he "benefited from it although it contains mistakes" while Ibn Ḥajar in his *Nukat 'alā Ibn al-Ṣalāḥ* said the author filled it with wrong rulings because of his inability to reconcile with what is incontrovertibly authentic the narrations that appeared, to him, to contradict the Sunna in the same manner as Ibn Ḥibbān.[134] Al-Dhahabī summarized it.

[133] Pointed out by al-Lacknawī, *al-Rafʿ*, Aḥmad al-Ghumārī, *Dar'*, and others.
[134] Cf. Abū Ghudda, marginalia on al-Lacknawī's *Rafʿ* (p. 321), al-Ghumārī, *Dar'* (p. 41-43).

- Ibn al-Jawzī's *al-Mawḍūʿāt al-Kubrā*, one of the largest, most influential, and least reliable encyclopedias of forgeries compiled from the four great early books of weak-narrator criticism – Ibn ʿAdī's *Kāmil* and Ibn Ḥibbān, al-ʿUqaylī, and al-Azdī's *Ḍuʿafāʾ* – in addition to Ibn Mardūyah's *Tafsīr*, al-Ṭabarānī's three *Muʿjams*, al-Dāraquṭnī's *Afrād*, al-Ḥākim's *Tārīkh*, al-Jawzaqānī's *Abāṭīl*, and the luxuriant, collected works of al-Khaṭīb, Ibn Shāhīn, and Abū Nuʿaym. Al-Dhahabī and Ibn Dirbās summarized it among others. Like the *Abāṭīl*, Ibn al-Jawzī's *Mawḍūʿāt* was faulted by the Ulema for its abundant flaws, especially Ibn Ḥajar and his student al-Suyūṭī who followed up with no less than four critiques (see below, paragraph on al-Suyūṭī and section on "The Status of Ibn al-Jawzī's *Mawḍūʿāt*").
- Ḍyāʾ al-Dīn Abū Ḥafṣ ʿUmar ibn Badr ibn Saʿīd al-Mawṣilī al-Ḥanafī's (557-622) thoroughly unreliable *al-Mughnī ʿan al-Ḥifẓi wal-Kitābi bi-Qawlihim Lam Yaṣiḥḥa Shayʾun fī Hādhā al-Bāb* in which he tried to compile all that the early Imāms had graded unsound into a forgery reference-book but failed according to al-Lacknawī, Abū Ghudda, and others before them such as Sirāj al-Dīn Ibn al-Mulaqqīn who rewrote a critical summary of his book; al-Suyūṭī as per his dismissal of the book in *Tadrīb al-Rāwī*; Ḥusām al-Dīn al-Maqdisī in *Intiqād al-Mughnī ʿan al-Ḥifẓi wal-Kitāb* which is in reality an epitome culled from *al-Tankīt wal-Ifāda* by Ibn Himmāt (see below); and Abū Isḥāq Ḥijāzī ibn Muḥammad ibn Sharīf al-Juwaynī al-Atharī who wrote *Faṣl al-Khiṭāb bi-Naqdi Kitāb al-Mughnī ʿan al-Ḥifẓi wal-Kitāb* – in print – in which he said that his own teacher Ḥāmid ibn Ibrāhīm ibn Aḥmad also wrote a refutation of the *Mughnī ʿan al-Ḥifẓ*.

- The Ḥanafī Lahore-born philologist of Baghdād Raḍī al-Dīn Ḥasan ibn Muḥammad al-ʿUmarī al-Ṣaghānī or al-Ṣāghānī's (d. 650) unreliably strict *Mawḍūʿāt Shihāb al-Akhbār lil-Quḍāʿī* – critiqued by Imām Zayn al-Dīn al-ʿIrāqī with his *Radd ʿalā al-Ṣaghānī fīl-Aḥādīth al-Mawḍūʿati fī Shihāb al-Akhbār* and, more recently, by Shaykh ʿAbd al-ʿAzīz al-Ghumārī in *al-Tahānī fīl-Taʿqīb ʿalā Mawḍūʿāt al-Ṣaghānī*; it may be an abridgment of his earlier *al-Durr al-Multaqaṭ fī Tabyīn al-Ghalaṭ wa-Nafī al-Laghaṭ*. Al-Qārī cites him often.
- Ibn al-Qayyim's *Naqd al-Manqūl wal-Miḥakk al-Mumayyiz bayn al-Mardūd wal-Maqbūl* in which he lists over two hundred ḥadīths that he considers forgeries from the perspective of content to begin, before considering the chains of transmission.
- The epilogue to the lexicographer Majd al-Dīn al-Fayrūzābādī's (d. 817) *Sifr al-Saʿāda* is also unreliably strict in its careless inclusion of non-forgeries and his imitation of Ibn Badr al-Mawṣilī as per al-Kattānī in the *Risāla Mustaṭrafa*, as shown by its critique *al-Tankīt wal-Ifāda fī Takhrīj Aḥādīth Khātimat Sifr al-Saʿāda* by Ibn Himmāt Shams al-Dīn Muḥammad ibn Ḥasan al-Dimashqī (1091-1175), ʿAbd al-Ḥaqq al-Dihlawī's *Sharḥ Sifr al-Saʿāda*, and al-Lacknawī's *Tuḥfat al-Kamala ʿalā Ḥawāshī Tuḥfat al-Ṭalaba*. Al-Qārī infrequently cites the *Sifr*.
- *Al-Ghummāz ʿalā al-Lummāz fīl-Mawḍūʿāt al-Mashhūrāt* by the Cairene Shāfiʿī Ḥasanī historian of Madīna Abū al-Ḥasan Nūr al-Dīn ʿAlī ibn ʿAbd Allāh ibn Aḥmad al-Samhūdī (844-911) which contains 340 entries with all-too-sparse rulings of one word or one line such as "weak," "weak-chained," etc.
- Al-Suyūṭī's four correctives on Ibn al-Jawzī: *al-Nukat al-Badīʿiyyāt ʿalā al-Mawḍūʿāt*; its abridgment *al-Taqṣībāt ʿalā al-Mawḍūʿāt*, known as the *Taʿaqqubāt*; *al-Laʾāliʾ al-Maṣnūʿa fīl-Aḥādīth al-Mawḍūʿa* in which he reviews all Ibn al-Jawzī's

entries; and its appendix *Dhayl al-Mawḍūʿāt*, the latter two frequently cited by al-Qārī who shares with al-Suyūṭī and Ibn ʿArrāq a lenient approach toward authenticating suspected reports. The *La'ālī'* was summarized by al-Zarqānī's student the centenarian Mālikī Sufi *Musnid* Abū al-Ḥasan al-Ḥurayshī (d. 1143).

- The great Shāfiʿī Damascene *Ḥāfiẓ* of Ṣāliḥiyya and author of the largest extant *Sīra*, Shams al-Dīn Muḥammad ibn Yūsuf ibn ʿAlī al-Shāmī's (d. 942) *al-Fawā'id al-Majmūʿa fīl-Aḥādīth al-Mawḍūʿa*.
- *Tanzīh al-Sharīʿati al-Marfūʿa ʿan al-Aḥādīth al-Shanīʿati al-Mawḍūʿa*, the best work in the genre according to our teacher Nūr al-Dīn ʿItr, by Imām Abū al-Ḥasan Saʿd al-Dīn ʿAlī ibn Muḥammad ibn ʿAlī ibn ʿAbd al-Raḥmān al-Kinānī, known as Ibn ʿArrāq (907-963), the Beiruti, Damascene, then Madīnan Shāfiʿī *faqīh*, expert in the canonical readings and inheritance laws, litterateur, and Akbarī Sufi who made coffee-drinking the fashion in Damascus although his erudite *faqīh* and *muqri'* father vehemently disapproved of it. He incorporated all al-Suyūṭī's corrections with Ibn al-Jawzī's entries in the *Mawḍūʿāt* and *ʿIlal*, adding his own critical supercommentary on both authors and including rulings from Ibn Dirbās, al-Dhahabī (his *Mīzān* and summaries of Ibn al-Jawzī and al-Jawzaqānī), al-ʿIrāqī (his *Amālī* and documentation of al-Ghazzālī's *Iḥyā'*), and Ibn Ḥajar (*Takhrīj al-Kashshāf, al-Talkhīṣ al-Ḥabīr, Tasdīd al-Qaws, Zahr al-Firdaws, al-Maṭālib al-ʿĀliya,* and *Lisān al-Mīzān*). He begins his book by listing the names of over two thousand established or suspected forgers (well over double Burhān al-Dīn al-Ḥalabī's (d. 841) 880 entries in a*l-Kashf al-Ḥathīth ʿamman Rumiya bi-Waḍʿ al-Ḥadīth)*. Al-Qārī shows no knowledge of this book.

- *Tadhkirat al-Mawḍūʿāt* by the Indian Jamāl al-Dīn Muḥammad Ṭāhir al-Ṣiddīqī al-Hindī al-Fattanī (d. 986) who also authored *Qānūn al-Mawḍūʿāt fī Dhikr al-Ḍuʿafā' wal-Waḍḍāʿīn*, both apparently unknown to al-Qārī.
- Al-Qārī's (d. 1014) major book of forgeries *al-Asrār al-Marfūʿa fil-Akhbār al-Mawḍūʿa*, known as *al-Mawḍūʿāt al-Kubrā*, and his minor book of forgeries titled *al-Maṣnūʿ fī Maʿrifat al-Ḥadīth al-Mawḍūʿ* – an earlier work known as the *Mawḍūʿāt al-Ṣughrā*.
- Al-Karmī's (d. 1033) unremarkable *al-Fawā'id al-Mawḍūʿa* which we mentioned in the previous section.
- Al-Saffārīnī (d. 1188) large *al-Durar al-Maṣnūʿāt fil-Aḥādīth al-Mawḍūʿāt*, an abridgment of Ibn al-Jawzī's *Mawḍūʿāt*.
- Al-Shawkānī's (d. 1250) *al-Fawā'id al-Majmūʿa fil-Aḥādīth al-Mawḍūʿa* which ranks with Ibn Ṭāhir, al-Jawzaqānī, Ibn al-Jawzī, al-Ṣaghānī, and al-Fayrūzābādī's works in its careless and uncritically imitative inclusion of non-forged and even *ṣaḥīḥ* and *ḥasan* reports among the forgeries according to al-Lacknawī in *Ẓafar al-Amānī*.
- *Al-Lu'lu' al-Marṣūʿ fīmā lā Aṣla lahu aw bi-aṣlihi Mawḍūʿ* by the Seal of Ḥadīth Scholars, our great-great GrandShaykh, the octogenarian Sufi *Musnid* of *Shām* and erudite expert in the Science of *isnād* Abū al-Maḥāsin Muḥammad ibn Khalīl al-Mashīshī al-Ḥasanī al-Qāwuqjī al-Ṭarābulsī (1224-1305) with 742 all-too-brief one-line entries.[135]
- Other recent works such as Imām ʿAbd al-Ḥayy Muḥammad ʿAbd al-Ḥalīm al-Lacknawī's (d. 1304) *al-Āthār al-Marfūʿa fī al-Akhbār al-Mawḍūʿa*; the two-volume *al-Kashf al-Ilāhī ʿan Shadīd al-Ḍaʿf wal-Mawḍūʿ wal-Wāhī* by Muḥammad ibn Muḥammad al-Ḥusaynī al-Ṭarābulsī al-Sandarūsī; *Taḥdhīr al-*

[135] Per its nice 1415/1994 edition at Dār al-Bashā'ir al-Islāmiyya by Fawwāz Aḥmad Zamarlī.

Muslimīn min al-Aḥādīth al-Mawḍūʿa ʿalā Sayyid al-Mursalīn ﷺ by Muḥammad al-Bashīr Ẓāfir al-Mālikī al-Azharī (d. 1325); the 2,000-folio *Jamʿ al-Aḥādīth al-Mawḍūʿa al-Muttafaq ʿalayhā wal-Mukhtalaf fīhā ʿalā Tartīb Muʿjam al-Ḥurūf* by ʿAdnān ʿAbd al-Raḥmān Barlādī; *al-Nukhbat al-Bahiyya fīl Aḥādīth al-Makdhūba ʿalā Khayr al-Bariyya* ﷺ by the Egyptian Mālikī *musnid* Abū ʿAbd Allah Muḥammad ibn Muḥammad known as al-Amīr al-Kabīr; and *al-Jidd al-Ḥathīth fī Bayān Mā Laysa bi-Ḥadīth* by Aḥmad ibn ʿAbd al-Karīm al-ʿĀmirī al-Ghazzī. Allah reward their efforts well!

The Status of Ibn al-Jawzī's *Mawḍūʿāt*

Ibn al-Ṣalāḥ said of Ibn al-Jawzī: "A contemporary that gathered together the forgeries in about two volumes went too far and included in them much that can never be proven to be a forgery and that should rather have been cited among the merely weak ḥadīths."[136]

The arch-Master of Ḥadīth (*Amīr al-Muʾminīn fil-Ḥadīth*), known as the absolute Shaykh al-Islām in the books of its Science, Imām Aḥmad ibn Ḥajar al-ʿAsqalānī, said in his *Qawl al-Musaddad* of al-Ḥākim's *Mustadrak* and Ibn al-Jawzī's *Mawḍūʿāt* that they each contained enough mistakes to make their general usefulness nil for other than specialists, hence, neither al-Ḥākim's ruling of *ṣaḥīḥ* [in the *Mustadrak*] nor Ibn al-Jawzī's ruling of *mawḍūʿ* [in the *Mawḍūʿāt*] should be relied upon without double-checking with someone else.

The *Mustadrak* contains about one hundred forgeries per al-Suyūṭī's *Taʿaqqubāt* as quoted by al-Kattānī in the *Risāla Mustaṭrafa* while the *Mawḍūʿāt* contains no less than three hundred erroneous entries as stated by al-Suyūṭī at the end of his *Taʿaqqubāt*! Ibn Ḥajar said: "He [Ibn al-Jawzī] has [wrongly]

[136] Ibn al-Ṣalāḥ, *ʿUlūm al-Ḥadīth*, chapter on the *Mawḍūʿ*.

included in his book of forgeries the *munkar* and weak ḥadīths that are acceptable in morals (*al-targhīb wal-tarhīb*) and a few fair ḥadīths as well, like the ḥadīth of *Ṣalāt al-Tasābīḥ* and that of reciting *Āyat al-Kursī* after the prayer, which is *ṣaḥīḥ*.... As for weak ḥadīths in absolute terms, there are many in his book.... Ibn al-Jawzī has another book titled *al-'Ilal al-Mutanāhiya fīl Aḥādīth al-Wāhiya* in which he cited many forgeries, just as he cited many merely flimsy reports in his book of forgeries. Yet, he incorrectly left out [from each book] ḥadīths of both kinds to the amount or more than what he did include!" [137]

Al-Dhahabī, al-Suyūṭī, Aḥmad al-Ghumārī, and Abū Ghudda said that Ibn al-Jawzī was fooled by the rejection of certain chains for certain ḥadīths in the books of narrator-criticism and took this to mean the ḥadīth itself was forged because of his ignorance of the *matn* and his failure to research it.[138]

In addition, Ibn al-Jawzī ignored his own rulings by including a large proportion of forgeries in his exhortative works.

Shaykh ʿAbd al-Fattāḥ Abū Ghudda said: "Our reliance is on Allah! Ibn al-Jawzī composed a great big book on ḥadīth forgeries so that jurists, preachers, and others may avoid them, then you will see him cite in his exhortative works forged hadīths and rejected stories without head nor tail, without shame or second thought. In the end one feels that Ibn al-Jawzī is two people and not one!... For this reason Ibn al-Athīr blamed him in his history entitled *al-Kāmil* with the words: 'Ibn al-Jawzī blamed him [al-Ghazzālī] for many things, among them his narration of unsound hadīths in his exhortations. O wonder that Ibn al-Jawzī should criticize him for that! For his own books and exhortative works are crammed full with them!' "[139] And the ḥadīth Master al-

[137] In *al-Nukat 'alā Ibn al-Ṣalāḥ* (2:848-850).

[138] Al-Dhahabī, cited in al-Suyūṭī's *Tadrīb* (1:329, chapter on the *mawḍūʿ*); al-Suyūṭī, *La'āli'* (1:106=1:117); Aḥmad al-Ghumārī, *al-Muthnawnī wal-Battār* (1:172) and *Dar'* (p. 91-95); Abū Ghudda, marginalia on al-Lacknawī's *Rafʿ* (p. 325-327).

Sakhāwī said in *Sharḥ al-Alfiyya*: 'Ibn al-Jawzī cited forgeries and their likes in high abundance in his exhortative works.'"[140]

Among the book-length critiques of Ibn al-Jawzī's failings in the *Mawḍūʿāt* is a work by Shaykh Muḥammad Ṣibghat Allah al-Madrāsī.

Al-Qārī's Major Dictionary of Forgeries

Al-Qārī's *al-Asrār al-Marfūʿa fil Akhbār al-Mawḍūʿa* is the second and, with 625 entries, the largest of two compilations he devoted to forgeries, the second being the earlier *al-Maṣnūʿ fī Maʿrifat al-Ḥadīth al-Mawḍūʿ* with 417 much sparser entries. The *Asrār* expands on the *Maṣnūʿ* both in the number of entries and in the treatment al-Qārī devotes to many of them. The all-too-small number of these entries is explained by the fact that the last part of the *Asrār* refers to many more forgeries obliquely, without devoting separate entries to them, by way of summarizing and commenting on Ibn al-Qayyim's *al-Manār al-Munīf.*

Al-Qārī devoted himself to *fiqh*, particularly *Ḥanafī* jurisprudence, and did not attain the rank of *Ḥāfiẓ* like his two principal sources, al-Sakhāwī and Ibn al-Qayyim. He shows no knowledge of some of the important early and late works on forgeries such as Ibn Ṭāhir al-Maqdisī's *Tadhkirat al-Mawḍūʿāt*, al-Jawzaqānī's *Abāṭīl*, Ibn ʿArrāq's *Tanzīh al-Sharīʿa*, and al-Fattanī's *Tadhkirat al-Mawḍūʿāt.*

Like his sources, al-Qārī often refers a ḥadīth to the *Iḥyā'*, one of the most acclaimed books in Islam which nevertheless contains a sizeable proportion of very weak or forged narrations.[141]

[139] Ibn al-Athīr, *al-Kāmil fil-Tārīkh* (Dār Ṣādir ed. 10:228=ʿIlmiyya ed. 9:240).

[140] ʿAbd al-Fattāḥ Abū Ghudda, notes to al-Lacknawī's *Rafʿ* (p. 420-421).

[141] Ibn al-Subkī and al-ʿIrāqī provided thorough documentations of those narrations and stressed that al-Ghazzālī did not excel in the field of ḥadīth cf. *Ṭabaqāt al-Shāfiʿiyya al-Kubrā* (6:287-389). For various reasons certain Mālikīs such as al-Ṭurṭūshī and al-Māzarī and Ḥanbalīs such as Ibn al-Jawzī and Ibn Taymiyya

Al-Qārī is lenient in his gradings and follows the criterion of many of the *Salaf* who retained chains missing a *Tābiʿī* link in narrations of merits (*faḍā'il, manāqib*) as in the ḥadīth Ibn Saʿd and Imām Aḥmad narrated from ʿĀ'isha ﷺ: "Three things of the world pleased the Messenger of Allah ﷺ: women, perfume, and food. He got two but missed one – he got women and perfume but missed food."

Al-Qārī said, "al-Suyūṭī said of this ḥadīth, 'Its chain is sound except that one transmitter was not named.' So then, its chain becomes fair."

He tends to authenticate the ḥadīths more than disauthenticate them and, in both cases, does not always hit the mark. The reason for this is that he takes certain assumptions as axioms and follows then consistently in his book when they are inaccurate to begin with. Among the examples for these methodological flaws are the following:

1. Al-Qārī's assumption that if a ḥadīth is cited by Imām al-Suyūṭī in *al-Jāmiʿ al-Ṣaghīr* it must necessarily not be forged because the latter made it his pre-condition for including it in the *Jāmiʿ*. This overlooks the possibility that al-Suyūṭī is not infallible in this and it is a fact that he fell short of his precondition and did include forgeries by the hundreds according to Aḥmad al-Ghumārī in *al-Mughīr 'alā al-Aḥādīth al-Mawḍūʿati fil-Jāmiʿ al-Ṣaghīr* ("The Raider on the Forgeries Contained in the *Jāmiʿ al-Ṣaghīr*").[142] (Al-Suyūṭī himself in the *La'ālī* makes the same false axiomatic assumption about any and all ḥadīths narrated

exaggerated the proportion of forgeries in the *Iḥyā'*. Two Ḥanafī ḥadīth Masters wrote superb documentations of its ḥadīths – Ibn Quṭlūbaghā and Murtaḍā al-Zabīdī – while the Damascene Muḥammad Amīn al-Suwaydī (d. 1246) compiled *al-Mawḍūʿāt fil-Iḥyā'*, also known as *al-Iʿtibār fī Ḥaml al-Asfār*.

[142] See also *al-Aḥādīth al-Mawḍūʿa min al-Jāmiʿ al-Kabīr wal-Jāmiʿ al-Azhar lil-Suyūṭī wal-Munāwī* by ʿAbbās Aḥmad Ṣaqr and Aḥmad ʿAbd al-Jawād.

by al-Bayhaqī in any of his books on the basis of al-Bayhaqī's identical purported criterion, as illustrated in al-Qārī's entry "The believer's heart is sweet, he loves sweetness.")

2. His axiom that the *mursal* is a proof for the *Jumhūr* and not just the *Fuqahā'*. See on this Shaykh Shu'ayb al-Arna'ūṭ's detailed survey of the views of the *Salaf* on this issue in his introduction to Abū Dāwūd's *Marāsīl*.
3. His idiosyncratic use of the term *thābit* to mean a ḥadīth that merely has a chain of transmission (*aṣl*) when in fact *thābit* is used by the scholars of ḥadīth as a synonym for *ṣaḥīḥ* as are *qawī* and *jayyid*.[143]
4. Similarly, al-Qārī understands *lā yathbut* to mean *lā aṣla lahu* when it means *lā yaṣiḥḥ*. In a *fiqhī* discussion *lā yathbut* and *lā yaṣiḥḥ* mean that the ḥadīth falls short of the rank of *ṣaḥīḥ* but in a ḥadīthic discussion of forgeries such terms mean the ḥadīth is forged.
5. His unheard-of assumption that it suffices for a ḥadīth to have a chain of transmission to preclude that it be forged.
6. His assumption that it suffices for a ḥadīth to be cited by one of the Daylamīs – father and son – (in the *Firdaws* or its documentation the *Musnad al-Firdaws*) to have an *aṣl* even if it is chainless.
7. He follows al-Zarkashī, Ibn 'Arrāq, and others in their misunderstanding of the term "inauthentic" (*lā yaṣiḥḥ*) to allow that a ḥadīth is not necessarily forged whereas in discussions of forgeries and strictly ḥadīthic, non-*fiqh* literature that term is strictly synonymous with "forged," "baseless," and other such descriptions used by the Masters in the books specifically devoted to forgeries as demonstrated by Abū Ghudda in his introduction to the *Maṣnū'* and elsewhere.

[143] Cf. the end of the chapter on the *ṣaḥīḥ* in Dr. 'Itr's *Manhaj al-Naqd*.

These flaws are illustrated in the following entries among many others:
- The entry for the saying, "Whoever plays chess is cursed" contains three major inaccuracies: the claim that the *mursal* is a proof for the *Jumhūr*; the deduction that a ḥadīth is not a forgery merely on the basis that al-Suyūṭī cites it in *al-Jāmiʿ al-Ṣaghīr*; and the claim that there are firmly-established ḥadīths blaming chess.
- The entry for the saying "To look at a beautiful face is worship" contains the claim that since al-Suyūṭī cites the saying, "Looking at a beautiful woman and greenery strengthens eyesight" in *al-Jāmiʿ al-Ṣaghīr*, it follows that it is not forged.
- The entry for the saying, "The traveller and his money are at risk." Al-Qārī states that "al-Daylamī narrates it from Abū Hurayra ؓ, from the Prophet ﷺ chainless," only to conclude, "So then, it is established and not forged"!
- The entry: "Whoever receives a present while he has company, the latter are his partners in it" where he says: "Ibn al-Jawzī wrongly included it in the *Mawḍūʿāt* since ʿAbd ibn Ḥumayd narrates it from Ibn ʿAbbās [ؓ] and others from ʿĀisha [ؓ]"!
- In the entry, "Whoever circumambulates this House seven times, prays two *rakʿas* behind the Station of Ibrāhīm, and drinks Zamzam water, all his sins shall be forgiven as many as they may be" al-Qārī cites al-Sakhāwī's ruling of *lā yaṣiḥḥ*, i.e. forged, but al-Qārī goes on,

> "Al-Sakhāwī's statement that the ḥadīth is inauthentic does not preclude its being weak or fair unless he meant to convey that it is unestablished (*lā yathbutu*). It seems al-Minnawfī understood the latter since he says, in his *Mukhtaṣar* [of al-Sakhāwī's *Maqāṣid*], 'It is a falsehood (*bāṭil*) without basis (*lā aṣla lahu*).'"

In reality both al-Sakhāwī and al-Minnawfī are asserting the same thing, namely, that the ḥadīth is forged; but al-Qārī follows two of his idiosyncrasies: first, he misunderstands al-Sakhāwī's statement to mean other than "forged"; second, he uses the terms "unestablished" and "without basis" indifferently.
– The entry, "The white rooster is my friend and the friend of my friend and the enemy of my enemy" where al-Qārī positively affirms that it is not forged without forwarding any proof.

Al-Qārī often discusses what he might call "sound meaning regardless of Prophetic authenticity"; this lengthens his text but improves its didactic benefits at the expense of ḥadīthic sharpness. For even if the Prophetic Ḥadīth is Divinely-revealed and incomparable to the rest of human discourse, it is not a precondition that a saying must be spoken by the Prophet ﷺ to be beneficial to humankind or *Sharīʿa*-worthy of discussion, explanation, and even recommendation.[144] Benefits are found in the sayings of the Companions and Successors, the Imāms of *fiqh*, the Sufis, the Israelite reports, the ancient philosophers and physicians, etc. As related the Holy Prophet ﷺ and from our liege-lord ʿAlī ibn Abī Ṭālib ؓ, "Wisdom is the lost property of the believer, wherever he finds it he has the right to take it."[145] Similarly, Imām Aḥmad said, "I seldom look into a book except I benefit." Hence al-Qārī's very frequent remark that a ḥadīth may be "baseless" (*lā aṣla lahu*) or "untrue (*ghayr ṣaḥīḥ*) in its phrasing (*mabnā*) or wording (*lafẓ*) but true (*ṣaḥīḥ*) in its meaning (*maʿnā*)."

---

[144] At the same time, our Sufi Masters tell us that not one single good teaching reaches us except it was revealed to and transmitted by our Prophet ﷺ first, whether in, before, or after his time as Imām al-Būṣīrī said in the *Burda*: "And each without exception takes from the Messenger of Allah ﷺ", while Shaykh Yūsuf al-Nabhānī said in *Saʿādat al-Dārayn*: "And every single favor in creation comes from Allah to him ﷺ, and from him to everything else."

[145] Narrated from Abū Hurayra from the Prophet ﷺ by al-Tirmidhī, Ibn Mājah and others; and as a saying of several Companions.

He takes this interesting stance notably when he discusses famous Sufi ḥadīths such as "I was a Treasure unknown..." and "Whoever knows himself knows his Lord" but also in many other entries such as "Among you women are those that spend half their lives not praying!"; "The Arabs are the leaders of the non-Arabs"; "The believer speaks truth and believes what he is told"; "The believer's back is a *qibla*"; "The best worship is the hardest one"; the wording, "when there was no Ādam nor water nor clay" in the entry, "I was a Prophet when Ādam was still between water and clay"; etc. This method also connects the meanings contained in those forgeries to firmly-established evidence from the Qur'ān and the Sunna as in the entry, "The believer is vulnerable and the disbeliever is covered" in which al-Qārī says:

> "Not a ḥadīth but its meaning is that a believer is exposed to tribulations as atonement for his sins while the disbeliever is safe from them and basks in prosperity so that his sins remain with him forever. Further, 'The world is the prison of the believer and the Paradise of the disbeliever.'"

Al-Qārī identifies the entry "the human devils surpass the *jinni* devils" as a saying of Mālik ibn Dīnār but goes on to link it to a Qur'anic verse and elucidates its benefits in typically exquisite fashion:

> "Its meaning may have been inferred from the saying of Allah Most High, {*Thus have We appointed unto every Prophet an adversary – devils of humankind and jinn*} (6:112), since He first mentioned the human devils before the *jinni* devils. This is also because the whispering of the *jinni* devil goes away upon one's taking refuge in Allah, contrary to the human Satans, and because the influence of the latter's company is heightened by the fact they share the same species with human beings."

Al-Qārī shines even when he is wrong. In the entry "A pious son makes the best husband" (*al-barru abarru bi-ahlih*), he misunderstands *barr* as "dry land" instead of "pious son" but typically investigates meaning to build an elaborate explanation on the basis of his misunderstanding (cf. entry, "Land is kindest to its own sons and daughters"):

> "It might be taken from the fact that land is mentioned before the sea in the verse {*He it is Who makes you to go on the land and the sea*} (10:22) and from the saying of the Most High, {*Have We not made the earth a receptacle both for the living and the dead*} (77:25-26), meaning, it embraces them the way a mother embraces her children, as indicated by the saying of the Most High, {*Thereof We created you and thereunto We return you*} (20:55)."

As a well-rounded work of general Muslim culture replete with doctrine, jurisprudence, sufism, philology, wit, and poetry, the *Asrār* is more interesting than any other manual of the forgery genre before it. Allah have mercy on its author and all our learned predecessors!

The "Disclaimed" - *Munkar* - Ḥadīth

Definitions

The *munkar* is similar to the *shādhdh* in that each of them describes a truly singular narration - one that comes only through X - hence its abnormality or aberrant quality (*shudhūdh*). The more X tends to be weak, the more reason such narration will be described as disclaimed (*munkar*). In later usage, each of the *shādhdh* and *munkar* category is itself sub-divided into two categories, the first of which is defined as stated above, the second entailing *mukhālafa* or irreconcilable difference with what is more authentically reported. *Munkar* and *shādhdh* may apply to text (*matn*) as well as chain (*sanad*).

Singular, uncorroborated chain or text not strong enough to be authenticated without corroboration (*fard lā yutābaʿ*).

/	\
The singular narrator is more or less trustworthy (*thiqa*) or at least truthful (*ṣadūq*). His ḥadīth is called *shādhdh* whether	The singular narrator is of unverified reliability (*mastūr*) or more or less weak (*ḍaʿīf*). His ḥadīth is *munkar* whether

/	\	/	\
it does not contradict others (*lā yukhālif*) (early usage, some calling it *munkar*)	or it contradicts others (*yukhālif*) (later usage, preferred by Ibn Ḥajar).	it does not contradict others (frequent usage)	or it contradicts others (later, most frequent usage, preferred by Ibn Ḥajar).

Imām Zayn al-Dīn al-ʿIrāqī said in *Alfiyyat al-Ḥadīth*: "And the *munkar* is the unheard-of stand-alone (*al-fard*) per al-Bardījī, in absolute terms; but the right [classification] for such narrations is to detail it just like the aberrant (*shādhdh*) which we discussed before.[146] For it shares its meaning; thus did the Shaykh [Ibn al-Ṣalāḥ] speak. For example 'Eat young dates with old dates,' etc;[147] or Mālik naming Ibn 'Uthmān ''Umar' [instead of ''Amr']:[148] I say, 'so what?'[149] or, again, the ḥadīth of his ﷺ removing his ring upon entering the privy and putting it down."[150]

The ḥadīth master Badr al-Dīn al-Ḥasanī states in his commentary on Abū al-ʿAbbās al-Lakhmī's poem on ḥadīth science,

[146] In *Fatḥ al-Mughīth*: The *shādhdh* is the trustworthy narrator's irreconcilable, solitary, uncorroborated contradiction of the whole trustworthy lot of the narrators or those stronger than him through addition or omission in the chain or text of a ḥadīth. Theirs is "retained" (*maḥfūẓ*) while his is "aberrant" (*shādhdh*).

[147] In *Fatḥ al-Mughīth*: Narrated [from 'Ā'isha by Ibn Mājah, al-Ḥākim, and Ibn al-Jawzī in the *Mawḍūʿāt*] exclusively through the honest but not quite reliable Abū Dhukayr Yaḥyā ibn Muḥammad ibn Qays al-Baṣrī as per al-Dāraquṭnī, Ibn 'Adī, and others while al-'Uqaylī said no-one corroborated him and it is unknown but for his narrating it; likewise al-Ḥākim: "It is among the stand-alone reports (*afrād*) of the Baṣrians from the Madīnans" hence graded *munkar* by al-Nasā'ī followed by Ibn al-Ṣalāḥ and Ibn Ḥajar, *Nukat* (2:680). The full wording of the ḥadīth is: "Eat *balaḥ* with *tamr*, eat the old with the new! For the devil is angered and says, 'The son of Ādam has lived to eat the old with the new!'"

[148] In the ḥadīth narrated from Usāma ibn Zayd in the Nine except al-Nasā'ī: "A Muslim does not inherit from a non-Muslim nor a non-Muslim from a Muslim." All the Masters and even Mālik's students other than Yaḥyā and Muḥammad ibn al-Ḥasan narrate it through 'Amr ibn 'Uthmān ibn 'Affān and not through his brother 'Umar except Mālik. The chain from Mālik, from al-Zuhrī reads "'Amr" in the *Risāla* edition of Abū Muṣ'ab al-Zuhrī's *Muwaṭṭa'* (2:539-540 §3061) and in our Shaykh Muḥammad 'Alawī al-Mālikī's edition – Allah have mercy on him! – of Ibn al-Qābisī's epitome (*talkhīṣ*) of Ibn al-Qāsim's *Muwaṭṭa'* (p. 126 §65). In *Fatḥ al-Mughīth*: Al-Nasā'ī said no-one corroborated Mālik on "'Umar" while Muslim and others even wrote it off as an error on his part but Mālik would motion with his hand when he said "'Umar" as if acknowledging they differed with him. He said, "Thus did we preserve it and thus is it written in my book, and we make mistakes – who is exempt of making them?"

Gharāmī Ṣaḥīḥ fī Anwā' al-Ḥadīth (verse 6): "*Munkar, ay mardūd*" [meaning "rejected"]. Similarly Ibn Kathīr in *Ikhtiṣār 'Ulūm al-Ḥadīth*.

Dr. Nūr al-Dīn 'Itr – Allah preserve him – wrote, "*Munkar* is used as a stand-alone term in two senses:

> (1) As settled upon by the later authorities, the *munkar* is what the weak narrator relates in contradiction of the trustworthy narrator and is very weak....
>
> (2) The *munkar* is a report with which a narrator singles himself out whether it contradicts others or not and even if he is trustworthy." [151]

Thus does al-Lacknawī also define it in the *Raf' wal-Takmīl*. However, if he is trustworthy then his report may be called *shādhdh* or *gharīb* rather than *munkar*. *Fatḥ al-Mughīth* states, in the chapter on the *munkar*: "They differ insofar as the narrator of the *shādhdh* is trustworthy (*thiqa*) or truthful (*ṣadūq*) without thorough accuracy (*ḍabṭ*), while the narrator of the *munkar* is

[149] In *Fatḥ al-Mughīth*: Both 'Amr ibn 'Uthman and his brother 'Umar are trustworthy so it makes no difference in the grading of the ḥadīth; and its *matn* may not be called *shādhdh* nor *munkar*. Ibn al-Ṣalāḥ cites it as an example of *munkar* in the chain exclusively because that quality may apply to the *isnād* as to the *matn*.

[150] Narrated in the four *Sunan* through Hammām ibn Yaḥyā, from Ibn Jurayj, from al-Zuhrī, from Anas. Abū Dāwūd said, "This is *munkar* as it is only recognized from Ibn Jurayj as narrated from Zyād ibn Sa'd, from al-Zuhrī, from Anas. The error in this is from Hammām and no-one else narrates it his way." In *Fatḥ al-Mughīth*: "Hammām is trustworthy and relied upon by the *Ṣaḥīḥ* compilers but he contradicted everybody. Nevertheless, Abū Dāwūd was not blessed to declare it disclaimed since Mūsā ibn Hārūn said, 'I do not rule it out that these are two different ḥadīths.' To this did Ibn Ḥibbān incline and he graded both of them sound.... At any rate the use of this ḥadīth as an example for the *munkar* and the use of Mālik's statement also, are only according to the method of Ibn al-Ṣalāḥ in not differentiating between the *munkar* and the *shādhdh*."

[151] In his notes on al-Nawawī's *Irshād* (p. 96) cf. al-Aḥmad Ghumārī infra.

weak because of poor memorization or ignorance [of correct narration] or the like." Al-Dhahabī said: "The singularity of the trustworthy narrator (*thiqa*) is counted as the *gharīb* while the singularity of the merely truthful narrator (*ṣadūq*) and those below him is counted as the *munkar*." [152]

Causes for which a Ḥadīth May Be Called *Munkar*

The grade of *munkar* can be caused by [1] a narrator (*al-rāwī*) that some declared weak rightly or wrongly, such as Suwayd ibn Sa'īd who is *thiqa* before his old age but whom Ibn Ma'īn lambasted as a criminal although Muslim retained him in his *Ṣaḥīḥ*; or by [2] a transmission (*al-riwāya*) some deem highly improbable, such as "al-Wāqidī from Ma'mar from al-Zuhrī" which resulted in Aḥmad no longer upholding al-Wāqidī as reliable although such transmission proved authentic; or by [3] the text transmitted (*al-marwī*) which struck some as implausible, such as al-Dhahabī rejecting the ḥadīth of Ukaydar the Roman king of Dūma's gift of a jar of ginger to Madīna although this it is quite possible and probable since such preserves or dried fruit continue to be one of the specialties of the Syro-Palestine region; or Ibn Ḥibbān rejecting the Prophet's ﷺ order to 'Abd Allah ibn 'Abd Allah ibn Ubay to have gold teeth made for himself although such a private dispensation does not contradict the general prohibition of the wearing of gold by men; or al-Dhahabī rejecting al-Tirmidhī's authentic narration of the two books the Prophet ﷺ showed the Companions, one containing the names, patronyms, and surnames of all the people of Paradise until the Day of Resurrection and the other those of the people of Hellfire because he surmised such books would be impossibly voluminous – a reasoning rejected by Ibn Ḥajar and others. [153]

[152] In *Mīzān al-I'tidāl*, chapter on 'Alī ibn al-Madīnī.

Munkar in the sense of "Forged"?

Shaykh ʿAbd al-Fattāḥ Abū Ghudda adds another meaning: "forged" (*al-mawḍūʿ al-kadhib al-muftarā*) in his introduction to al-Qārī's *Maṣnūʿ*.[154] Ibn Ḥajar said unambiguously: "The *munkar* is other than the *mawḍūʿ*"[155] and he differentiates between them time and again: "Ibn al-Jawzī cited the '*balaḥ* and *tamr*' ḥadīth[156] among the forgeries but the correct ruling is what al-Nasāʾī said, followed by Ibn al-Ṣalāḥ, that it is *munkar* in view of its singularity from a weak narrator";[157] "He [Ibn al-Jawzī] has [wrongly] included in his book of forgeries the *munkar* and weak ḥadīths...."[158]

This can be reconciled [1] if Abū Ghudda means the terminology of certain specific post-5th century scholars as Aḥmad al-Ghumārī noted (see below) and [2] if he means the use of *munkar* in conjunction with a more explicit statement as in the expressions "*munkar* and a lie," "a *munkar* falsehood or forgery," "*munkar*, and the one who made it up is..." etc. Abū Ghudda himself notes[159] that al-Suyūṭī cautioned in *Bulūgh al-Maʾmūl fī Khidmat al-Rasūl* ﷺ that the scholars may use *munkar* in the sense of a single-chained (*gharīb*) ḥadīth as when al-Dhahabī in the *Mīzān* calls many sound reports "*munkar*," even some in the two *Ṣaḥīḥs*,[160] or Ibn ʿAdī[161] saying of Sallām ibn Sulaymān al-Madāʾinī,

[153] Cf. al-Ghumārī, *Darʾ al-Ḍaʿf ʿan Ḥadīth Man ʿAshiqa fa-ʿAff* (p. 36-48).

[154] In *al-Maṣnūʿ* (p. 20 n. and p. 42 n. 6) cf. his notes on the *Rafʿ* (p. 211 n. 1).

[155] In *al-Qawl al-Musaddad* (p. 79).

[156] See note 147.

[157] In *al-Nukat ʿalā Ibn al-Ṣalāḥ* (2:680).

[158] *Nukat* (2:848).

[159] In the *Rafʿ* (p. 200 n. 2).

[160] *Al-Ḥāwī lil-Fatāwī* (2:210).

[161] Ibn ʿAdī is Abū Aḥmad ʿAbd Allah ibn ʿAdī ibn ʿAbd Allah ibn Muḥammad ibn Mubārak ibn al-Qaṭṭān al-Jurjānī (277-365), the Imām, keen ḥadīth Master who travelled the world, and author of *al-Kāmil fīl-Jarḥ wal-Taʿdīl* in five large volumes, an unprecedented encyclopedia of weak narrators. He heard Bahlūl ibn Isḥāq al-Tanūkhī, Muḥammad ibn ʿUthmān ibn Abi Suwayd, Muḥammad ibn

"His narrations are *munkar* but they are all *ḥasan* ḥadīths."[162] In *Tadrīb al-Rāwī*, chapter on the *maqlūb*, al-Suyūṭī differentiates between the *munkar* and the forged:

> "The worst type of weak ḥadīth is the forgery (*al-mawḍūʿ*), followed by the discarded (*al-matrūk*), then the disclaimed (*munkar*), then the defective (*muʿallal*), then the inserted (*mudraj*), then the topsy-turvy (*al-maqlūb*) then the inconsistent (*muḍṭarib*). Thus did Shaykh al-Islām [=Ibn Ḥajar al-ʿAsqalānī] arrange them." [163]

Al-Suyūṭī elsewhere said:

> "Ibn ʿAsākir's ruling of *munkar* on the ḥadīth [of the declaration of belief on the part of the Prophet's parents when they were temporarily brought back to life in front of him ﷺ] is a categorical proof for what I say, namely, that it is *ḍaʿīf* and not forged, since the *munkar* is a sub-class of the *ḍaʿīf* and there is a difference between the *munkar* and the *mawḍūʿ* as is well-known in ḥadīth science.... and the *ḍaʿīf* is a rank above the *munkar* and better in state. It is also better than another rank which stands below the *munkar*, namely, the *matrūk*. The latter is also a sub-class of the non-forged *ḍaʿīf*."[164]

Yaḥyā al-Marwazī, Anas ibn al-Salām, al-Nasā'ī, al-Firyābī, Abū Yaʿlā al-Mawṣilī, al-Baghawī, Ibn Khuzayma, etc. He lived a long time and his chain of transmission became quite short. He specialized in narrator-criticism, ḥadīth authentication and criticism, until he became a foremost expert in this science despite weakness in his grammar. Al-Dāraquṭnī praised his book as sufficient for knowledge of the weak narrators. Ibn ʿAsākir and others declared him trustworthy and praised his mastership and memorization. Apparently he was Shāfiʿi and compiled a book based on the chapter-headings of al-Muzanī's *Mukhtaṣar*. His method in the *Kāmil* is to mention every narrator that was ever criticized rightly or wrongly. Al-Dhahabī integrated it into *Mīzān al-Iʿtidāl* and expanded upon it, criticizing him at times for citing undeserving entries. Cf. al-Dhahabī, *Siyar* (16:154).

[162] Al-Sakhāwī, *Fatḥ al-Mughīth*, chapter on the *munkar*.

[163] Cf. Ṭāhir al-Jazā'irī, *Tawjīh al-Naẓar ilā Uṣūl al-Athar* (2:597).

Al-Zarqānī in *Sharḥ al-Mawāhib* cites it and applies the same reasoning toward Ibn Kathīr's words, "*munkar jiddan*."[165]

Shaykh Aḥmad al-Ghumārī said:

> "When the early authorities declare a ḥadīth *munkar* it does not indicate that it is false nor a forgery unlike what Ibn al-Qayyim concluded [with reference to the ḥadīth "Whoever falls passionately in love but remains chaste..."], who relied upon their having declared it *munkar*. For "*munkar*" in their usage and conventions differs from "*munkar*" in the terminology of the later scholars, by whom we mean those of the fifth century and later.
>
> "The later scholars use "*munkar*" in two senses: the first – and the one by which they usually define it – is "that by which a weak narrator contradicts the trustworthy one." The second meaning – and the one they use in their discourse – is "what is thoroughly flimsy or forged" (*wāhin aw mawḍūʿ*). Hence you find them saying, "This is a *ḥadīthun munkarun mawḍūʿ*," or "This is a *ḥadīth munkar* and the culprit for it is So-and-so," as you can frequently read in the likes of al-Khaṭīb, Ibn ʿAsākir, Ibn al-Najjār, Ibn al-Jawzī, and al-Dhahabī who is the seal of those that very frequently use the term *munkar* to refer to a forgery.
>
> "As for the early authorities, they also use the term *munkar* in two meanings. One of them is "that with which a narrator singles himself out even if he is trustworthy" as defined by [Aḥmad ibn Hārūn ibn Rawḥ] al-Bardījī (d. 301)[166] in the leaves

[164] In *al-Fawāʾid al-Kāmina fī Īmān al-Sayyida Āmina = al-Taʿẓīm wal-Minna bi-anna Wāliday al-Muṣṭafā fīl-Janna* (Muṣṭafā ʿĀshūr 1988 Ryadh ed. p. 44-45).

[165] Cf. Imām Aḥmad Riḍā Khan, *Munīr al-ʿAyn* (p. 16).

[166] He defined the *munkar* as "the unheard-of stand-alone were it not for its narrator" (*al-fard al-ladhī lā yuʿraf matnuhu min ghayri rāwīh*) in al-Suyūṭī's *Tadrīb al-Rāwī* (1:238).

he gathered on the subject of ḥadīth terminology, and the other is "that with which an unknown-status (*mastūr*) or weak (*ḍaʿīf*) narrator singles himself out." Some of them might also use the term *munkar* and mean by it the terminally unreliable narrator that has very few narrations (*al-sāqiṭ al-wāhī ʿalā qilla*)."[167]

The above remarks do not address "blameworthiness of meaning" (*nakārat al-maʿnā*) by which *munkar* is also sometimes used to mean forged as in Ibn ʿAdī's familiar expression, "So-and-so does not narrate any ḥadīth of blameworthy content (*munkar al-matn*)."[168] Shaykh ʿAbd Allah al-Ghumārī said: "When a ḥadīth is reprehensible in meaning (*munkaran fil-maʿnā*) it is forged even if its chain meets the criterion of the *Ṣaḥīḥ*. In fact, there would be a hidden defect in its chain in such a scenario."[169]

It goes without saying that reprehensibility is a far more subjective criterion than the criteria applied to the chain although Ibn al-Jawzī, Ibn al-Qayyim, and others did attempt to itemize the signs of forgery in relation to *matn* implausibility, among them:

- nonsense as in the report, "Do not eat the pumpkin before you slaughter it";
- disproportional rewards or punishments;
- anachronism as in the pseudo-Prophetic ḥadīths mentioning the *muṣḥaf* or Abū Ḥanīfa;
- extravagant praise or blame for a tribe, person ("My daughter Fāṭima is pure and purified, no trace of blood can be seen from her whether of menses or in giving birth")[170], locality, time

[167] Aḥmad al-Ghumārī, *Dar' al-Ḍaʿf ʿan Ḥadīth Man ʿAshiqa fa- ʿAff* (p. 49-50).
[168] Ibn ʿAdī, *Kāmil* (1:208, 1:310, 1:387, 2:384, 4:88).
[169] ʿAbd Allah al-Ghumārī, notes on al-Sakhāwī's *Maqāṣid al-Ḥasana* (p. 193).
[170] Cf. Ibn al-Jawzī, *Mawḍūʿāt* (1:421), Ibn Ḥajar, *Lisān* (3:238), al-Suyūṭī, *La'āli'* (1:400), Ibn ʿArrāq, *Tanzīh* (1:413-414).

(such as the reports emphasizing the month of Rajab compiled by Ibn Ḥajar in his monograph *Tabyīn al- ʿAjab fīmā Warada fī Rajab*), food ("Cheese is a disease and walnuts a cure," "Egg-plant fulfills whatever [need] it is eaten for"), celibacy ("The best of you after the year 200 are the wifeless and childless"), school-teachers ("The worst of you are those who teach young pupils") etc.

– literary artificiality illustrated by

(a) poor or strained language as in the account of the Prophetic ascension known as *Miʿrāj Ibn ʿAbbās* or the saying, "*Sharīʿa* is my words, *Ṭarīqa* is my actions, *Ḥaqīqa* is my state, *Maʿrifa* is my capital, *ʿAql* is the basis of my *Dīn*..."[171]

(b) long speeches bursting at the seams with figures of rhetoric, internal rhymes or learned expressions such as *Nahj al-Balāgha*, a 5th-century forgery.

(c) "priamels" or numbered lists cataloguing types of levels such as creation in the "ḥadīth of Jābir" on the light of the Prophet ﷺ; or merits with rewards and/or defects with punishments as in the long pseudo-ḥadīth of Ibn ʿAbbās on the merits of each *Sūra* (said to be forged by Nūḥ ibn Abī Maryam) and the *Munabbihāt ʿalā al-Istiʿdād li-Yawm al-Maʿād lil-Nuṣḥi wal-Widād* ("Admonitions for Preparation for the Day of the Return for Advice and Love") compiled by Zayn al-Quḍāt Aḥmad ibn Muḥammad al-Ḥijjī or al-Ḥajrī or Ḥujurī's (d. ?) and falsely attributed to Ibn Ḥajar al-ʿAsqalānī although it is replete with sourceless, chainless, ungraded reports in the most patent contrast with the masterly style that shines like the sun in all his works.[172]

[171] Cited chainless from the 5th century onward as a Prophetic saying narrated from ʿAlī ؓ in the *Iḥyā'* (4:361) and *Shifā* (p. 191 §347) as well as *Nahj al-Balāgha*. Neither al-ʿIrāqī nor Ibn Ḥajar found any chain for it while al-Suyūṭī declared it a forgery in *Manāhil al-Ṣafā* (§322) as did al-Fattanī in *Tadhkirat al-Mawḍūʿāt*.

Abū Ghudda's Examples of *Munkar* to Mean *Mawḍu*ʿ

Shaykh ʿAbd al-Fattāḥ Abū Ghudda cites thirty examples of what he says are uses of the term *munkar* to mean "forged" from four books: Ibn al-Jawzī's *Mawḍūʿāt* (1 example), al-Dhahabī's *Mīzān al-Iʿtidāl* (4 examples), Ibn ʿArrāq's *Tanzīh al-Sharīʿa* (19 examples), and al-Qārī's *Maṣnūʿ* (6 examples). He introduces his list of citations with the words, "The scholars frequently use the term *munkar* to mean the *mawḍūʿ*, indicating thereby the blameworthiness (*nakāra*) of its meaning together with the weakness of its chain and the lack of its veracity (*buṭlān thubūtih*)." He then cites the page numbers for the thirty passages he believes prove his claim, some of which we examine below:

In Ibn ʿArrāq's *Tanzīh al-Sharīʿa*:

- Al-Khaṭīb's statement "*munkar jiddan*" about the forged ḥadīth "The Qur'ān is the Speech of Allah neither creator nor created." (1:134 §5)
- Ibn al-Najjār's statement "*munkar*" about the forged ḥadīth, "O ʿAlī, the Qur'ān is the Speech of Allah uncreated." (1:135 §7).
- Ibn ʿAsākir's statement, "al-Khaṭīb wrote these two [ḥadīths forged] by al-Ahwāzī[173] in astonishment at their blameworthyness (*nakāra*) and they are false" about the narrations "I saw my Lord on the Day of *Nafar* [10 Dhūl-Ḥijja] on a red camel" and "Every *Jumuʿa* Allah descends wrapped in a cloak" (1:146 §35).

[172] Cf. the catalogue of Arabic manuscripts of the library of Sarajevo (§ 334) and as referenced by Ḥajji Khalīfa in *Kashf al-Ẓunūn* (2:1848) while other manuscripts misattribute it to Ibn Ḥajar al-Haytamī or leave the author unmentioned. See Shākir Maḥmūd ʿAbd al-Munʿim's two-volume 1997 doctoral thesis published at Mu'assasat al-Risāla, Beirut under the title *Ibn Ḥajar al-ʿAsqalānī: Muṣannafātuhu wa-Dirāsatun fi Manhajihi wa-Mawāridihi fi Kitābihi al-Iṣāba* (1:394-395).

[173] Abū ʿAlī al-Aḥwazī is the *Ḥanbalī* anthropomorphist that concocted the accusations against al-Ashʿarī that prompted Ibn ʿAsākir to write his masterpiece *Tabyīn Kadhib al-Muftarī fīmā Nasabahu ilā al-Imām Abī al-Ḥasan al-Ashʿarī*.

- Al-Khaṭīb's statement "*munkar*" about the forged ḥadīth, "Allah says, *Lā ilāha illa Allah* is My Word... and the Qur'ān is My Speech and issued from Me" (1:148 §40).
- Al-Khaṭīb's statement "*munkar*" about the forged ḥadīth, "Allah has three angels, one in charge of the *Ka'ba*..." (1:170 §2).
- Al-Khaṭīb's statement "*munkar jiddan*" about the forged ḥadīth, "Do not beat your children for their weeping..." (1:171 §6).
- The editor 'Abd Allah al-Ghumārī's statements equating the *munkar* in meaning with the forged (1:193 n.).
- Al-Bayhaqī's statement "*munkar*, and the culprit for this may be So-and-so" about the forgery in which the Prophet ﷺ says to Ibn Mas'ūd, "Always look into the *muṣḥaf* for I had ophthalmia and Gibrīl gave me the same advice" (1:308 §81).
- Al-Dhahabī's statement "*munkar*" of the ḥadīth that Gibrīl brought the Prophet ﷺ a bunch of grapes (*qiṭf*) and said, "Allah greets you and sent me to you with this bunch of grapes for you to eat"[174] (1:334 §20 although Ibn 'Arrāq argues that al-Dhahabī's statement means or should mean other than "forged" cf. §19).
- Al-Dhahabī's statement "*munkar*" in the *Mīzān* of the forgery in which Gibrīl brings Abū Bakr water for *wuḍū'* and Mīkā'īl brings him a towel (1:341 §1, Ibn 'Arrāq prefers al-Dhahabī's more explicit ruling of "*kadhib*" in his *Mughnī* in keeping with his view that *munkar* is an inappropriate term for "forged").
- Al-Khaṭīb's statement "*munkar*" about the forgery, "'Alī is the best of human beings, whoever doubts it commits disbelief" (1:353-354 §39).

[174] The narrator of this ḥadīth became known as "Ḥafṣ the bunch-man."

More Precisions on the Sources of the Above Examples

Al-Khaṭīb:

Al-Khaṭīb may use *munkar* in a way that suggests he means "forged" when he says (3:307), for example, "This ḥadīth is false and forged (*bāṭil mawḍū'*)... and the one before it is also *munkar*"; on closer look, however, the second ḥadīth – "Generosity is a tree in paradise" – is not as definitely forged as the former, and Allah knows best. Al-Khaṭīb applies the grading *munkar* to a ḥadīth about 30 times and the grading *mawḍū'* about 20 in *Tārīkh Baghdād*. A review of his usage indicates the following:

- He uses *munkar jiddan* for ḥadīths which prove forged beyond doubt per later critical reference-works (3:168, 4:59, 4:85, 4:376, 7:128, 9:434, 11:337, 13:42)[175] except once, in reference to a highly implausible chain for an otherwise authentic ḥadīth (12:467)[176]. He does seem to mean forged in those cases.
- Where the text happens to be utterly singular, the high implausibility of its chain leads to the certitude of its forgery as in al-Khaṭīb's statement, "When he read the ḥadīth I had strong doubts about it (*istankartuhu*) and expressed my wonder about it. I said that such a ḥadīth was extremely odd (*gharībun jiddan*) through that path and that I conclude it is a falsehood (*wa-urāhu bāṭilan*)" (3:96).[177]
- He uses *munkar* for chains and/or texts of ḥadīths that vary from being indisputably forged (1:259, 3:304, 4:81, 4:157, 7:403,

[175] "If you are a Prophet, tell me what I have in my possession. – If I tell you, will you affirm the testimony of faith?..."; "Whoever hopes that prices will rise in my Community..."; "Whoever feeds his brother a mouthful of sweet..."; "The bearers of knowledge in the world are the caliphs of Prophets..."; "Whoever wears a helmet for *jihād*..."; "We seven of Banū al-Muṭṭalib..."; "Do not beat your children for their weeping..."; "When the orphan weeps his tears fall...."

[176] Ḥadīth of the Prophet ﷺ joining prayers during the campaign of Tabūk.

[177] "Whoever takes the hand of someone afflicted, Allah takes his hand."

7:421, 12:423, 13:122)[178], debatably forged (3:222, 4:158, 5:13),[179] weak (2:51, 3:267, 5:296, 11:338),[180] and even fair (7:263),[181] sound (5:367, 8:370, 11:36),[182] or *mutawātir* (8:370)![183] In the latter three or four categories it is abundantly clear that he uses *munkar* in only one of the three senses claimed by Abū Ghudda: neither "the blameworthiness (*nakāra*) of its meaning" nor "the lack of its veracity (*buṭlān thubūtih*)" but only "the weakness of its chain."

- When he wants to say a ḥadīth is *mawḍūʿ* – in its chain, its text, or both – he calls it just that (2:203, 2:247, 2:289, 3:98, 3:290-291, 3:307, 3:410, 4:209, 7:135, 8:44, 8:165, 9:49, 10:356, 10:373, 13:32, 13:271, 13:335).[184]

[178] "The night I was taken up to the heaven I saw on the gate of Paradise…"; "Whoever associates in partnership with a covenantee (*dhimmī*) and humbles himself before him…"; "Whoever learns the Qur'ān and memorizes it, Allah shall enter him into Paradise and give him intercession for ten of his relatives…"; "Allah has three angels, one in charge of the *Kaʿba*…"; "Cheese is a disease and walnuts a cure…"; "ʿAlī is the best of human beings, whoever doubts it commits disbelief"; "Paying due rights and keeping trusts is our Religion…"; "There will be no rider besides us on the Day of Resurrection…."

[179] "What is this camel? O ʿAlī, fear Allah regarding worldly possessions…"; "When an innovator dies, Islam gains a new victory"; "When I was taken up to the heaven Gibrīl brought me to *Sidrat al-Muntahā* and bathed me in light…."

[180] "If you are pleased to make your prayer pure, put forward the best among you"; "The Prophet ﷺ prayed over an adultress and her daughter"; "When I was taken up to the heaven and I reached the fourth heaven, an apple fell into my lap…"; "On the Day of Resurrection the people will be made to stand…."

[181] "Do you have qualms about denouncing the openly corrupt man?! (*atariʿūn ʿan dhikr al-fājir*)…."

[182] "Two types of my Community have no part in Islam: the Murji'a and the Qadariyya"; "There is no marriage without guardian"; "Your Lord [in al-Bukhārī and al-Dārimī: A man] built a house and prepared a banquet…"

[183] "Whoever harms a covenanted citizen (*dhimmī*), I will personally accuse him on the Day of Resurrection!"

[184] "I asked Allah not to answer the supplication of the lover against the beloved"; "Allah says, 'Son of Ādam, I am your indispensable need…' "; "A man will come

- Al-Khaṭīb also means "forged" when he says *laysa bi-thābit* – "it is unestablished" - about three times (4:376, 7:421, 12:331).[185] Al-Dhahabī takes strong exception to what he deems an understatement that does not, in his understanding, denote outright forgeries but merely ḥadīths that fall short of the rank of *ṣaḥīḥ*.[186] Al-Dhahabī would be right if he were discussing a *fiqh*-oriented ruling, such as Imām Aḥmad's statement that there is no *thābit* ḥadīth stipulating *Basmala* at the time of ablutions – *i.e.*, only *ḥasan*. However, al-Khaṭīb's ruling of "unestablished" here uses a different convention, namely a twofold, "either authentic or forged" convention used by Ibn al-Jawzī and others. Abū Ghudda has shown beyond the shadow of a doubt – after Imām al-Kawtharī's citation of the ḥadīth Master Ibn Himmāt al-Dimashqī – that such a term does indeed mean "forged" in ḥadīth-oriented literature as opposed to *fiqh*.[187]

after me named al-Nu'mān ibn Thābit, Abū Ḥanīfa..."; "Whoever takes the hand of someone afflicted, Allah takes his hand"; "Allah curse your killer [O al-Ḥusayn]..." "Allah gave preference to the Messengers over the angels brought near..."; "On the Day of Resurrection the scholars of ḥadīth will come, inkwells in hand..."; Mukarram ibn Aḥmad's *Faḍā'il Abī Ḥanīfa*; "The night of my wedding to the Messenger of Allah, he embraced me..."; "Allah revealed to the world, 'Serve whoever serves Me...'"; "I saw marjoram growing under the Throne"; "The Throne shook at the death of Sa'd" [*ṣaḥīḥ* with a forged chain]; "I am the Seal of Prophets and you, 'Alī, are the Seal of Saints"; "Pursuing *'ilm* is an obligation upon every Muslim" [*ḥasan* with a forged chain]; "Whoever loves me, let him love 'Alī; and whoever angers 'Alī has angered me..."; "Every *Jumu'a* night Allah delivers 100,000 people from the Fire except the hater of Abū Bakr and 'Umar..."; "There will be in my Community a man named al-Nu'mān, his nickname is Abū Ḥanīfa...."

[185] "The bearers of knowledge in the world are the caliphs of Prophets..."; "'Alī is the best of human beings, whoever doubts it commits disbelief"; "My daughter Fāṭima is a human houri, she never got menses...."

[186] *Mīzān* (s.v. al-Ḥasan ibn Muḥammad ibn Yaḥyā al-'Alawī).

[187] Abū Ghudda, introduction to al-Qārī's *Maṣnū'* (p. 29-30): "Al-Dhahabī lost sight of the rule and was overhasty to correct al-Khaṭīb." In this oversight al-Dhahabī joins a list of lesser Masters such as al-Zarkashī, al-Qārī, and Ibn 'Arrāq – Allah have mercy on all of them and continue to benefit the *Umma* with them.

Al-Dhahabī:

Al-Dhahabī says *khabar munkar* for the following among others in the *Mīzān* – most apparently in the sense of forgery:

- the report, "The Hour will not rise before Allah will not have been worshipped for a hundred years on the earth" (*s.v.* Abān ibn Khālid).
- the report from Ibn ʿAbbās that the Prophet ﷺ supposedly said at the funeral of Abū Ṭālib, "May direct relatives embrace you and may you be rewarded with goodness, my uncle!" (*s.v.* Ibrāhīm ibn ʿAbd al-Raḥmān al-Khwārizmī).
- the report that ʿAlī supposedly said, "People gave *bayʿa* to Abū Bakr although I am worthier..." (*s.v.* al-Ḥārith ibn Muḥammad).
- the report, "There is no Mahdī but ʿĪsā ibn Maryam" (*s.v.* Muḥammad ibn Khālid al-Janadī).
- the report, "The believers and their children are in the heaven while the disbelievers and their children are in the fire" (*s.v.* Muḥammad ibn ʿUthmān, "an unknown").
- the report, "I was given superiority to people in four things: generosity, courage, frequent coitus, and fierceness in combat" (*s.v.* Marwān ibn ʿUthmān ibn Abī Saʿīd).
- the report that as the Prophet ﷺ was praying he replied to someone's greeting lest the greeter take offense (*s.v.* Abū Bakr al-ʿUmarī, "an unknown").
- the report that ʿĀ'isha gave a dīnār to al-Ḥasan and al-Ḥusayn and split her tunic in half for each of them (*s.v.* Jābir ibn Yazīd ibn al-Ḥārith).
- the report that al-Khaḍir and Ilyās – upon our Prophet and them blessings and peace – meet every year in the *Ḥajj* season at ʿArafa (*s.v.* al-Ḥasan ibn Razīn).

Al-Dhahabī much less frequently uses *munkar* to question a certain chain for an otherwise authentic hadīth cf. "My Community is not taken to task for fleeting thoughts" (*s.v.* Ayyūb ibn Manṣūr ibn ʿAlī) and in the notice of ʿAbd al-Mu'min ibn Sālim ibn Maymūn.

The Term *Munkar al-Ḥadīth*

As for the term *munkar al-ḥadīth* the early scholars use it for a narrator that singles himself out in narrating certain ḥadīths or is condemned for *fisq* but not lying[188] among the categories of the "rejected ḥadīth" (*al-mardūd*) while al-Bukhārī means it in the worst negative sense and Muslim in his *Muqaddima* identifies it with matrūk when one's narrations are mostly *munkar*.[189] This is also the usage of al-Khaṭīb in *Tārīkh Baghdād* and he equates it with *ḍaʿīf jiddan* and *matrūk* although Abū Ḥātim equates it with the "nearly *matrūk*." Shaykh Nūr al-Dīn ʿItr defines *munkar al-ḥadīth* as "The narrator who narrates *munkar* ḥadīths and singles himself out or contravenes others thereby; his narrations are taken into consideration in the methodology of other than al-Bukhārī."[190]

[188] Cf. Ibn al-Ḥanbalī's *Qafw al-Athar* (p. 74).
[189] Cf. Ibn Ḥajar, *Nukat* (2:675), al-Lacknawī, *Rafʿ Īqāẓ* 7, al-Tahānawī's *Qawāʿid fī ʿUlūm al-Ḥadīth* (p. 274) etc.
[190] ʿItr, *Muʿjam al-Muṣṭalaḥāt al-Ḥadīthiyya* (p. 108).

From The Critical Method in the Sciences of Ḥadīth
by Shaykh Nūr al-Dīn ʿItr

The disclaimed and the recognized narration *(Al-Munkar wal-Maʿrūf)*:

The expressions of the scholars vary in defining the *munkar* to the point that the observer is unsure what it means exactly. Careful scrutiny yields a clear determination that this diversity is caused by the difference in purposes for each side when they use that terminology. After such scrutiny we found that there were two ways (*maslakayn*) among the Ulema as follows:

> The first way applies the term *munkar* to a particular type of divergence, namely, the weak narrator's report in contravention of the trustworthy narrator. This division is the opposite of the "recognized narration" (*al-maʿrūf*), which is the ḥadīth of the trustworthy narrator in contravention of that of the weak narrator. The above convention is followed by many of the ḥadīth scholars and is standard terminology among the later scholars. The *ḥāfiẓ* Ibn Ḥajar uses it in *al-Nukhba* and its commentary.

Over-generalization on the part of the early scholars in the [terminology of the] *munkar* and the resolution of the problem inherent in its multiple usages:

> The second way overgeneralizes in the use of the term *munkar* and apply it to whatever a narrator is alone in narrating (*tafarrada bih*), whether or not he contravenes others and even if he is trustworthy. There are many different illustrations for this. In each of these cases the ḥadīth scholars applied the term *munkar*. This is the way of many of the early authorities. Following are examples of what we find them saying:

1. Imām Aḥmad said of Aflaḥ ibn Ḥumayd al-Anṣārī – one of the trustworthy narrators of the two *Ṣaḥīḥs*: "Aflaḥ narrates two *munkar* ḥadīths: that the Prophet ﷺ bled his sacrificial animal as a pre-slaughter marking, and the ḥadīth 'The consecration-place of the people of Iraq is Dhātu 'Irqin.'"[191] So Imām Aḥmad named these two ḥadīths *munkar* due to Aflaḥ singling himself out with their narration although he is trustworthy.
2. The ḥadīth of Ibn al-Zubayr al-Makkī who said: "I asked Jābir about the [prohibition of the] sale of the wildcat and the dog and he replied, 'The Prophet ﷺ strongly forbade us this.'" Thus did Muslim narrate it while al-Nasā'ī said, "Ibrāhīm ibn al-Ḥasan narrated to me saying, Ḥajjāj ibn Muḥammad told us, from Ḥammād ibn Salama, from Abū al-Zubayr, from Jābir ibn 'Abd Allah, that the Messenger of Allah ﷺ forbade the sale of dogs and wildcats except hunting dogs." Abū 'Abd al-Raḥmān [al-Nasā'ī] said, "This is *munkar*." This is a chain of trustworthy narrators but it alone narrates the phrase "except hunting dogs." Hence al-Nasā'ī said of it that it is *munkar*. It is possible to put this in the category of the *shādhdh* because this addition actually contravenes [what is established].
3. Al-Tirmidhī said (in the "Chapter of what is related concerning giving *salām* before [all other] talk"), "Al-Faḍl ibn al-Ṣabāḥ Baghdādī narrated to us: Sa'īd ibn Zakariyyā narrated to us, from 'Anbasa ibn 'Abd al-Raḥmān, from Muḥammad ibn Zādhān, from Muḥammad ibn al-Munkadir, from Jābir ibn 'Abd Allah who said: The Messenger of Allah ﷺ said, '*Salām* comes before [all other] talk'..." Abū 'Īsā [al-Tirmidhī] said, "This is a *munkar* ḥadīth, we do not know it except through this particular chain (*min hādhā al-wajh*); and I heard Muḥammad [ibn Ismā'īl al-Bukhārī] say, ''Anbasa ibn 'Abd al-Raḥmān is weak in ḥadīth and forgetful (*dhāhib*) while Muḥammad ibn Zādhān is a disclaimed-ḥadīth narrator (*munkar al-ḥadīth*).'"

[191] In Ibn Ḥajar, *Hadī al-Sārī* (2:117).

Thus, Abū ʿĪsā al-Tirmidhī graded the ḥadīth *munkar* and it is narrated with a chain containing two weak narrators, together with its not being known through any other chain.

4. The ḥadīth of Abū Hurayra that "the Prophet ﷺ used to clip his nails and cut his moustache on the day of Jumuʿa before coming out to the Prayer." Al-Bazzār and al-Ṭabarānī narrated it in *al-Awsaṭ* (*Majmaʿ al-Zawā'id* 2:170-171) and its chain contains Ibrāhīm ibn Qudāma al-Jumaḥī – "he is not known." Hence al-Dhahabī said, "This is a *munkar* report" (In the *Mīzān*, entry for Ibrāhīm ibn Qudāma [1:53]. See also our book *al-Ṣalawāt al-Khāṣṣa* p. 17). This is a rare example of the use of this term by later scholars.

The status of the *munkar* according to its various usages:

As for the status or grading (*ḥukm*) of the *munkar*, in the context of the first nomenclature it is very weak because its narrator is weak and it is made weaker by its contravention [of other reports and/or narrators]. In the context of the second nomenclature which applies the term to unique reports (*al-fard*) as well as the aberrant (*al-shādhdh*), its status is the same as for the singular report (*al-gharīb*) with regard to both text and chain and the absolutely unique report (*al-fard al-muṭlaq*): it could be sound, it could be fair, and it could be weak.

Hence it is required from everyone that peers into the books of the *Muḥaddithūn* to understand well and realize how the word *munkar* is used and not act in haste then proceed to weaken something that does not deserve weakening or speak without knowledge as happened with one of our contemporaries.[192] Their statement, "The most *munkar* that So-and-so narrates" does not mean its weakness!

[192] He means Nāṣir al-Albānī.

Al-Suyūṭī said (in *Tadrīb al-Rāwī* p. 153=1:241): "Among their expressions is 'The most *munkar* that So-and-so narrates is this,' even when that ḥadīth is far from weak. Ibn ʿAdī said, 'The most *munkar* that Burayd ibn ʿAbd Allah narrated is, 'When Allah desires good for a nation, He seizes their Prophet before seizing them.' That ḥadīth is in *Ṣaḥīḥ Muslim*. And al-Dhahabī said [in the *Mīzān*], 'The most *munkar* ḥadīth that al-Walīd ibn Muslim narrates is that of the memorization of the Qur'ān' but it is in al-Tirmidhī who declared it fair while al-Ḥākim declared it sound by the criterion of the Two Shaykhs" (See the detailed study of this ḥadīth in *al-Ṣalawāt al-Khāṣṣa* p. 246-253).[193]

★ ★ ★

In recapitulation, as Shaykh Aḥmad al-Ghumārī said: "In the usage of the early authorities *nakāra* has no precise definition (*ḥaddun maḥdūd*) nor a firm reference-text concerning it (*aṣlun yurjaʿu ilayhi fīhā*), nor a reliable rule by which to declare it (*qāʿidatun yuʿtamadu ʿalayhā fil-ḥukmi bihā*)."[194] And Allah knows best.

[193] ʿItr, *Manhaj al-Naqd fī ʿUlūm al-Ḥadīth* (p. 430-433).
[194] In *Dar' al-Ḍaʿf ʿan Ḥadīth Man ʿAshiqa fa-ʿAff* (p. 35).

The Use of Weak Ḥadīths in Islam

It is the Consensus of the Ulema that weak ḥadīths can be narrated and put into practice in Islam according to al-Bayhaqī, Ibn ʿAbd al-Barr, al-Nawawī, Ibn Taymiyya, al-Qārī, and ʿAlawī ibn ʿAbbās al-Mālikī in *al-Manhal al-Laṭīf fī ʿUlūm al-Ḥadīth*, provided certain conditions are met.[195] Ibn al-Ṣalāḥ, al-Nawawī, and al-ʿIrāqī's sole conditions were that

[1] the ḥadīth be related to good deeds (*faḍā'il al-aʿmāl*) without bearing on legal rulings and doctrine and

[2] the ḥadīth not be forged.

After them, Ibn Daqīq al-ʿĪd, al-Zarkashī, and Ibn Ḥajar added three further conditions: that the ḥadīth not be very weak;[196] that it be subsumed under a principle already established in the Law; and that one not positively believe that the Prophet ﷺ said or did it.

195 Cf. al-Bayhaqī, *Dalā'il al-Nubuwwa* (1:33-34); Ibn ʿAbd al-Barr, *Tamhīd* (1:127); al-Nawawī, *Majmūʿ* (5:63), *Rawḍat al-Ṭālibīn* (2:138), *Irshād Ṭullāb al-Ḥaqā'iq* (p. 107-108), *Sharḥ Ṣaḥīḥ Muslim* (introduction), *Adhkār* (introduction p. 5) cf. Ibn ʿAllān, *Futūḥāt al-Rabbāniyya* (1:84); Ibn Taymiyya, *Sharḥ al-ʿUmda* (1:171), *Majmūʿ al-Fatāwā* (18:26, 18:65-66), and *Miswaddat Āl Taymiyya* (p. 233, 246, 461); al-Qārī, *Sharḥ al-Shifā* (2:91), and *Mirqāt* (2:381); ʿItr, *Manhaj al-Naqd* (p. 291-296), and *Uṣūl al-Jarḥ wal-Taʿdīl* (p. 140-143) Possibly the sole dissenting view among the authorities is that of al-Kawtharī in his *Maqālāt* (p. 139-140=p. 45), with whom Abū Ghudda took issue for that reason in *Ẓafar al-Amānī* (p.185)

196 This condition is not retained by the subsequent commentators on Ibn al-Ṣalāḥ and al-Nawawī such as al-Suyūṭī and al-Ṣanʿānī. Furthermore it is mostly ignored in practice: al-Bukhārī uses very weak ḥadīths on many occasions in *al-Adab al-Mufrad* as do Imām Aḥmad in the *Musnad*, Ibn al-Mubārak, Ibn Abī ʿĀsim, Hannād, and Aḥmad in their *Zuhd* books, al-Nawawī in *al-Adhkār*, Ibn Taymiyya, Ibn al-Qayyim, al-Dhahabī, and Ibn Rajab in their books on *faḍā'il*, al-Mundhirī in *al-Targhīb*, al-Maqdisī in *Faḍā'il al-Aʿmāl*, al-Shawkānī in *Tuḥfat al-Dhākirīn*, etc., and Ibn Ḥajar himself in his "Forty Ḥadīths Prohibiting the Muslim from Insulting His Brother Muslim" while al-Sakhāwī in *al-Qawl al-Badīʿ* (p. 432) says of a certain ḥadīth: "In sum, it is a very weak ḥadīth (*ḍaʿīf jiddan*) that is written in meritorious deeds (*yuktabu fī faḍā'il al-aʿmāl*), but as for its being forged, no, it is not [forged]."

Ibn al-Mubārak said, "One may narrate from him [a weak narrator] to a certain extent or those ḥadīths pertaining to good conduct (*adab*), admonition (*maw'iẓa*), and simple living (*zuhd*)."[197]

This conditional rule for narrating – and practicing – weak ḥadīths is in conformity with the unanimous view of the *Salaf* who permitted their use *in faḍā'il al-a'māl* as well as *manāqib*, *tafsīr*, and history including *sīra*, as opposed to *'aqīda* or the rulings pertaining to *ḥalāl* and *ḥarām*. This is stated or practiced by Sufyān al-Thawrī, Ibn 'Uyayna, 'Alī ibn al-Madīnī, Yaḥyā ibn Ma'īn, 'Abd al-Raḥmān ibn Mahdī, Aḥmad, Ibn Abī Ḥātim, al-Bukhārī in other than the *Ṣaḥīḥ*, al-Tirmidhī, and many others.[198] Ibn al-Ṣalāḥ said in his *'Ulūm al-Ḥadīth*:

> "Know that the forgery is the very worst of the weak ḥadīths and that it is not licit for anyone that knows a ḥadīth is forged to narrate it in any sense whatsoever except by showing, at the time, that it is forged, contrary to other types of weak ḥadīths,[199] which are possibly true in an unapparent way. It is permitted to narrate the latter in [matters of] encouragement [to good deeds] and deterrence [from evil ones.]....
>
> Among the experts of ḥadīth and other than them, it is allowed to lower the standards in the transmission chains and to narrate all kinds of weak ḥadīth other than the forgeries without attention to showing that they are weak, except with regard to the Divine Attributes and the rulings of the Law in the licit and the illict and other [rulings] besides these two. This

[197] Narrated by Ibn Abī Ḥātim in *Muqaddimat al-Jarḥ wal-Ta'dīl* (2:30) and cited by Ibn Rajab in *Sharḥ 'Ilal al-Tirmidhī* (1:73).
[198] Cf. al-Khaṭīb, *Kifāya* (p. 162-163=133-134), Ibn Abī Ḥātim, *Muqaddimat al-Jarḥ* (2:30-38), Ibn Rajab, *Sharḥ 'Ilal al-Tirmidhī* (1:73), Ibn Ḥajar, end of *al-Nukat 'alā Ibn al-Ṣalāḥ* (2:887-888), al-Suyūṭī, *Tadrīb*, al-Lacknawī, *al-Ajwibat al-Fāḍila*, etc.
[199] Because the forgery is ranked as the lowest type of weak ḥadīth.

> is the case, for example, in exhortations and [didactic] story-telling, meritorious deeds, all the varieties of encouragement and deterrence, and all that is un-connected with legal rulings and doctrinal beliefs. Among those from whom we narrate such a stipulation are ʿAbd al-Raḥmān ibn Mahdī and Aḥmad ibn Ḥanbal – Allah be well-pleased with both of them!"[200]

Imām al-Suyūṭī cites the above in the second section of his *Taḥdhīr al-Khawāṣṣ* on "The Prohibition of Narrating False Ḥadīths and Attributing them to Him ﷺ" then says:

> "On this the ulema of ḥadīth concur one and all and they categorically affirm that it is impermissible to narrate a forgery in any sense whatsoever except together with the exposition of its being forged, contrary to the weak ḥadīth which it is permissible to narrate in other than legal rulings and doctrine. Among those who have categorically affirmed this is Shaykh al-Islām Muḥyī al-Dīn al-Nawawī in his two books *al-Irshād* and *al-Taqrīb*, Qāḍī al-Quḍāt Badr al-Dīn Ibn Jamāʿa in *al-Manhal al-Rawī [fī ʿUlūm al-Ḥadīth al-Nabawī]*, al-Ṭībī in *al-Khulāṣa [fī ʿUlūm al-Ḥadīth]*, Shaykh al-Islām Sirāj al-Dīn al-Bulqīnī in *Maḥāsin al-Iṣṭilāḥ [fī Taḍmīn Ibn al-Ṣalāḥ]*, and the ḥadīth master of his time, Shaykh Zayn al-Dīn Abū al-Faḍl ʿAbd al-Raḥīm al-ʿIrāqī in his *Alfiyya* and its commentary."

The *Alfiyya* states,

> *They did not permit [the forgery] to be mentioned in any way*
> *By a learned person* [201] *as long as he fails to expose its status.*

[200] Ibn al-Ṣalāḥ, *ʿUlūm al-Ḥadīth*, chapters on the twenty-first type of ḥadīth ("The *mawḍūʿ*") and the twenty-second ("The *maqlūb*").
[201] *I.e.* "let alone the general public."

Then he said,

> *And they lowered standards in narrating other than the forged*[202]
> *Without having to show its weakness, but this they deem*
> *A must in what pertains to legal rulings and doctrines*
> *As related from Ibn Mahdī and several others.*

Al-Qārī cites some of the above in his introduction to the *Asrār* and adds, "I say: the ḥadīth Master of his time, al-ʿAsqalānī, has declared it explicitly in his commentary on his own *Nukhba*."

The dissents reported from Yaḥyā ibn Maʿīn, al-Bukhārī, Muslim, Ibn Ḥazm, Ibn al-ʿArabī al-Mālikī and al-Shawkānī are inaccurate. The correct position of Imām Muslim in the introduction to his *Ṣaḥīḥ* is that he forbade the use of forgers and other abandoned narrators, not of truthful weak ones, in conformity with the position of Aḥmad and the rest of the *Salaf*.[203] Muslim also says:

> "The sound reports from the trustworthy (*thiqāt*) narrators and those whose reliability is convincing are more than that we should be forced to transmit reports from those who are not trustworthy and whose reliability is not convincing."

The difference is clear between saying we are not forced to use weak narrators and saying that one cannot transmit anything from them. A proof of this is his use of the weak narration from ʿĀʾisha: "Treat people according to their ranks" and the fact that his strictness in narrators drops a notch or two in the ḥadīths of *raqāʾiq* or *faḍāʾil al-aʿmāl* in the *Ṣaḥīḥ*, as in the case of Shaddād ibn Saʿīd Abū Ṭalḥa al-Rāsibī or al-Walīd ibn Abī Walīd, as does al-Bukhārī's in his also.

[202] Corrupted to read '*narrating the forged*' in al-Ṣabbāgh's edition of the *Taḥdhīr*!
[203] Cf. al-Nawawī, *Sharḥ Ṣaḥīḥ Muslim, Muqaddima*; Ibn al-Qayyim, *Iʿlām al-Muwaqqiʿīn* (1:31); al-Sakhāwī, *al-Qawl al-Badīʿ* (p. 474); and ʿItr, Notes on Ibn Rajab's *Sharḥ ʿIlal al-Tirmidhī* (1:75-76).

Al-Bukhārī uses an even lesser criterion for narrations pertaining to *Faḍā'il* in his *Adab al-Mufrad.*

The claim about Ibn Maʿīn began with Ibn Sayyid al-Nās in his introduction to *'Uyūn al-Athar* and was imitated by others since, although it is contradicted by the early sources we cited.

The similar claim that Ibn al-ʿArabī was opposed to the use of weak ḥadīths in absolute terms is put to rest by his own statement about a certain weak ḥadīth: "Its chain is unknown, but it is preferable to put it into practice...."[204]

As for Ibn Ḥazm's statement against the use of weak narrations in absolute terms[205]: he elsewhere states preferring the use of weak ḥadīth over the use of juridical opinion (*ra'ī*), as does Ibn al-ʿArabī himself.[206] Finally, al-Shawkānī in *Nayl al-Awṭār* recommends putting into practice the ḥadīth on the preferable timings of cupping despite its severe weakness. And Allah knows best.

[204] Ibn al-ʿArabī, *'Āriḍat al-Aḥwadhī* (10:205) cf. *Fatḥ al-Bārī* (10:606) as cited by Muḥammad ʿAwwāma in his marginalia on *al-Qawl al-Badīʿ* (p. 472).

[205] In *al-Fiṣal fil-Milal wal-Niḥal* (2:83=2:69).

[206] Cf. Ibn Ḥazm, *al-Iḥkām* (6:225-226) and Ibn al-ʿArabī, *al-Maḥṣūl* (p. 98) and *Marāqī al-Zulaf* as cited in Ibn ʿArrāq, *Tanzīh al-Sharīʿa* (2:209-210).

Weak Ḥadīths in *Ṣaḥīḥ al-Bukhārī*?

Ibrāhīm ibn Maʿqil said: "I heard Muḥammad ibn Ismāʿīl al-Bukhārī say: 'I was with Isḥāq ibn Rāhūyah when a man said: 'Why don't you compile an epitome (*mukhtaṣar*) of the prophetic ways?' This stayed with me and was the reason why I compiled this book (the *Ṣaḥīḥ*)."[207] Al-Dhahabī said: "It has been narrated through two firm channels of transmission that al-Bukhārī said: 'I extracted this book from about 600,000 ḥadīths, and I compiled it over sixteen years, and I made it a plea for what lies between myself and Allah.'"[208] Al-Firabrī said: "Muḥammad ibn Ismāʿīl said to me: 'I never included in the *Ṣaḥīḥ* a ḥadīth except I made a major ablution (*ghusl*) and prayed two *rakʿat* beforehand.'"

Al-Nawawī said: "The scholars have agreed that the soundest of all ḥadīth compilations are the two *Ṣaḥīḥs* of al-Bukhārī and Muslim, and their vast majority have agreed that the soundest and most beneficial of the two was al-Bukhārī's." He continued: "The totality of its ḥadīths are 7,275 with the repetitions and about 4,000 without."

[207] M.M. Azamī writes: "Al-Bukhārī did not claim that what he left out were the spurious, nor that there were no authentic traditions outside his collection. On the contrary, he said: 'I only included in my book *al-Jāmiʿ* those that were authentic, and I left out many more authentic traditions than this to avoid unnecessary length.' He had no intention of collecting all the authentic traditions. He only wanted to compile a manual of *Ḥadīth* according to the wishes of his shaykh Isḥāq ibn Rūhāyah, and his function is quite clear from the title of his book *Al-Jāmiʿ, al-Musnad, al-Ṣaḥīḥ, al-Mukhtaṣar, Min Umūri Rasūl Allah wa-Sunanihi, wa-Ayyāmih* ('The Compendium of Sound Narrations Linked Back With Uninterrupted Chains and Epitomized of the Matters of the Messenger of Allah, His Ways, and His Times'). The word *al-mukhtaṣar*, epitome, itself explains that al-Bukhārī did not make any attempt at a comprehensive collection." *Studies in Early Ḥadīth Literature* (p. 304-305). This should be understood by those who ask: "If ḥadīth x is not in al-Bukhārī nor Muslim then how can it be authentic?"

[208] Narrated by al-Khaṭīb, *al-Jāmiʿ li-Akhlāq al-Rāwī* (2:270-271 §1613).

In his *Kitāb al-Tatabbu*ʿ al-Dāraquṭnī argues for the weakness of 78 ḥadiths in *al-Bukhārī*, 100 in *Muslim*, and 32 in both based mostly on *isnād* criticism.

Al-Nawawī said: "The two *Ṣaḥīḥs* differ from all other books only in respect to the fact that what is in them is *ṣaḥīḥ* and does not require investigation."[209] Ibn al-Ṣalāḥ said:"Whatever only al-Bukhārī or only Muslim narrates enters [also] into the category of what is definitely *ṣaḥīḥ*... except a few letters, which some of the expert critics objected to, such as al-Dāraquṭnī and others – and these are known to the specialists."[210] He said this after stating that what they agree upon is 'definitely *ṣaḥīḥ*' (*maqṭūʿun bişiḥḥatihi*) for the Umma. Imām al-Nawawī objected to the terms 'definitely *ṣaḥīḥ*' while granting all that is in the *Ṣaḥīḥayn* the level of 'strongly presumed [*ṣaḥīḥ*]' until it becomes *mutawātir* (*yufīdu al-ẓanna mā lam yatawātar*) as is the rule with all *ṣaḥīḥ* lone-narrated (*āḥād*) ḥadīths.[211] But Ibn Kathīr differed: "I am with Ibn al-Ṣalāḥ in his conclusion and directives, and Allah knows best."[212] Al-Suyūṭī in *Tadrīb al-Rāwī* cites Ibn Kathīr's words verbatim then states: "And this is also my choice and none other."[213] It is also the choice of Ibn Ḥajar. Al-Suyūṭī states: "Shaykh al-Islām said: 'What al-Nawawī mentioned in *Sharḥ Ṣaḥīḥ Muslim* is based on the perspective of the majority (*al-aktharīn*); as for that of the verifying authorities (*al-muḥaqqiqīn*), then no. For the verifying authorities also agree with Ibn al-Ṣalāḥ'"[214] (By "Shaykh al-Islām"

[209] Al-Nawawī, Introduction to his *Sharḥ Ṣaḥīḥ Muslim* (1:20): *"Innamā yaftariqu al-Ṣaḥīḥāni ʿan ghayrihimā min al-kutub fī kawni mā fīhimā ṣaḥīḥan lā yuḥtāju ilā al-naẓari fīḥ."*

[210] Ibn al-Ṣalāḥ, *ʿUlūm al-Ḥadīth*, chapter on the *ṣaḥīḥ* ḥadīth (Dār al-Fikr ed. p.29): *"Mā infarada bihi al-Bukhārī aw Muslimun mundarijun fī qābili mā yuqṭaʿu bi-ṣiḥḥatihi... siwā aḥrufin yasīratin takallama ʿalayhā baʿḍu ahli al-naqdi min al-Ḥuffāẓ kal-Dāraquṭnī wa-ghayrih, wa-hiya maʿrūfatun ʿinda ahli hādha al-sha'n."*

[211] Al-Nawawī, *Taqrīb wal-Taysīr* (p. 70) and *Sharḥ Ṣaḥīḥ Muslim* (1:20).

[212] Ibn Kathīr, chapter on the *ṣaḥīḥ* ḥadīth in *Ikhtiṣār ʿUlūm al-Ḥadīth* (p. 45).

[213] Al-Suyūṭī, *Tadrīb al-Rāwī* (Dār al-Kalim al-Ṭayyib ed. 1:145).

al-Suyūṭī means the spotless *Ḥāfiẓ* and immaculate *Imām* Ibn Ḥajar al-ʿAsqalānī and his book *al-Nukat ʿalā Ibn al-Ṣalāḥ*.[215]) This is because of the standing of the two *Ṣaḥīḥs* in the *Umma* and because none of the past *Imāms* in Islam ever declared explicitly and rightly that all they had gathered in their respective books was *ṣaḥīḥ* except al-Bukhārī and Muslim, and the verifying experts have confirmed their claim.

Al-Suyūṭī goes on to quote in detail – mostly from *Hadī al-Sārī* – the refutations of Ibn Ḥajar to al-Dāraquṭnī's criticism, showing that, in effect, the latter fails to invalidate the view of the *Ṣaḥiḥayn* as 100% *ṣaḥīḥ*.[216] The fact is that they are all *ṣaḥīḥ* but not all of them reach the same high degree of *ṣaḥīḥ*.

This is in essence what al-Dhahabī concluded concerning the few narrators of the *Ṣaḥiḥayn* whose grading was questioned: The narration of one such as those, does not go below the rank of *ḥasan* which we might call the lowest rank of the *ṣaḥīḥ*.[217] Shaykh Abū Ghudda comments in the margin: "This is an explicit confirmation that al-Bukhārī and Muslim did not confine themselves, in the narrations of their respective books, only to narrate ḥadīths that have the highest degree of *ṣiḥḥa*." Then again in his

[214] *Tadrīb al-Rāwī* (1:143).

[215] Cf. Ibn Ḥajar, *al-Nukat ʿalā Ibn al-Ṣalāḥ* (1:371). See also his words from his *Sharḥ Nukhbat al-Fikar* (p. 230-231) to the effect that the foremost ḥadīth expert's examination of and familiarity with any given *āḥād* ḥadīth may take him to the conclusion that it is *qaṭʿī al-thubūt* – categorically established as *ṣaḥīḥ*, i.e. in effect of *mutawātir*-like authenticity – unlike the feel of the rest of the scholars with regard to the same ḥadīth. The knowledge of the expert is named by Dr. ʿItr, after Ibn al-Ṣalāḥ, "non-absolutely-binding study-based knowledge reaching certainty" (*al-ʿilm al-naẓarī al-yaqīnī ghayr al-ḍarūrī* and he places it midway between *al-ʿilm al-yaqīnī al-qaṭʿī al-ḍarūrī* which is absolutely binding, and *ʿilm ghalabat al-ẓann*, which is relatively binding. From his unpublished inaugural lecture to the Preparatory Class of Abū al-Nūr Institute, Damascus, October 1997.

[216] Cf. Abū Ghudda, Appendix to al-Dhahabī's *Mūqiẓa* (p.141-145)

[217] Al-Dhahabī, *al-Mūqiẓa* (p. 80).

appendix (p. 144) he states: "Our Shaykh, the *'Allāma* Aḥmad Shākir – Allah have mercy on him – stated: 'The truth without doubt among the verifiers of those who have knowledge of the sciences of ḥadīth... is that the ḥadīths of the two *Ṣaḥīḥs* are all *ṣaḥīḥ* and there is not in a single one of them a cause for true disparagement or weakness. What al-Dāraquṭnī and others criticized is only on the basis that it did not reach the high criterion which each of them defined in their respective books. As for the [criterion of] soundness (*siḥḥa*) of the ḥadīths in themselves, then both of them lived up to it.

Dr. Badī' al-Sayyid al-Laḥḥām in his edition of Ibn Kathīr's *Ikhtiṣār 'Ulūm al-Ḥadīth* (p. 44-45) also closes the discussion on the topic of the *Ṣaḥīḥayn* with the same words but without attributing them to Shākir. Abū Ghudda concludes (p. 145): "All these texts show that most of what is in *Ṣaḥīḥ al-Bukhārī* and *Ṣaḥīḥ Muslim* is of the highest degree of the *ṣaḥīḥ*, and that some of what is in them is not of the highest degree of the *ṣaḥīḥ*."

More to the point, our teacher Dr. Nūr al-Dīn 'Itr said in his manual *Manhaj al-Naqd fī 'Ulūm al-Ḥadīth*: "The ruling concerning the ḥadīths of the two *Ṣaḥīḥs* is that they are all *ṣaḥīḥ*."[218]

All those mentioned above – Ibn al-Ṣalāḥ, al-Nawawī, al-Dhahabī, Ibn Kathīr, Ibn Ḥajar, al-Suyūṭī, Aḥmad Shākir, Abū Ghudda, 'Itr, al-Laḥḥām – agreed on the fact that all of what is in al-Bukhārī and Muslim is *ṣaḥīḥ*, and, apart from al-Nawawī's duly recorded dissent, the *muḥaqqiqūn* such as Ibn al-Ṣalāḥ, Ibn Kathīr, Ibn Ḥajar, and al-Suyūṭī consider all the ḥadīths contained in them *maqṭū'un biṣiḥḥatihi* i.e. of the same probative force as *mutawātir* ḥadīth. Further examination of the positions of the major ḥadīth masters might add more names to this distinguished list.

[218] 'Itr, *Manhaj al-Naqd fī 'Ulūm al-Ḥadīth* (3rd ed. p. 254).

The questions are sometimes asked (1) whether all the Ulema of ḥadīth agree that all the ḥadīths in *al-Bukhārī* and *Muslim* are *ṣaḥīḥ* or (2) if there are any scholars who consider them to contain some weak narrations, and (3) whether one who believes that the *Ṣaḥīḥayn* are not 100% *ṣaḥīḥ* is an innovator.

As was just shown, some of the greatest ḥadīth authorities answered yes to the first question. Imām al-Ḥaramayn (Ibn al-Juwaynī) even said that if a man swore on pains of divorce that all that is in al-Bukhārī and Muslim is *ṣaḥīḥ* his marriage would be safe.[219] But Imām al-Dāraquṭnī said a small number may not reach that level so the answer to the second question has to be yes. Yet the objections were refuted one by one by Ibn Ḥajar at the beginning of *Fatḥ al-Bārī* and Imām al-Nawawī at the beginning of *Sharḥ Ṣaḥīḥ Muslim*. The short formula "whether the *Ṣaḥīḥayn* are or not 100% *ṣaḥīḥ*" remains tenuous and misleading, for the *Umma* far and wide – meaning the Consensus of the *Fuqahā'* generation after generation – have been satisfied that they are.

This conclusion excludes the chainless, broken-chained reports, or unattibuted reports sometimes adduced by al-Bukhārī in his chapter-titles or appended to certain narrations. An example of the latter is the so-called "suicide ḥadīth" – one of al-Zuhrī's unattributive narrations (*balāghāt*) which is actually broken-chained and therefore weak. It does not meet the criteria of ḥadīth authenticity used by the ḥadīth Masters, even less that of al-Bukhārī who mentioned it only to show its discrepancy with two other chains whose versions omit the attempted suicide story, and Allah knows best.[220]

[219] See Sirāj al-Dīn's *Sharḥ al-Bayqūniyya* (p. 46)

[220] Cf. *Fatḥ* (12:359-360), Abū Shuhba, *al-Sīra al-Nabawiyya* (1:265-266), Mūsā Shahīn, *Fatḥ al-Mun'im* (2:337), al-Albānī, *Difā' 'an al-Ḥadīth wal-Sīra* (p. 41-42), and Sa'd al-Mirṣafi in *Ḥadīth Bid' al-Waḥī fil-Mīzān* (p. 75- 85).

The above conclusion is proof that the position that everything that is found in the two *Ṣaḥīḥs* is rigorously sound refers only to full-chained reports positively attributed to the Prophet ﷺ – and Allah knows best.[221]

[221] See more on this issue at http://webpages.marshall.edu/~laher1/bkhr_mslm.html.

Lone-Narrator Reports (*Āḥād*)

The lone-narrator report (*khabar al-wāḥid*) lexically means something narrated by only one person, and in ḥadīth nomenclature, any report that does not reach the conditions of mass narration (*tawātur*), whether narrated by one, two, or more narrators.[222] *Āḥād* reports can either be *ṣaḥīḥ*, *ḥasan*, or *ḍaʿīf*. Thus, their being lone-narrator reports is not an evaluation of the authenticity of the ḥadīth but rather a description of how it reached us.

Ahl al-Sunna concur, unlike the *Muʿtazila*, that the lone-narrator reports that are authenticated – "acceptable" (*maqbūl*) in ḥadīth nomenclature – are obligatory to believe and put into practice. Al-Qārī relates, on this point, the consensus of the Companions and the Successors.[223] Where Scholars differ is whether the same ḥadīths convey absolute certainty of knowledge (*al-ʿilm al-yaqīnī*) or only the compelling assumption of truth (*al-ẓann al-ghālib*). These two categories differ insofar as obligatory practice and belief based on certainty of knowledge cannot be denied except on pains of apostasy, while the denial of obligatory practice and belief based on reports compellingly assumed to be true does not constitute apostasy but constitutes sin. The scholars do concur that if one disbelieves in a sound lone-narrator report one commits a grave transgression (*fisq*) and is even considered misguided (*ḍāll*), but does not leave the fold of Islam: "If one disbelieves in them [*āḥād* reports], we do not say to him: 'Repent [of your *kufr*]!'"[224] This is clearly unlike disbelief in a mass-transmitted report or in a verse of the Qur'ān.

[222] Al-Qārī, *Sharḥ Sharḥ Nukhbat al-Fikar* (p. 209). Cf. Ibn al-Ṣalāḥ, *'Ulūm al-Ḥadīth* (p. 10); *Uṣūl al-Shāshī* (p. 272); Ibn Ḥazm, *al-Iḥkām* (1:108). Imām al-Qarafī in *Sharḥ Tanqīḥ al-Uṣūl fī Ikhtiṣār al-Maḥṣul fil-Uṣūl* (p. 356) defines it as "the report of a singular or group of upright (*'adl*) reporters that leads to conjecture (*ẓann*)."
[223] Al-Qārī, *op. cit.* (p. 211).
[224] Al-Shāfiʿī, *al-Risāla* (p. 460-461).

Ibn Khafīf said in *Al-ʿAqīda al-Ṣaḥīḥa*:

> 89. Lone-narrator reports (*āḥād*) make practice obligatory, but not knowledge (*yūjib al-ʿamal lā al-ʿilm*), while mass-narrated (*mutawātir*) reports make both knowledge and practice obligatory.

The meaning of the above position is that it is obligatory to integrate the content of an accepted lone-narrator report into one's Islamic practice and belief; however, such a report does not impose the certainty of knowledge of a mass-transmitted report.

Assumption of truth carries various degrees of strength, the highest of which, according to Ibn Ḥajar and others, constitute "iron-clad inductive knowledge" (*ʿilm naẓarī yaqīnī*) because of various external indicators (*qarāʾin*). For example, if a lone-narrated ḥadīth is narrated in the two *Ṣaḥīḥs*, has several (non-discrepant) chains of transmission, and counts among its narrators great Imāms such as Mālik and al-Shāfiʿī, "then it would not be far-fetched to declare it categorically true, and Allah knows best."[225] At the same time Ibn Ḥajar warned: "All the types of non-*mutawātir* ḥadīth which we have mentioned do not result in [certainty of] knowledge regarding their veracity except to the Scholar of ḥadīth who has reached the level of expertise, knows the situations of the narrators, and is fully acquainted with the minute defects of ḥadīth."[226]

Thus certain indices or parallels raise the accepted lone-narrated ḥadīth closer or up to the level of definitive, obligatory knowledge as already illustrated by Ibn Ḥajar's words, and as stated by the scholars of *uṣūl*.[227] Among these factors are those mentioned by Ibn Ḥajar – the acceptance of the report by the

[225] Ibn Ḥajar, *Sharḥ Nukhbat al-Fikar* (p. 232).
[226] Cf. note 215.
[227] Cf. al-Ghazzālī, *al-Mustaṣfā* (1:135-136); al-Āmidī, *al-Iḥkām fī Uṣūl al-Aḥkām*, Part 1, section entitled *Fī Ḥaqīqat al-Khabar al-Wāḥid*.

entire Community, lack of discrepancy among its various narrations, and soundness of their chains of transmission. Examples of such ḥadīths are those that concern the punishment of the grave.[228]

All of the scholars further agree, as already stated, that a non-mass-narrated accepted ḥadīth, although merely *ẓannī al-thubūt*, possesses the following properties:

- Belief in it is obligatory (*al-taṣdīq bihi wājib*)
- Denying it is a grave transgression (*inkāruhu fisq*)

Beyond the above, the scholars differ on the point brought up by Ibn Khafīf. Some have held that we are obliged only to assume as true accepted lone-narrator reports, although they do make belief and practice obligatory since such assumption is compelling (*yufīd al-ẓann al-ghālib*) and thus precludes doubt. This is the position of Ibn Khafīf and the Ashʿarīs, in conformity with the vast majority (*al-jumhūr*) of *Ahl al-Sunna* as stated by Ibn ʿAbd al-Barr:

> "What the majority of the people of knowledge believe is as follows: Some hold that the lone-narrated ḥadīth make practice obligatory but not knowledge (*yūjib al-ʿamal dūna al-ʿilm*). This is the position of al-Shāfiʿī and the vast majority of the jurists and the scholars of principles. To them, the lone-narrated ḥadīth does not make knowledge obligatory except on oath, providing definite preclusion of falsehood, and if there is no disagreement concerning it."[229]

[228] Cf. al-Sarakhsī, *al-Uṣūl* (1:329-330 *Bāb fī Qabūl Akhbār al-Āḥād*); al-Pazdawī, *al-Uṣūl* (1:696). Yet many Masters consider the narrations of the punishment of the grave to have *mutawātir* status: Abū Manṣūr al-Baghdādī (a major Ashʿarī authority) at the end of *al-Farq bayn al-Firaq* and Abū Maymūn al-Nasafī (a major Māturīdī authority) in *Tabṣirat al-Adilla* both said there is consensus that the denier of the punishment of the grave is an apostate (and not just a corrupt innovator), while al-Kattānī entered it in his *Naẓm al-Mutanāthir*.

An illustration for the acceptance of lone-narrated ḥadīths on provision of oath is given by ʿAlī ibn Abī Ṭālib ﷺ: "When I heard something from the Messenger of Allah, Allah would benefit me with it as He wished; but when someone other than him narrated it to me, I would make him swear to it; if he took an oath, I would believe him." [230]

Ibn ʿAbd al-Barr goes on to say that part of the Scholars of ḥadīth and some of the Scholars of principles consider that lone-narrated ḥadīths make both external knowledge[231] and practice obligatory. He concludes: "Our position is that they make practice obligatory but not knowledge... and that is the position of most jurists and ḥadīth scholars."[232] It is also the position of al-Bukhārī and Aḥmad as well as later scholars including al-Kawtharī.[233]

Their position on doctrinal matters conveyed by *āḥād* reports is given by al-Bayhaqī:

> "The perspicuous scholars (*ahl al-naẓar*) among our [Ashʿarī] companions relinquish the use of lone-narrated reports as proofs in the Divine Attributes if such reports do not have a foundation in the Qur'ān or in scholarly Consensus. Instead, they interpret them figuratively."[234]

[229] Ibn ʿAbd al-Barr, *al-Tamhīd* (1:7).
[230] See notes 280-281.
[231] By external knowledge is meant knowledge of obligations and prohibitions as opposed to internal knowledge which concerns doctrine, and Allah knows best.
[232] Ibn ʿAbd al-Barr, *al-Tamhīd* (1:7).
[233] Cf. al-Ghazzālī, *al-Mustaṣfā*, Ibn al-Ṣalāḥ, *'Ulūm al-Ḥadīth*, al-ʿIrāqī, *Sharḥ 'Ulūm al-Ḥadīth*, Ibn Kathīr, *Ikhtiṣār 'Ulūm al-Ḥadīth*, al-Nawawī, *Sharḥ Muqaddima Muslim*, al-Qāsimī, *Qawāʿid al-Taḥdīth*, and the contemporary authorities such as Abū Zahra, Muḥammad al-Khudarī, al-Ghazālī, and al-Qaraḍāwī, all as quoted from Sāmer Islambūlī's *al-Āḥād, al-Naskh, al-Ijmāʿ* (p. 27-30). Also see al-Khaṭīb, *al-Kifāya* (p. 34-48) and ʿAbd al-Qāhir al-Baghdādī, *Uṣūl al-Dīn* (p. 12). "Any proof in the chapter of doctrine can only be from the revealed Book or the well-known sound ḥadīths." Al-Kawtharī, commentary on al-Subkī's *al-Sayf al-Ṣaqīl* (p. 173 n.).

Others dissented, such as Ibn al-Qayyim and, lately, al-Albānī, claiming that not only are *āḥād*-based belief and practice obligatory, but we are also obliged to know them as categorically true (*yufīd al-ʿilm al-qaṭʿī*) and they consider them part of obligatory doctrinal knowledge.[235] These classifications can be summarized in the following table:[236]

Āḥād sound report on *ʿaqīda*	Those who say: "It imparts knowledge"	Those who say: "It does not impart it"
Its transmission chain? Belief in it? Its rejection? What does it impart?	Assumed veracity Obligatory Grave transgression Definitive knowledge (al-Albānī)	Assumed veracity Obligatory Grave transgression Compelling assumption (*al-jumhūr*)

The position that sound *āḥād* impart definitive knowledge is a weak position since it blurs the unanimous, vital distinction between *mutawātir* and qur'ānic reports on the one hand, and all other reports. An additional inconsistency of that position is its contradictory labeling of lone-narrated reports as "assumed" in the veracity of their transmission chains and yet "categorical" in the knowledge they impart. Some have reacted to these errors with another weak stand which consists in dismissing any and all *āḥād* reports as something one is free to reject, especially in the chapter of doctrine. Hence, Dr. Nūr al-Dīn ʿItr characterized these contemporary positions with regard to *āḥād* ḥadīths as straddling two extremes: "Some exaggerate in accepting the sound lone-narrated ḥadīth to the point that they seem to think none but they put it into practice, while others exaggerate to the point that they seem to consider the lone-narrated ḥadīth as nothing binding."[237]

[234] Al-Bayhaqī, *al-Asmā' wal-Ṣifāt* (Kawtharī ed. p. 357, Ḥāshidī ed. 2:201).
[235] Cf. Ibn al-Qayyim, al-Albānī in his essay entitled "The Lone-Narrated Ḥadīth is a Proof in Itself," and those who followed them, refuted by Islambulī.
[236] Adapted from Islambūlī's *al-Āḥād* (p. 41).

Finally, the Consensus of the scholarly Community of *Ahl al-Sunna* take precedence over the lone-narrated ḥadīth in the hierarchy of juridical sources in the Religion. Al-Shāfiʿī said: "Consensus is greater than a lone-narrated ḥadīth."[238] Al-Khaṭīb explained: "This means that when Consensus is opposed by a lone-narrated ḥadīth, the latter cannot be cited as proof."[239]

In recapitulation,[240] although lone-narrator ḥadīths do not form a basis for certitude, they are valid to be used under specific conditions. Following are some of the conditions that were laid down by the Ulema:

- They have to be accepted by the *Umma*.[241]
- They should not contradict a definite text. Al-Shawkānī said in *Irshād al-Fuḥūl*: "This point has its origin with the *Salaf*." ʿĀʾisha rejected the ḥadīth that "the dead person gets punished if his family weeps over him" because it contradicted verses 38-39 of Sūrat al-Najm.
- They must not go against the Consensus of *Ahl al-Madīna* according to the Mālikī School, for whom that Consensus takes precedence over lone-narrator reports.
- They must not contradict facts proven conclusively by the mind.[242]

The *Jumhūr* therefore agreed that, provided certain conditions, lone-narrator reports were a source of legislation – but not doctrine – in Islam. Al-Khaṭīb al-Baghdādī said in the *Kifāya*: "A lone-narrated report cannot be independently relied upon in an

---

[237] From the inaugural lecture to the Preparatory Class of Abū al-Nūr Institute, Damascus, October 1997.
[238] *Siyar Aʿlām al-Nubalāʾ* (Risāla ed.10:20), *Ḥilya* (9:105), Ibn Abī Ḥātim's *Ādāb al-Shāfiʿī* (p. 231) and others.
[239] Al-Khaṭīb al-Baghdādī, *Al-Faqīh wal-Mutafaqqih* (1:132).
[240] Some of the material cited from this point was adapted from Iyād Hilal's article, "Khabr Ahaad and the ʿAqeedah" in *Khalifʿornia Journal*, January-June, 1997 issue.
[241] Cf. Ibn Taymiyya, *Miswadda* (p. 243).
[242] Cf. al-Shawkānī, al-Shāṭibī, and ʿAbd al-Qāhir al-Baghdādī, *Uṣūl al-Dīn* (p. 23).

issue where absolute knowledge is required because it cannot be proven beyond the shadow of a doubt that this is what the Prophet ﷺ said. However, a [sound] lone-narrated report must be accepted in the legal rulings such as penalties, moonsighting, *ḥajj*, *zakāt*, inheritance, prayer, prohibiting the illicit, etc." To reject such reports as a source of the *Sharī ʿa* constitutes a denial of the greatest part of the Religion!

The disagreement of the scholars was not over the general use of those reports, but rather over the conditions that justified or nullified the use of one particular ḥadīth. A similar debate does not exist regarding the *mutawātir*, because it is conclusively proven to be from the Prophet ﷺ. The lone-narrator report's margin of error comes from the fact that although the reporters of the *ṣaḥīḥ* ḥadīth are credible as individuals, they are not infallible.

Following are the conclusions of some of the scholars on that basis:

- Al-Kamāl ibn al-Humām: "Most jurists and ḥadīth scholars say that the *khabar al-wāḥid* does not produce certainty at all."[243]
- Al-Āmidī stated: "The Scholars of the *Umma* said that the *khabar al-wāḥid* produces conjecture (*ẓann*) except for some of the Ẓāhiris and Aḥmad ibn Ḥanbal according to one of two narrations from him."[244]
- According to Ibn Qudāma in *Rawḍat al-Nāẓir* (1:202-4) and al-Ṭūfī in *al-Bulbul* (p. 35), two opinions are related from Imām Aḥmad concerning the issue of whether *āḥād* ḥadīths convey *ʿilm*: [1] No; it is the preponderant (*aẓhar*) opinion and held by most; [2] Yes; it is an opinion held by a group of *Ahl al-ḥadīth* and Ẓāhirīs; this is understood only for reports that have "external indicators" (*qarāʾin*) [cf. Ibn al-Mibrad's *Ghāyat al-Sūl* (p. 211-12) and al-Turkī, *Uṣūl Madhhab al-Imām Aḥmad* (p. 250)].

[243] In *al-Taḥrīr* (2:368).
[244] In *al-Iḥkām* (2:49-50).

It is also said that the second opinion applies to statements transmitted by a scholar agreed to be upright, trustworthy, and expert, when it is transmitted to us through multiple chains and the *Umma* has accepted it, such as the narrations of Abū Bakr and ʿUmar ☙, and the like. In any case, the Ḥanbalī School one and all hold the first opinion and respond to the second opinion by saying that if this were indeed so, we would believe every single report we ever hear, not a single report could disagree with the other, it would be possible for an *āḥād* report to abrogate the Qurʾān or a *mutawātir* ḥadīth, it would be permissible for a judge to pass judgment based on a single witness's report; upright and corrupt narrators would be indifferent (as in *tawātur* reports) – all of which is false. In conclusion, Imām Aḥmad's two narrations do not really contradict one another, and while some externalists did allow that lone-narrated reports convey absolute knowledge, nevertheless, this can only be when there are some forms of external indicators and not a single Ḥanbalī has been cited to say or practice otherwise.

– Ibn Taymiyya quotes Ibn ʿAbd al-Barr's summary already mentioned: "The majority said that it dictates action, not certainty, and it is the opinion of al-Shāfiʿī and the majority of the jurists." Ibn Taymiyya adds: "The lone-narrator report makes action obligatory and is most likely to be true, short of certainty, according to the majority." He then cites al-Juwaynī and Ibn al-Bāqillānī in support of this opinion.[245]

– Al-Shāṭibī: "Anything related to *Uṣūl al-Dīn* must be conclusive." "A proof is either lone or mass-transmitted. If it is lone-narrated then it obviously does not dictate absolute certitude." "If any conclusive proof conflicts with a conjectural proof, the conclusive proof is binding."[246]

---

[245] In *Miswaddat Āl Taymiyya* (p. 236-244).

- 'Abd al-'Alī al-Anṣārī: "Most Scholars of *uṣūl*, including the three Imāms (Abū Ḥanīfa, al-Shāfi'ī, and Mālik) hold that the lone-narrator report produces conjecture only. This holds whether the report is supported by external indicators (*qarā'in*) or not."[247]
- Al-Shawkānī said something similar as does our teacher Dr. Nūr al-Dīn 'Itr in his *Manhaj al-Naqd fī 'Ulūm al-Ḥadīth.*[248]
- Al-Lacknawī said: "The attainment of absolutely obligatory knowledge (*'ilm ḍarūrī*) is of the exclusive attributes of the mass-transmitted report. As for the *āḥād* and widespread reports (*mashāhīr*) which are supported by external indicators (*qarā'in*) they do not convey other than inductive knowledge (*'ilm naẓarī*). It is also said that they do not convey knowledge at all. Ibn Ḥajar said: 'The truth is it is a difference in terminology [only]. Whoever lets it be called *'ilm* qualifies it as inductive and whoever refuses to call it *'ilm* reserves the latter label for the mass-transmitted exclusively, saying that any other type only conveys conjecture (*ẓann*).'"[249]

Hence Imām al-Bayhaqī said regarding reports on doctrine:

> "The rule is that every Divine Attribute mentioned in the Book or authentically conveyed in mass-narrated (*mutawātir*) reports or in lone-narrated ones (*āḥād*) but having an origin (*aṣl*) in the Book, or being inferable from one of its meanings: we affirm such an Attribute and we let it pass as stated in its external wording, without addressing modality. As for what is not mentioned in the Book, nor originates in mass-narrated reports, nor derives from the meanings of the Book, at the same time being conveyed in lone-narrated reports: if, by letting it

[246] In *al-Muwāfaqāt* (1:29-36 and 2:15).
[247] In *Fawātiḥ al-Raḥamūt fī Sharḥ Musallam al-Thubūt* (2:121).
[248] Al-Shawkānī, *Irshād al-Fuḥūl* (p. 48-49), 'Itr, *Manhaj al-Naqd* (p. 245).
[249] Al-Lacknawī, *Ẓafar al-Amānī* (p. 42)

pass according to its external meaning, we end up likening Allah to creation, then we interpret that meaning on linguistic bases so as to eliminate any anthropomorphism."[250]

Isnād-Criticism of the First Four Caliphs

The major Companions usually did not accept lone-narrated reports but may have done so at times because the Prophet ﷺ himself did when he questioned the man who said he had seen the new moon of *Ramaḍān*: "Do you bear witness that there is no God except Allah and that Muḥammad is the Messenger of Allah?" When he replied in the affirmative, the Prophet ﷺ accepted his news.[251]

When Abū Bakr ؓ asked: "How much does the grandmother inherit?" Al-Mughīra ibn Shuʿba said, "I bear witness that the Messenger of Allah ﷺ gave her one sixth." Abū Bakr said, "Does anyone else know this?" Then Muḥammad ibn Maslama came forward with the same report.[252]

Al-Ḥākim said: "The first to ascertain that no lie be attributed to the Messenger of Allah ﷺ was Abū Bakr."[253] Al-Dhahabī said: "Abū Bakr was the first to take precautions before accepting reports."[254]

When ʿUmar asked the people if they had heard anything concerning blood-money for the stillborn, al-Mughīra ibn Shuʿba said: "I witnessed the Messenger of Allah ﷺ order the emancipation of a male or female slave [as payment] for it." ʿUmar said, "Bring me someone to witness [to the same] with you," after which Muḥammad ibn Maslama again came forth and witnessed to the same.[255] Even so, ʿUmar seems to have sought

[250] *Al-Asmā' wal-Ṣifāt* (Kawtharī ed. p. 353; Ḥāshidī ed. 2:194-195).
[251] With a fair chain from Ibn ʿAbbās by al-Tirmidhī, Abū Dāwūd, and al-Dārimī.
[252] In the *Muwaṭṭa'* and *Sunan* cf. ʿAjāj al-Khaṭīb, *al-Sunna Qabl al-Tadwīn* (p. 112).
[253] Al-Ḥākim, *Madkhal ilā Maʿrifati Kitāb al-Iklīl* (p. 116 §200) toward the end.
[254] Al-Dhahabī, *Tadhkirat al-Ḥuffāẓ* (1:2-3) cf. al-Aʿẓamī, *Manhaj al-Naqd ʿind al-Muḥaddithīn* (p. 50).

further assurance since Ṭāwūs also narrated that when ʿUmar asked, "I adjure by Allah any man who heard from the Messenger of Allah ﷺ something about the foetus?" Ḥamal ibn Mālik ibn al-Nābigha got up and said, "I was between two women of mine – meaning two wives – and one of them hit the other one with a tent-pole killing her and her unborn child, whereupon the Messenger of Allah ﷺ ordered that she pay one tenth of the blood money or [the emancipation of] a slave for the foetus, and that she be killed for killing the woman." ʿUmar said, "Had I not heard it I would have ruled something else."[256]

ʿAbd Allah ibn ʿAmr ibn Umayya al-Ḍamrī narrated from his father that ʿUmar passed the latter as he was haggling over the price of a wool or silk garment. ʿUmar asked, "What is this?" He replied, "I wish to buy it and give it away as a charity." He bought it and gave it to his wife, saying, "I heard the Messenger of Allah ﷺ say, 'Whatever you give the womenfolk [of your household] it is a *ṣadaqa*.'" ʿUmar said, "Who will witness [to this] with you?" He went to ʿĀ'isha and stood behind the door. She asked, "Who is this?" He replied, "ʿAmr." She said, "What brings you?" He said, "I heard the Messenger of Allah ﷺ say, 'Whatever you give the womenfolk it is a *ṣadaqa*.'" She said, "Yes."[257]

Mālik ibn Aws said: "I heard ʿUmar say to ʿAbd al-Raḥmān ibn ʿAwf, Ṭalḥa, al-Zubayr, and Saʿd: 'I adjure by Allah by Whom stand the heaven and the earth! Do you all know for sure that the Messenger of Allah ﷺ said, "We [Prophets] do not bequeath inheritance; whatever we leave behind is charity (*ṣadaqa*)?"' They all said, '*Allahumma!* Yes.'"[258]

[255] Narrated by al-Bukhārī and Muslim cf. al-Aʿẓamī, *Manhaj al-Naqd* (p. 51) and ʿAjāj al-Khaṭīb, *al-Sunna Qabl al-Tadwīn* (p. 114).

[256] Narrated from Ḥamal in the *Sunan* and *Musnad* and from al-Mughīra ibn Shuʿba in the *Ṣaḥīḥayn* cf. al-Aʿẓamī, *Manhaj al-Naqd* (p. 54).

[257] Narrated by al-Bayhaqī in *Sunan al-Kubrā* (4:178) cf. al-Aʿẓamī, *Manhaj al-Naqd* (p. 52-53).

The Two Shaykhs – Abū Bakr and ʿUmar ※ – went to inordinate lengths in their suspicion of fraud in ḥadīth reports. Abū Bakr had the written record of all the ḥadīths he had in his possession burnt lest a mistake slip into them. It is related that ʿĀʾisha said: "My father gathered the ḥadīth from the Messenger of Allah ﷺ and it was five hundred ḥadīths. He spent one night tossing and turning and this worried me. I said, 'Are you tossing and turning because of some ailment or have you heard some bad news?" In the morning he said, "Daughter, bring me the ḥadīths you have with you." I brought them, then he called for fire and burnt them. He said, "I fear lest I die with those [ḥadīths] still in your possession and there might be among them ḥadīths from someone I trusted and believed, but it was not as he said to me, and I would have imitated him [in his error]."[259]

Abū Mūsā al-Ashʿarī visited ʿUmar one day but the latter was busy with the *Anṣār* so Abū Mūsā left. Later, when ʿUmar asked him why he had left he replied: "I asked permission to enter thrice but was denied so I left, since the Messenger of Allah ﷺ said: 'When one of you asks permission to enter thrice and is denied, let him leave.'" Umar said: "I swear by Allah that you are going to have to prove this beyond doubt or I shall make you sore! Has anyone among you heard this from the Prophet ﷺ ?" Ubay ibn Kaʿb said, "I swear by Allah that none but the youngest here shall stand by you!" Abū Saʿīd al-Khudrī said: "I was the youngest, so I stood by him and told ʿUmar that the Prophet ﷺ had indeed said that." ʿUmar said to Abū Mūsā, "Truly I do not question your truthfulness, but I feared lest people start attributing things to the Messenger of Allah ﷺ !"[260]

---

[258] Narrated by Aḥmad with a sound chain cf. ʿAjāj al-Khaṭīb, *al-Sunna Qabl al-Tadwīn* (p. 115).

[259] Narrated by al-Ḥākim as stated by Ibn Kathīr in the *Musnad al-Ṣiddīq* inside his *Jāmiʿ al-Asānīd* and cited by al-Muḥibb al-Ṭabarī in *al-Riyāḍ al-Naḍira* (2:144 §612) and al-Dhahabī in *Tadhkirat al-Ḥuffāẓ* (1:5 *lā yaṣiḥḥ*).

Sālim Abū al-Naḍr narrated that ʿUmar asked al-ʿAbbās to sell or donate his house so the Prophet's ﷺ mosque could be expanded and accommodate the large number of the Muslims but al-ʿAbbās refused. They went to Ubay ibn Kaʿb for arbitration whereupon the latter narrated that the Prophet ﷺ said: "Allah revealed to Dāwūd, 'O Dāwūd, build for me a house where I shall be remembered and mentioned.' Dāwūd designed the plan for Bayt al-Maqdis but squarely in the middle was the house of one of the Israelites. Dāwūd asked him to sell it to him but the man refused, after which Dāwūd thought to take it from him. Allah revealed to him, 'Dāwūd, I asked you to build for me a house where I shall be remembered and mentioned but you want to enter robbery into my house! Your punishment is that you will not build it.' Dāwūd said, 'Lord! One of my offspring then.' He said, 'One of your offspring.' " ʿUmar grabbed Ubay by the ties of his garments and said, "I brought you something but your brought a greater [problem] by far! You shall take back what you said!" Then he dragged him until he brought him into the mosque and stood him before a circle of the Companions of the Messenger of Allah ﷺ, among them Abū Dharr, saying, "I adjure by Allah any man that heard the Messenger of Allah ﷺ say the ḥadīth of Bayt al-Maqdis in which Allah commanded Dāwūd to build it, to mention that ḥadīth!" Abū Dharr said, " I heard it from the Messenger of Allah ﷺ!" Another man said, "So did I!" Another also said, "So did I!" Then ʿUmar let go of Ubay. The latter turned to him and said, "ʿUmar, do you suspect me [of lying] about the ḥadīth of the Messenger of Allah?" He replied, "Abū al-Mundhir, no, I swear by Allah that I do not suspect you about it but I hated that the ḥadīth of the Messenger of Allah ﷺ not be exposed in full view." Then he said to al-ʿAbbās, "Go, I

[260] Narrated by al-Bukhārī and Muslim cf. al-Aʿẓamī, *Manhaj al-Naqd* (p. 51) and ʿAjāj al-Khaṭīb, *al-Sunna Qabl al-Tadwīn* (p. 113-114).

shall not pester you about your house." The latter said, "Now that you do this, I have given it as a charity to the Muslims by which I shall expand for them their mosque; but as for you challenging me over it, never!" Then ʿUmar designed for them their present-day edifice and built it out of the Muslim treasury.[261]

Even with two witnesses ʿUmar sometimes did not accept a report. When al-ʿAbbās came to him saying, "The Messenger of Allah ﷺ gave me al-Baḥrayn [present-day Aḥsā'] as my allotment," ʿUmar asked, "Who knows this?" He said, "al-Mughīra ibn Shuʿba." The latter came and bore witness to it. Even so, ʿUmar did not accede to his demand, as if he were not accepting his testimony, whereupon al-ʿAbbās told him some harsh words. ʿUmar said, "ʿAbd Allah, take your father's hand...."[262]

Yet, the standard for verifying authenticity was often met even without seeking a second witness. ʿUmar received Abū Wāqid al-Laythī's sole report that in the two ʿEids the Prophet ﷺ used to recite Sūrat Qāf and Sūrat al-Qamar.[263] Similarly, when he heard ʿAbd al-Raḥmān ibn ʿAwf's sole report that there was plague in Syro-Palestine, ʿUmar turned back the entire Muslim army rather than enter it.[264] He also began to take the *jizya* from the Zoroastrians after hearing the same ʿAbd al-Raḥmān ibn ʿAwf's sole report from the Prophet ﷺ to that effect with regard to the Zoroastrians of Hajar.[265] He also received ʿAbd al-Raḥmān's sole report from the Prophet ﷺ that "If one of you has doubts in his *ṣalāt* whether he prayed one or two *rakʿas*, let him count it as one; if he does not know whether he prayed two or three, let him count them as two; and if he does not know whether he prayed

[261] Narrated by Ibn Saʿd in his *Ṭabaqāt* (4:13-14, 3:203) cf. al-Aʿẓamī, *Manhaj al-Naqd* (p. 52) and ʿAjāj al-Khaṭīb, *al-Sunna Qabl al-Tadwīn* (p. 115).
[262] Narrated by Ibn Saʿd (4:14) cf. al-Aʿẓamī, *Manhaj al-Naqd* (p. 53).
[263] Narrated by Muslim cf. al-Aʿẓamī, *Manhaj* (p. 56).
[264] Narrated by al-Shāfiʿī in the *Risāla* (p. 429) cf. al-Aʿẓamī, *Manhaj* (p. 54).
[265] Narrated by al-Shāfiʿī in the *Risāla* (p. 431) cf. al-Aʿẓamī, *Manhaj* (p. 54).

three or four, let him count them as three. Then, let him prostrate after he has finished his prayer, while he is still sitting and before he gives *salām*, two prostrations."[266] In another version ʿUmar even adds, "Narrate then, for you are the well-agreed upright one in our view!"[267] ʿUthmān in his time gave ʿAbd al-Raḥmān ibn ʿAwf a similar commendation (see below). Al-Khaṭīb explained that the attribute "upright" signifies honesty while the attribute "well-agreed" refers to accuracy.

Another time, when ʿUmar used to say that the blood money (*diyya*) all went to the male blood relatives (*ʿāqila*) and a woman got nothing from her husband's blood money, al-Ḍaḥḥāk ibn Sufyān told him that the Messenger of Allah ﷺ wrote him to let the wife of Ushaym al-Ḍabbābī inherit his *diyya*. Hearing this, ʿUmar changed to the latter position.[268]

When a man from Thaqīf asked him, "Can a woman who visited the House then entered menses leave before purity?" ʿUmar said no but the Thaqafī said, "The Messenger of Allah ﷺ said other than you." Hearing this, ʿUmar got up and hit him with his birch, saying, "Why do you all ask me about something for which the Messenger of Allah ﷺ already gave a reply?"[269]

Another time, when ʿUmar heard that Zayd ibn Thābit said no major ablution (*ghusl*) is required if there was mere penetration without ejaculation, he called him and said, "You little foe of himself! Is this what you are telling people?" He protested that he was not making it up but heard it from his uncles Rifāʿa ibn Rāfiʿ al-Zuraqī and Abū Ayyūb al-Anṣārī. Then ʿUmar asked

[266] Narrated by al-Tirmidhī (*ḥasan gharīb ṣaḥīḥ*) and Aḥmad.
[267] Narrated by al-Ḥākim (1:325), al-Bayhaqī in his *Sunan* (2:332), al-Khaṭīb in the *Kifāya* (p. 108), and Ibn ʿAsākir.
[268] Narrated by al-Shāfiʿī in the *Risāla* (p. 426) cf. Muḥammad Ḥamīd Allāh, *al-Wathā'iq al-Siyāsiyya* (§228) in al-Aʿẓamī, *Manhaj al-Naqd* (p. 53).
[269] Al-Bayhaqī, *Madkhal*, al-Khaṭīb, *al-Faqīh wal-Mutafaqqih* (1:207-208) cf. Ibn Ḥazm, *Iḥkām* (6:807), al-Suyūṭī, *Miftāḥ al-Janna* (p. 91), al-Aʿẓamī, *Manhaj* (p. 55).

confirmation from the Companions. When they differed, ʿAlī told him, "Send the question to the wives of the Prophet ﷺ," whereupon ʿĀ'isha responded, "If one circumcised part (*al-khitān*) penetrates the other circumcised part (i.e. the male and female genitals) then *ghusl* is necessary." ʿUmar said, "Let me not know anyone that does it now then does not make *ghusl* except I shall make an example of him!"[270]

Another time, when Umm Salama narrated that the Prophet ﷺ said, "Of [those I treat today as] my Companions there will be those whom I shall never see nor shall they ever see me after I die." ʿUmar said, "I adjure you by Allah! Am I one of them?" She replied, "No, and I shall not ever exonerate anyone else after you."[271] But he seems to have asked Ḥudhayfa the very same question and gotten the same reply when he remarked to Ḥudhayfa that he sometimes refrained from praying the funeral prayer over one of the deceased so the latter told him that the Prophet ﷺ had revealed to him the names of twelve of the hypocrites, whereupon ʿUmar asked Ḥudhayfa, "I adjure you by Allah! Tell me, am I one of them?" Ḥudhayfa replied, "No, and I will not tell anyone anything further after this."[272]

Another time, when ʿUmar was splashed by some blood from chickens that had been slaughtered and had dripped down a spout onto him as he was on his way to Jumuʿa he ordered that the spout be removed. Al-ʿAbbās came to him and said, "I swear by Allah that this was definitely the spot the Messenger of Allah

[270] Al-Ṭaḥāwī in *Sharḥ Mushkil al-Āthār* (§3965) cf. al-Zarkashī, *al-Ijāba li-Īrād mā Istadrakathu ʿĀ'ishatu ʿalā al-Ṣaḥāba* (2nd ḥadīth of 2nd chapter) and al-Aʿẓamī, *Manhaj al-Naqd* (p. 55); and from Saʿīd ibn al-Musayyab by al-Tirmidhī (*ḥasan ṣaḥīḥ*), al-Nasā'ī, Ibn Mājah, and Aḥmad.

[271] Yaʿqūb ibn Shayba in his *Musnad ʿUmar* cf. al-Aʿẓamī, *Manhaj* (p. 55).

[272] Narrated by al-Ṭabarī in his *Tafsīr* (11:11), al-Bazzār through trustworthy narrators according to al-Haythamī (3:42), al-Bayhaqī in his *Sunan al-Kubrā* (8:200), al-Azdī in *Musnad al-Rabīʿ* (p. 361 §929), and Ibn Abī Shayba (7:481).

ﷺ himself placed it," whereupon ʿUmar said, "I bid you to climb on my back until you place it back in the spot where the Messenger of Allah ﷺ placed it." Al-ʿAbbās did just that.[273]

ʿUmar even ordered his son ʿAbd Allah: "When Saʿd [ibn Abī Waqqāṣ] narrates something to you, do not reject it!" But this was prompted by ʿAbd Allah's questioning a widely known, mass-transmitted report among the Companions, namely the *sunna* of wiping on the leather socks.[274] And ʿUmar's exclusive reliance on Ibn ʿAbbās over the senior veterans of Badr in the explanation of Sūrat al-Naṣr is well-known.[275]

Similarly did our liege-lord ʿUthmān follow the sole report of al-Furayʿa bint Mālik ibn Sinān on the widow's home waiting-period (*ʿidda*) after he summoned and asked her, then applied what she had replied in his own rulings.[276]

Another time, when al-Zubayr said, "ʿAbd al-Raḥmān ibn ʿAwf claims that the Messenger of Allah ﷺ allotted him such-and-such a land," ʿUthmān replied, "ʿAbd al-Raḥmān is an agreeable witness whether for or against himself."[277]

Another time, he performed his ablution in the presence of an assembly of the Companions and said, "Thus did I see the Messenger of Allah ﷺ make his ablution; all of you here, is it just so?" They all said yes.[278]

Similarly, Abū Ayyūb said before Muʿāwiya and ʿUqba ibn ʿĀmir: "I heard the Messenger of Allah ﷺ say, 'Whoever makes his ablution just as he was commanded and prays just as he was

[273] Narrated by Ibn Saʿd (4:12) cf. al-Aʿẓamī, *Manhaj al-Naqd* (p. 56).
[274] Narrated by Aḥmad cf. al-Aʿẓamī, *Manhaj al-Naqd* (p. 54).
[275] Narrated by al-Bukhārī, al-Tirmidhī, and Aḥmad.
[276] Narrated by Mālik, al-Tirmidhī, and Abū Dāwūd cf. al-Aʿẓamī, *Manhaj* (p. 57).
[277] Narrated by Aḥmad with a sound chain, al-Khaṭīb in the *Kifāya* (p. 108), and al-Bayhaqī in the *Sunan al-Kubrā* (10:124).
[278] Narrated by Aḥmad with a sound chain cf. ʿAjāj al-Khaṭīb, *al-Sunna Qabl al-Tadwīn* (p. 116).

commanded, all his past actions are forgiven.' Is it just so, ʿUqba?" He said yes. And the Tābiʿī al-Ḥakam asked Ibn ʿAbbās which day he should fast. " *ʿĀshūrā*'" he replied, "When you see the new moon of Muḥarram, get ready and arise fasting on the ninth." Al-Ḥakam said, "Is this the way Muḥammad ﷺ fasted it?" Ibn ʿAbbās said yes.[279]

ʿAlī said: "When I heard something from the Messenger of Allah ﷺ, Allah would benefit me with it as He wished; but when someone other than him narrated it to me, I would make him swear to it; if he took an oath, I would believe him. And Abū Bakr said to me – and Abū Bakr tells the truth: 'I heard the Messenger of Allah ﷺ say, "None sins but then rises, purifies himself and prays, then asks forgiveness of Allah except Allah forgives him. Then he recited this verse, {*Yet whoso does evil or wrongs his own soul, then seeks pardon of Allah, will find Allah Forgiving, Merciful*} (4:110)."[280] Al-Bukhārī questioned the veracity of this report because its sole narrator from ʿAlī, the little-known *Tābiʿī* Asmā' ibn al-Ḥakam al-Fazārī or al-Sulamī, does not narrate anything else in all ḥadīth literature, nor was the practice of putting narrators under oath current among the Companions. Except for al-Bazzār, neither the earlier nor the later authorities endorsed those objections beginning with al-Bukhārī's student Imām al-Tirmidhī

[279] Narrated by Muslim, Abū Dāwūd, al-Tirmidhī, and Aḥmad.

[280] Narrated by al-Tirmidhī (*ḥasan*), Abū Dāwūd, al-Nasā'ī in the *Kubrā* and *ʿAmal al-Yawm wal-Layla*, Aḥmad in the *Musnad* and *Faḍā'il al-Ṣaḥāba* (1:159 §142), Ibn Abī Shayba, Ibn al-Mubārak in *al-Zuhd*, Abū Yaʿlā, al-Ḥumaydī, and al-Ṭayālisī in their *Musnads*, al-Ṭabarānī in the *Awsaṭ*, Ibn ʿAdī who declared it *ḥasan* or *ṣaḥīḥ* in the *Kāmil*, Ibn Ḥibbān in his *Ṣaḥīḥ* (2:389-390 §623 *isnād ḥasan*), al-Ismāʿīlī in *Muʿjam al-Shuyūkh*, al-Maqdisī in the *Mukhtāra*, al-ʿAlā'ī who declared it *thābit* in *Jāmiʿ al-Taḥṣīl*, al-Dhahabī who declared its chain fair (*ḥasan*) in *Tadhkirat al-Ḥuffāẓ*, al-Haythamī in *Mawārid al-Ẓam'ān*, and Ibn Ḥajar who declared its chain "good" (*jayyid*) in *Tahdhīb al-Tahdhīb*. Al-Bayhaqī narrates it in the *Shuʿab* through a completely different chain from ʿAlī. Cited in the books of *Tafsīr* for the verse cited. Ibn Kathīr declares it *ṣaḥīḥ* in his *Tafsīr*.

who declared the ḥadīth fair while Ibn ʿAdī, Ibn Ḥibbān, al-ʿAlāʾī, Ḍyāʾ al-Dīn al-Maqdisī, al-Dhahabī, Ibn Kathīr, al-Haythamī, and Ibn Ḥajar all authenticate it.[281]

Similarly, Ibn ʿAbbās said: "If a trustworthy source tells us of a *fatwā* by ʿAlī, we do not seek any further concerning it."[282]

All the above evidence shows that the Companions already fully distinguished between reliable and unreliable sources. The double-checking in some cases was a reconfirmation of the element of accuracy (*ḍabṭ*) since the uprightness (*ʿadl*) was not being called into question in any of the examples given. All the Companions without exception are trustworthy sources according to the saying of Allah: {*You are the best community that has been raised up for mankind*} (3:110) and several other verses and ḥadīths to that effect,[283] hence the absolute Consensus to that

[281] M.M. al-Aʿẓamī erred in declaring this narration "inauthentic" in his *Manhaj al-Naqd ʿind al-Muḥaddithīn* (p. 57) due to his imitating al-Muʿallimī's claims in *al-Anwār al-Kāshifa* (p. 68) that the sole narrator of this ḥadīth, the *Tābiʿī* Asmāʾ ibn al-Ḥakam al-Fazārī or al-Sulamī, is unknown – also a claim of al-Bazzār's but long since rejected by Mūsā ibn Hārūn as cited in *Tahdhīb al-Tahdhīb* – and that al-Bukhārī questioned this ḥadīth in *al-Tārīkh al-Kabīr* (2:54), but none of the subsequent masters confirmed him. Similarly al-Arnaʾūṭ in his *Taḥrīr al-Taqrīb* incorrectly rejects Ibn Ḥajar's assessment of Asmāʾ in the *Taqrīb* as *ṣadūq*: "*Bal majhūl*" on the grounds that he could not verify Mūsā ibn Hārūn's statement that Asmāʾ is not unknown because both ʿAlī ibn Rabīʿa and al-Rukayn ibn al-Rabīʿ narrate from him: "We could not find among the early authors of biography books someone that mentioned that al-Rukayn narrated from him." It is more than enough ʿAbd al-Razzāq (1:434) and Ibn Abī Shayba (2:144) do! A further inconsistency is that al-Arnaʾūṭ himself grades this ḥadīth fair in his edition of Ibn Ḥibbān's *Ṣaḥīḥ*; how could that be if he considers Asmāʾ unknown and no one else narrates it? As for the objection that "none of the other Companions asked others to swear before accepting their reports" it proves nothing, moreover, swearing or asking others to swear while narrating ḥadīth is part of the practices of ḥadīth Scholars as per *Fatḥ al-Mughīth*.

[282] Narrated by Ibn Saʿd (2:339), Ibn ʿAbd al-Barr in *al-Istīʿāb* (3:39-40), and al-Suyūṭī in *Tārīkh al-Khulafāʾ*.

effect among *Ahl al-Sunna* according to Imām al-Ḥaramayn as cited by al-Shawkānī in *Irshād al-Fuḥūl* and others. Yet it is correct to say that some were more upright than others, and some were definitely more accurate and meticulous in their transmission than others.

Al-Dhahabī mentions the version of the ḥadīth of *sahū* which ʿUmar prefaces by saying to ʿAbd al-Raḥmān ibn ʿAwf, "Tell us, for you are in our view the well-agreed upright one" and comments:

> "Therefore, the Companions of the Messenger of Allah ﷺ, even if they are upright, nevertheless, some of them are more upright than others and more firmly established (*fa-baʿḍuhum aʿdalu min baʿḍin wa-athbat*). Here, for example, ʿUmar was satisfied with the reporting of ʿAbd al-Raḥmān while in the report of seeking permission [to enter] he said [to Abū Mūsā], "Bring someone to witness with you." As for ʿAlī ibn Abī Ṭālib he said, "Whenever someone narrated something to me from the Messenger of Allah ﷺ I would make him swear to it; but Abū Bakr narrated to me – and Abū Bakr tells the truth.... So ʿAlī did not need to make the Ṣiddīq swear an oath. And Allah knows best."[284]

Our liege-lord ʿUmar was also careful to prevent the dissemination of unverified – chainless – knowledge that was to proliferate after his time. He said: "Whoever finds a book containing knowledge that he did not hear from a person of learning, let him dip it in water until its ink is diluted."[285]

[283] This evidence was listed by al-Khaṭīb in *al-Kifāya* (1358H ed. p. 46-49) and Ibn Ḥajar in *al-Iṣāba* (1:10-11).
[284] *Siyar* (Fikr ed. 3:46= Risāla ed. 1: 72-73).
[285] See note 109.

This hyperbolic rule typifies the conveyance of knowledge in Islam and was encapsulated in Ibn al-Mubārak's historical principle: "The *isnād* is an integral part of the Religion, otherwise anyone can say anything."[286] This is the reason why bookish knowledge is not accepted in Islam from the earliest times until the present because it does not qualify as verified knowledge.

Weak Arguments for the Necessary Acceptance of Lone-Narrated Reports in Doctrine

Some of those that affirm that the lone-narrated ḥadīth can serve as a basis for doctrine – such as Nāṣir al-Albānī[287] – adduce the verse, {*O believers! If a depraved person brings you any news, verify it*} (49:6), to conclude that if someone other than a depraved person brings news, such as a trustworthy person, then we need not verify it and, even in issues of doctrine, the report of the lone trustworthy person is acceptable or even the total stranger as long as we do not know for sure that he is a *fāsiq*. Al-Jaṣṣāṣ pre-empted this view in *Aḥkām al-Qur'ān* (3:399): "The claim that verification is only for the news of the *fāsiq* and that verifying the news of the trustworthy is out is absurd, because mentioning one item from a list of items does not mean that the other items are excluded from the rule."

In fact, the context of revelation for the above verse provides a proof against the use of lone-narrated reports. The Prophet ﷺ had sent al-Walīd ibn ʿUqba ibn Abī Muʿīṭ to the Banū Muṣṭalaq

[286] Narrated by Muslim (introduction to his *Ṣaḥīḥ)* and al-Khaṭīb in his *Tārīkh* (6:166). Ibn al-Subkī in *Ṭabaqāt al-Shāfiʿiyya al-Kubrā* (1:314) mentions this and similar statements of the *Salaf*: "The *isnād* is the believer's weapon" (Sufyān al-Thawrī); "Religion does not disappear except with the disappearance of the *isnād*" (al-Awzāʿī); "Every religion has its knights, and the knights of this Religion are the bearers of *isnāds*" (Yazīd ibn Zurayʿ); "Pursuing the highest *isnād* [i.e. the shortest chain with the least narrator-links] is part of the Religion" (Aḥmad ibn Ḥanbal).

[287] In his *Wujūb Akhdhi Aḥādīth al-Āḥād fil-ʿAqīda.*

and he came back with the news they had left Islam, but then the Prophet ﷺ sent Khālid ibn Walīd to verify this news. When the latter sent back word that they were still Muslims, the verse was revealed, as in al-Qurṭubī and others.

Some adduce the fact that "Allah Most High sent only one Messenger to every nation" or the Prophethood of our liege-lord Ādam ﷺ as an indication that lone-narrated reports are independently probative in doctrine. This argument ignores the agreed-upon preconditional doctrine of Prophetic infallibillity in delivering the Message, whereby the word of a single Prophet ﷺ (in the office of delivering the Divine Message) carries more weight than that of the entire non-Prophetic human and *jinn* population from the beginning of creation to the end!

Additionally, Prophethood is supported by miracles which Allah Most High tasked the people to receive as proofs of Divine support for their Prophets. As for the claim that "only the Qur'ān is the miracle that was presented as a proof for Muḥammad's ﷺ prophethood," it conveniently ignores the fact that the Qur'ān consists in several thousand verses, each of which forms a separate miracle! Further, there were countless other miracles besides as established in the compilations of *Sīra*, *Shamā'il*, *Khaṣā'iṣ*, and al-Nabhānī's monumental encyclopedia of the miracles of the Prophet ﷺ titled *Ḥujjat Allah 'alā al- 'Ālamīn*.

Some adduce the fact that the Prophet ﷺ would send lone individuals to the rulers of other nations as emissaries and missionaries of Islam and as governors and that this model was followed by the early community, such as when 'Uthmān ؓ unified the community over a single *muṣḥaf* by sending copies to the various lands and, with each copy, a single person to instruct the people in proper recitation and explanation. The reply in all this is that the Prophet's ﷺ seal and that of his Caliphs after his time precisely played the role of a witness to the veracity of the lone emissary, i.e. a virtual second emissary confirming the first. In addition, the message in question was not new but familiar, and could be verified independently. The outwardly lone-narrated report of the change in *qibla* similarly combines the fact that the Prophet ﷺ used proven emissaries as well as the very public and easily verifiable nature of the news. This is established beyond doubt in the Prophet's ﷺ ḥadīth on the conveyance of *Sūrat Barā'a* to the Quraysh: "None may convey [this news] on my part except myself or a man from me (*i.e.* my household)."[288]

As for those that claim that the last two verses of *Sūrat al-Tawba* were integrated into the Qur'ān on the sole basis of lone-narrated reports the reply is that this claim is a lie, these verses were integrated on the basis of mass transmission just as the rest of the Qur'ān was and had been memorized by many of the Companions. The reports mention that Zayd ibn Thābit had difficulty finding the last two verses of *al-Tawba*, verses he used to hear from the Messenger of Allah ﷺ, until he finally found them written with Khuzayma ibn Thābit al-Anṣārī who swore to having received them from the Prophet ﷺ. This shows that at least Zayd, Khuzayma, and ʿUmar knew those verses if not more people among the *Ṣaḥāba*, certainly not just Khuzayma, but the latter had them written down and this is what Zayd was looking for. In addition, Ubay ibn Kaʿb confirmed having heard the Prophet ﷺ reciting them and ʿUthmān swore an oath witnessing to that effect.[289] And Allah knows best.

[288] Narrated by Aḥmad at the very beginning of his *Musnad*, Abū Yaʿlā (1:100 §104), al-Ṭabarī in his *Tafsīr* (10:65), and Ibn Ḥibbān (15:16-17 §6644), cf. Ibn Ḥajar, *Fatḥ al-Bārī* (8:318).

[289] Cf. Ibn Abī Dāwūd, *Maṣāḥif* (1:158-172 §24-25, §29, §33, 1:201-202 §71, and 1:221-225 §96-98) and Ibn Ḥajar, *Fatḥ al-Bārī* (8:518, 9:12-15).

Ḥadīth Narration *ad Sensum vs. ad Litteram* (*al-riwāyatu bil-ma'nā aw bil-lafẓ*)

The Ḥanafī Ḥadīth Master Murtaḍā al-Zabīdī began his great commentary on the *Iḥyā'* with an explanation that al-Ghazzālī's method of ḥadīth citation – conveying the general meaning without ascertaining the exact wording – had a basis in the practice of the Companions and *Salaf*:

"The verification of the wording of narrations was not an obligation for al-Ghazzālī – Allah have mercy on him! He would convey the general meaning, conscious of the different significations of the words and their mutual conflict with one another, avoiding what would constitute interpolation or arbitrary rendering of one term with another.

"A number of the Companions have permitted the conveyance of Prophetic ḥadīths in their meanings (*riwāya bil-ma'nā*) rather than their very wordings (*riwāya bil-alfāẓ*). Among them: 'Alī, Ibn 'Abbās, Anas ibn Mālik, Abū al-Dardā', Wāthila ibn al-Asqa', and Abū Hurayra ﷺ.[290] Also, a greater number of the Successors, among them: the Imām of Imāms al-Ḥasan al-Baṣrī, al-Sha'bī, 'Amr ibn Dīnār, Ibrāhīm al-Nakha'ī, Mujāhid, and 'Ikrima....

"Ibn Sīrīn said: 'I would hear a ḥadīth from ten different people, the meaning remaining one but the wordings differing.'[291]

[290] Al-Khaṭīb in *al-Jāmi' fī Akhlāq al-Rāwī* (2:24, 2:26-28) mentions Ibn Mas'ūd, Abū al-Dardā', Anas, 'Ā'isha, 'Amr ibn Dīnār, 'Amir al-Sha'bī, Ibrāhīm al-Nakha'ī, Ibn Abī Nujayh, 'Amr ibn Murra, Ja'far ibn Muḥammad ibn 'Alī, Sufyān ibn 'Uyayna, and Yaḥyā ibn Sa'īd al-Qaṭṭān as allowing the narration of Prophetic ḥadīth other than in its precise original wording. He narrates examples from Ibn Mas'ūd (§1113), Abū al-Dardā' (§1114-1115), and Anas (§1116-1117) to that effect. He also narrates the prohibition of narrating Prophetic ḥadīths other than in their precise original wording from Wakī' (2:24 §11108), and Mālik (2:25 §1110-1111). Al-Khaṭīb documents this subject at length in *al-Kifāya* (p. 203-211).

[291] Also narrated from Abū al-Aḥwaṣ Muḥammad ibn al-Haytham by al-Khaṭīb in *al-Jāmi' li-Akhlāq al-Rāwī* (2:21 §1099).

"Similarly, the Companions' wordings in their narrations from the Prophet ﷺ have differed one from another. Some of them, for example, will narrate a complete version; others will narrate the gist of the meaning; others will narrate an abridged version; others yet replace certain words with their synonyms, deeming that they have considerable leeway as long as they do not contradict the original meaning. None of them intends a lie, and all of them aim for truthfulness and the report of what he has heard: that is why they had leeway. They used to say: 'Mendacity is only when one deliberately intends to lie.'[292]

"'Imrān ibn Muslim [al-Qaṣīr] narrated that a man said to al-Ḥasan [al-Baṣrī]: "O Abū Sa'īd! When you narrate a ḥadīth you put it in better and more eloquent terms than when one of us narrates it." He replied: "There is no harm in that as long as you have fully expressed its meaning."[293] Al-Naḍr ibn Shumayl (d. 208) said: "Hushaym (d. 183) used to make a lot of mistakes in Arabic, so I adorned his narrations for you with a fine garment" – meaning, he arabized it, since al-Naḍr was a philologist (*naḥwī*).[294] Sufyān [al-Thawrī] used to say: "When you see a man show strictness in the wordings of ḥadīth, know that he is advertising himself." It is narrated that a certain man began to question Yaḥyā ibn Sa'īd al-Qaṭṭān (d. 198) about a specific wording inside a ḥadīth. Yaḥyā said to him: "*Yā Fulān!* There is not in the whole world anything more sublime than the Book of Allah, yet He has permitted that its words be recited in seven different dialects. So do not be so strict!"[295]

[292] See on this chapter al-Khaṭīb, *al-Kifāya* (1986 ed. p. 239-247= Madīna ed. p.204-211).

[293] Al-Khaṭīb, *al-Kifāya* (1986 ed. p. 243=Madīna ed. p. 207), *al-Jāmi'* (2:22 §1101-1102). Cf. al-Shāfi'ī – without naming al-Ḥasan or al-Zuhrī – in *al-Risāla* (p. 275).

[294] Ismā'īl ibn Umayya said: "We used to correct Nāfi' ['Umar's freedman] if he made mistakes of language [in his narrations] but he would refuse and say: 'Nothing but exactly what I heard.'" Cited by al-Dhahabī in the *Siyar* (5:567).

"In the Ḥadīth Master al-Suyūṭī's commentary on [al-Nawawī's] *al-Taqrīb*, in the fourth part of the twenty-sixth heading,[296] the gist of what he said is as follows:

> 'If a narrator is not an expert in the wordings and in what shifts their meanings to something else, there is no permission for him to narrate what he heard in terms of meaning only. There is no disagreement concerning this. He must relate the exact wording he has heard. If he is an expert in the matter, [opinions have differed:] a large group of the experts of ḥadīth, *fiqh*, and *uṣūl* said that it is not permitted for him to narrate in other than the exact same words. This is the position of Ibn Sīrīn, Tha'lab, and Abū Bakr al-Rāzī the Ḥanafī scholar.[297] It is also narrated as Ibn 'Umar 's position [as illustrated in the reports of 'Ubayd ibn 'Umayr al-Marwazī quoted above].'

"At any rate, the vast majority of the *Salaf* and *Khalaf* from the various groups, among them the Four Imāms, permit narration in terms of meaning in all the above cases provided one adduces the meaning.[298] The practice of the Companions and *Salaf*

[295] Cf. al-Shāfi'ī, *al-Risāla* (p. 274).

[296] Al-Suyūṭī, *Tadrīb al-Rāwī fī Sharḥ Taqrīb al-Nawāwī* (1:532-539).

[297] Cf. al-Khaṭīb in al-*Kifāya* (1986 ed. p. 242=Madīna ed. p. 207) who also names Ibrāhīm ibn Maysara, al-Qāsim ibn Muḥammad, Rajā' ibn Ḥaywa, and Ibn Ṭāwus.

[298] Al-Suyūṭī, *Tadrīb al-Rāwī* (1:532-533, cf. *Taqrīb* p. 77-78). Al-Nawawī continues in his *Taqrīb* (p. 78 = *Tadrīb* 1:538): "This holds true in other than ḥadīth compilations (*muṣannafāt*). The alteration of a ḥadīth compilation is impermissible, even if in the same sense. Also, it is imperative for the one who narrates in terms of meaning to say, at the conclusion of his narration: 'or something near it' – *aw kamā qāl, aw naḥwahu, aw shibhahu* – or other such expressions." Al-Suyūṭī adduces proofs that this was the practice of Ibn Mas'ūd, Abū al-Dardā', and Anas ibn Mālik. Further proofs to this effect are adduced by al-Tirmidhī in *al-'Ilal* and its commentary by Ibn Rajab entitled *Sharḥ 'Ilal al-Tirmidhī* (1:145-152), al-Khaṭīb, *al-Kifāya* (1986 ed. p. 232-247 = Madīna ed. p. 198-211), and al-Qāḍī 'Iyāḍ in *al-Ilmā'* (p. 174-178). See also Ibn Ḥajar's discussion and its commentary by al-Qārī in *Sharḥ Sharḥ Nukhbat al-Fikar* (p. 497-502).

witnesses to this dispensation as shown by their narrating a single report in different wordings.

"There is a Ḥadīth of the Prophet ﷺ relevant to the issue narrated by Ibn Mandah in *Maʿrifat al-Ṣaḥāba* and al-Ṭabarānī in *al-Kabīr* from ʿAbd Allah ibn Sulaymān ibn Aktham[299] al-Laythī [= ʿAbd Allah ibn Sulaym ibn Ukayma][300] who said: 'I said: 'Messenger of Allah! Verily, when I hear a ḥadīth from you I am unable to narrate it again just as I heard it from you.' That is, he adds or omits something. The Prophet ﷺ replied: 'As long as you do not make licit the illicit or make illicit the licit, and as long as you adduce the meaning, there is no harm in that.'[301]

[299] This is a misspelling in al-Zabīdī's text.

[300] As stated by Ibn Ḥajar in *al-Iṣāba* and *Taʿjīl al-Manfaʿa*. Al-Ḥusayni erred in *al-Ikmāl* (p. 565 §1211) when he identified the Ibn Ukayma cited in Aḥmad's *Musnad* as ʿAbd Allah ibn Sulaym ibn Ukayma, since the Ibn Ukayma of the *Sunan*, the *Muwaṭṭa'*, and Aḥmad's *Musnad* is named by al-Tirmidhī in the *Sunan* – and others – as ʿUmara or ʿAmmār ibn Ukayma al-Laythī. Muslim in his *Ṣaḥīḥ* (3:1566), Ibn Ḥibbān (5:158, 13:238-239), Abū Yaʿlā, *al-Musnad* (12:348), and Ibn ʿAbd al-Barr, *al-Tamhīd* (17:237) further identify him as ʿAmr ibn Muslim ibn ʿAmmār ibn Ukayma al-Laythī, all agreeing that he is not a Companion, but a Successor who narrated from both Abū Hurayra and Saʿīd ibn al-Musayyab. As for al-Ṭabarānī's narrator ʿAbd Allah ibn Sulaym(an) ibn Ukayma – he is unknown.

[301] Narrated from ʿAbd Allah ibn Sulaymān ibn Ukayma by al-Ṭabarānī in *al-Kabīr* (7:100 §6491, 117) and Ibn Qāniʿ (d. 351) in *Muʿjam al-Ṣaḥāba* (3:17), both with a chain containing two unknown narrators – Yaʿqūb ibn ʿAbd Allah ibn Sulaym(an) ibn Ukayma and his father ʿAbd Allah ibn Sulaym(an) – as stated by al-Haythamī (1:154), cf. al-Sakhāwī, *Fatḥ al-Mughīth* (3:145). Also narrated by al-Jawraqānī (d. 543) in *al Abāṭil* (1:90-97) where he said: "This ḥadīth is null and void (*bāṭil*), and there is inconsistency (*iḍṭirāb*) in its chain." Still, al-Khaṭīb adduced it through two similar chains in his discussion of the permissibility of narration in terms of meaning in *al-Kifāya* (1986 ed. p. 234 = Madīna ed. p. 198), as well as al-Qārī in *Sharḥ Sharḥ Nukhbat al-Fikar* (p. 498). Also narrated from Salama ibn al-Akwaʿ by Ibn ʿAsākir as stated by Ibn Ḥamza al-Ḥusaynī in *al-Bayān wal-Taʿrīf* (2:77-78). Ibn Ḥajar narrates it in *al-Iṣāba* (3:166 §3436, 6:341 §8532) and says: "Ibn al-Jawzī included it among the forgeries, blaming al-Walīd ibn Salama for it, but it is not as he claimed. For Ibn Mandah narrated it [in *Maʿrifat al-Ṣaḥāba*] through another way from ʿUmar ibn Ibrāhīm, from

When this was mentioned to al-Ḥasan he said: 'Were it not for this, we would never narrate anything.'[302]

"Al-Shāfi'ī [303] adduced as his proof [for the same position] the ḥadīth, "The Qur'ān was revealed in seven dialects."[304]

"Al-Bayhaqī narrated from Makḥūl that he and Abū al-Azhar went to see Wāthila ibn al-Asqa' and said to him: 'Narrate to us a Ḥadīth of the Prophet ﷺ in which there is no omission, no addition, and nothing forgotten.' He replied: 'Has any of you recited anything from the Qur'ān?' They said: 'Yes, but we have not memorized it very well. We sometimes add 'and' or the letter *alif*, or omit something.' He said: 'If you cannot memorize

Muḥammad ibn Isḥāq ibn Ukayma, from his father, from his grandfather, in similar terms. However, 'Umar is a contemporary of al-Walīd. Ibn Mandah narrated it through another way from 'Umar ibn Ibrāhīm, saying: 'from Muḥammad ibn Isḥāq ibn 'Abd Allah ibn Sulaym.' He added 'Abd Allah in his lineage. Then he cited it under 'Abd Allah's entry with this chain. It was also narrated by Abū al-Qāsim ibn Mandah in his book *al-Waṣiyya* through two chains going back to al-Walīd ibn Salama, 'from Isḥāq ibn Ya'qūb ibn 'Abd Allah ibn Ukayma, from his father, from his grandfather.' There are other discrepancies.... Abū Mūsā in *al-Dhayl* and Ibn Mardūyah also narrated it in *Kitāb al-'Ilm*, both through 'Abdān al-Marwazī.... I believe some reshuffling took place and that the correct chain is: Muḥammad ibn Isḥāq, from 'Abd Allah ibn Sulaym ibn Ukayma, from his father, from his grandfather." In *Ta'jīl al-Manfa'a* (p. 531 §1440) Ibn Ḥajar declares Ibn Madah's chains "flimsy" (*wāhiya*). Thus he considers the ḥadīth weak, but not forged. Its content is confirmed by two other ḥadīths of the Prophet ﷺ adduced by al-Khaṭīb, the first: "As long as one adduces the meaning, let him narrate it," and the second: "I did not mean to prohibit that [one should narrate *ad sensum*], but only that whoever falsely claims that I said something which I did not say, and his purpose is to shame me and smear Islam – or: to smear me and shame Islam." Narrated respectively from Ibn Mas'ūd and an unnamed Companion by al-Khaṭīb in *al-Kifāya* (1986 ed. p. 234-235 = Madīna ed. p. 198). From Abū Hurayra: "The Prophet ﷺ was asked about a man who narrates something he said while interchanging the position of clauses or words, and the Prophet ﷺ replied: 'There is no harm in it as long as he adduces the meaning.'" Narrated by al-Ḥakīm al-Tirmidhī in *Nawādir al-Uṣūl* (p. 389). So the mass-transmitted ḥadīth narrated in unconditional terms from Salama ibn al-Akwa' by al-Bukhārī in his *Ṣaḥīḥ* (book of *'Ilm*): "Whoever says that I said something which I did not say, let him prepare himself for his seat in the Fire" must be understood the Qur'ān which is written down before you, adding and omitting something from it, then how about narrations which we heard from the Prophet ﷺ, some of them only once? Suffice yourself, whenever we narrate them to you, with the general meaning!'[305] He narrated something similar from Jābir ibn ʿAbd Allah in *al-Madkhal*: 'Ḥudhayfa said to us: "We are Bedouin Arabs, we may cite a saying without its proper order."' He also narrated from Shuʿayb ibn al-Hajjab: 'I visited al-Ḥasan together with ʿAbdān. We said to him: "Abū Saʿīd! Someone may narrate a ḥadīth in which he adds or from which he omits something." He replied: "Lying is only when someone deliberately intends this."'[306]... [He also narrated something similar from Ibrāhīm al-Nakhaʿī,[307] al-Shaʿbī,[308] al-Zuhrī,[309] Sufyān,[310] ʿAmr ibn Dīnār,[311] and Wakīʿ.[312]]"

End of quotation from al-Suyūṭī and Ḥāfiẓ al-Zabīdī's text.[313]

in terms of those other ḥadīths. This is confirmed by the comments of the Companions and Successors related by al-Zabīdī and the practice of the *Salaf* as demonstrated by al-Ḥakīm al-Tirmidhī (p. 389-390, *Aṣl* §268) as quoted in full by al-Qāsimī in *Qawāʿid al-Taḥdīth* (p. 223-224), and Allah knows best.

[302] Narrated by al-Khaṭīb: *Jāmiʿ* (2:21-22 §1100), *al-Kifāya* (Madīna ed. p. 207).

[303] In *al-Risāla* (p. 274).

[304] Narrated from ʿUmar and Ibn ʿAbbās by al-Bukhārī, Muslim, and Aḥmad, and also from Ubay ibn Kaʿb in the *Sunan*.

[305] Narrated by al-Khaṭīb in *al-Jāmiʿ* (2:20-21 §1098) and *al-Kifāya* (1986 ed. p. 239 = Madīna ed. p. 204). Al-Khaṭīb also narrates something identical from Qutayba. In al-Ḥakīm al-Tirmidhī's version in *Nawādir al-Uṣūl* (p. 389) Makḥūl asks: "Has any of you stood in prayer at length at night?"

[306] Narrated by al-Khaṭīb in *al-Kifāya* (1986 ed. p. 244 = Madīna ed. p. 208).

[307] See note 290.

[308] *Ibid.*

[309] Al-Khaṭīb, *al-Jāmiʿ* (2:22 §1103).

[310] Al-Khaṭīb, *al-Jāmiʿ* (2:23 §1104-1106).

[311] See note 290.

[312] Also Ḥammād ibn Zayd as narrated in al-Khaṭīb, *al-Jāmiʿ* (2:23-24 §1107). However, the reports indicate that Wakīʿ, like Mālik, forbade *al-riwāya bil-lafẓ* and insisted on the precise original wording, cf. n. 290.

The Imāms of Ḥadīth are unanimous in accepting the "narration in meaning" **on condition that the narrator master the Arabic language and his narration not present an aberration or anomaly (*shudhūdh*)**, among other conditions.[314] Al-Zabīdī's documentation of the majority position that it is permissible to narrate the ḥadīths of the Prophet ﷺ in their meanings rather than their wordings is also the position of Ibn al-Ṣalāḥ in his *Muqaddima*, but the latter avers that **the dispensation no longer applies at a time when the ḥadīths are available to all in published books.**[315] Shaykh Nūr al-Dīn ʿItr adopts the latter position: "The last word on this subject is to prohibit ḥadīth narration in the sense of meaning only, because the narrations have all been compiled in the manuals of ḥadīth, eliminating the need for such a dispensation."[316]

[313] Al-Zabīdī, *Itḥāf al-Sādat al-Muttaqīn* (1:48-49).
[314] ʿItr, *Manhaj al-Naqd* (p. 227-230).
[315] Ibn al-Ṣalāḥ, *ʿUlūm al-Ḥadīth* (p. 214).
[316] Nūr al-Dīn ʿItr, ed., Ibn Ḥajar, *Sharḥ al-Nukhba Nuzhat al-Naẓar fī Tawḍīḥ Nukhbat al-Fikar* (p. 95 n. 1). Cf. al-Qāsimī's *Qawāʿid al-Taḥdīth* (p. 223-225) and Ṭāhir al-Jazāʾirī's *Tawjīh al-Naẓar* (p. 298-312).

Ḥadīth Authentication by *Kashf*

In nine parts: Definitions – Status of One That Denies *Kashf* – Status of *Kashf* – Proofs for *Kashf* and *Kashf*-Authentication – Seeing the Prophet ﷺ in Dream – Three Visions of Ibn ʿAbbās – Seeing the Prophet ﷺ and Authenticating Ḥadīth – Canonization of *Ṣaḥīḥ al-Bukhārī* by *Kashf* – *Kashf*-Authentication of *Ijmāʿ*

Definitions: *Kashf, Ilhām, Firāsa, Waḥī, Fatḥ*

The spiritual disclosure known as *kashf* or *mukāshafa* – "unveiling" – denotes a type of experiential knowledge that may or may not be available through normal means but that was reached by or granted to a non-prophet through an extraordinary Divine gift (*karāma*) generically known as *ilhām* – "inspiration" – or *firāsa* – "insight" – although the latter also denotes a kind of accurate sagacious premonition. *Kashf*, *ilhām*, and *firāsa* are different from *waḥī* – "revelation" – which is the Divine address reserved for Prophets although the word is also used, in the Qur'ān, for non-Prophets in the sense of inspiration. *Ilhām* might be termed the general angelic opposite of *waswasa* or satanic whispering, *kashf* the specific manifestation of *ilhām* that usually results in a qualitative (albeit reversible) jump in learning, experience, or spiritual state. This event is either visionary as in the *mushāhada* – "vision" – or auditory as in the *mukhāṭaba* – "address" – and is synonymous, in the terminology of spiritual literature, with *fatḥ* – "major opening" – all of which can take place either in dream (*bil-ru'yā*) or awake (*yaqaẓatan*).

Legal Status of One That Denies *Kashf* in Islam

The reality of *kashf*, *ilhām*, *firāsa*, *waḥī*, and *fatḥ* is firmly established. Whoever denies the reality of *waḥī* commits apostasy while whoever denies the reality of any of the rest borders on or commits heresy. Typical naysayers fall mute at the words of their putative Imām, Shaykh Aḥmad ibn Taymiyya in *al-Furqān*: "It is definitely established that the Friends of Allah receive extraordinary addresses and visionary disclosures."[317]

He again states more explicitly in his *'Aqīda Wāsiṭiyya*:

> "Also of the foundational credal principles (*uṣūl*) of *Ahl al-Sunna* is the confirmation (*taṣdīq*) of the miraculous gifts of the friends of Allah and whatever suspension of the laws of nature Allah causes at their hands (*wamā yujrī Allahu 'alā aydīhim min khawāriq al-'ādāt*) with all kinds of knowledge and spiritual unveilings (*fī anwā' al-'ulūm wal-mukāshafāt*), and all kinds of powers and influences (*wa-anwā' al-qudra wal-ta'thīrāt*) such as those reported from the ancient communities, [for example] in the cave (*al-kahf*) and others, and as reported from the early beginnings of this community regarding the Companions and the Followers and from every generation of Muslims after that, and these miracles will not cease to take place in this community until the day of resurrection (*wa-hiya mawjūdatun fīhā ilā yawm al-qiyāma*)."[318]

Legal Status of *Kashf* and Related Issues

Sahl al-Tustarī recited: "The hearts of Knowers have eyes / that see what onlookers cannot see" (*Qulūb al-'ārifīna lahā 'uyūn / tarā mā lā yarāhu al-nāẓirūn*). Shaykh 'Abd al-Qādir al-Gīlānī said in Discourse 9 of *Futūḥ al-Ghayb*: "To the *awliyā'* and *abdāl* are disclosed such workings of Allah in the course of *kashf* and *mushāhada* as overwhelm the reasoning power of man and shatter into pieces all habits and customs." Hence, the highly

[317] "*Faqad thabata anna li-awliyā' Allahi mukhāṭabātun wa-mukāshafāt.*" In *al-Furqān bayna Awliyā' al-Shayṭān wa-Awliyā' al-Raḥmān* (p. 52).
[318] *Al-'Aqīdat al-Wāsiṭiyya* (Cairo: al-Maṭba'at al-Salafiyya, 1346) p. 33-34.

subjective nature of these unusual phenomena dictates that they must pass the test of the *Sharī'a* before they are accepted. Shaykh Abū al-Ḥasan al-Shādhilī gave this luminous rule of thumb: "Whenever your spiritual disclosure clashes with the Book or the Sunna, hold fast to the Book and the Sunna and discard spiritual disclosure. Tell yourself: truly, Allah has guaranteed for me immunity from error regarding the Book and the Sunna but He has not guaranteed it for me with regard to spiritual disclosure."[319]

Ibn Taymiyya repeats after him: "The one that receives angelic communication, inspiration, and disclosure in this *Umma* must weigh all this against the Book and the Sunna. If they agree then what he has experienced is truthful; if they disagree he pays no attention to what he has experienced."[320]

Then Ibn Ḥajar in *Fatḥ al-Bārī*: "The Muslim who is communicated to (*muḥaddathun*), if his existence is ascertained, what befalls him is not used as basis for a legal judgment, and he is obliged to evaluate it with the Qur'ān; if it conforms to it or to the Sunna, he acts upon it, otherwise he leaves it."[321]

[319] *"Idhā 'āraḍa kashfuka al-Kitāba wal-Sunna, fa-tamassak bil-Kitābi wal-Sunna wa-du'i al-kashf. Wa-qul li-nafsika: inna Allahu qad ḍamana lī al-'iṣmata fīl-Kitābi wal-Sunna wa-lam yaḍmanhā liya fī jānibi al-kashf."* In al-Taftazānī, *Madkhalun ilā al-Taṣawwuf* (p. 240). Thus if the inspiration came to the heart of the *walī*, for example, to give the Holy Prophet ﷺ the name of al-Raḥmān, he would know with certainty that he must reject such inspiration because the Book, the Sunna, and the *Ijmā'* of *Ahl al-Sunna wal-Jamā'a* reject it and consider it impermissible.

[320] *"Fal-muḥaddath al-mulham al-mukāshaf min hādhihi al-umma yajibu 'alayhi an yazina dhālika bil-Kitābi wal-Sunna; fa-in wāfaqa dhālika ṣadaqa mā warada 'alayh; wa-in khālafa: lam yaltafit ilayh."* In *Majmū' al-Fatāwā* (24:377).

[321] Ibn Ḥajar, *Fatḥ al-Bārī* (7:62-63 §3689).

Proofs for *Kashf* and *Kashf*-Authentication from the Qur'ān and Sunna

Allah Most High said, {*Therein lie portents for those who read the signs*} (15:75) and He said, {*Then found they one of Our slaves, unto whom We had given mercy from Us, and had taught him knowledge from Our presence*} (18:65), *i.e.* al-Khaḍir by Consensus of the Ulema of *Tafsīr*. According to Aḥmad ibn Taymiyya, "The majority hold that he [al-Khaḍir] was not a prophet."[322] Ibn Ḥajar and al-Suyūṭī squarely contradict him in *al-Zahr al-Naḍir fī Naba' al-Khaḍir* and *al-Wajh al-Naḍir fī Tarjīḥ Nubuwwat al-Khaḍir* respectively.

The Prophet ﷺ said: "Beware the insight (*firāsa*) of the believer for he sees with the light of Allah."[323]

[322] *Majmū' al-Fatāwā* (4:338).

[323] A sound (*ṣaḥīḥ*) ḥadīth narrated through Yaḥyā ibn Ma'īn from Abū Umāma al-Bāhilī by al-Ṭabarānī, *al-Kabīr* (8:121) and *Musnad al-Shāmiyyīn* (2:407) with a fair chain according to al-Haythamī (10:268); Ibn 'Abd al-Barr, *Jāmi' Bayān al-'Ilm* (1:677 §1197) with a fair chain per al-Zuhayrī; al-Ḥakīm al-Tirmidhī, *Nawādir al-Uṣūl*; Ibn 'Adī, *Kāmil* (4:1523, 6:2401); Abū Nu'aym, *Ḥilyat al-Awliyā'* (6:118) and *al-Arba'īn 'alā Madhhab al-Mutaḥaqqiqīn min al-Ṣūfiyya* (p. 104); al-Khaṭīb, *al-Tārīkh* (5:99); al-Bayhaqī, *al-Zuhd al-Kabīr* (p. 159-160 §358); al-Suyūṭī, *al-La'ālī'* (2:329-330) who declared it fair as did al-Shawkānī in *al-Fawā'id al-Majmū'a* (p. 243-244); and through the trustworthy ḥadīth Master Muḥammad ibn 'Awf al-Ḥimṣī by al-Quḍā'ī, *Musnad al-Shihāb* (1:387=1:476). The slight defect (*'illa*) of Abū Umāma's chain revolves around al-Bukhārī's shaykh the narrator 'Abd Allah ibn Ṣāliḥ al-Juhanī [cf. al-Dhahabī, *Mīzān* (2:440-445 §4383); al-Arna'ūṭ said of him in *Taḥrīr al-Taqrīb* (2:222 §3388): "Truthful (*ṣadūq*), his memorization is somewhat lacking, but of fair narrations in follow-ups (*mutāba'āt*)."] However, Maḥmūd Mamdūḥ in his monograph *Bishārat al-Mu'min bi-Taṣḥīḥ Ḥadīth Ittaqū Firāsat al-Mu'min* argues the ḥadīth is *ṣaḥīḥ* as it is established that 'Abd Allah ibn Ṣāliḥ narrated it to Yaḥyā ibn Ma'īn and Muḥammad ibn 'Awf from his written record, and Ibn Ḥajar said of him in *al-Taqrīb* (p. 308 §3388) "He is solid when narrating from his book" (*thabtun fī kitābih*) and again in his introduction to *Fatḥ al-Bārī* titled *Hadī al-Sārī* (p. 414): "Whatever comes from him through the narration of the major experts such as Yaḥyā ibn Ma'īn, al-Bukhārī, Abū Zur'a, and Abū Ḥātim, is from his sound

The Prophet ﷺ also said: "Allah has servants who know [what lies hidden] through reading the signs" (*tawassum*).[324]

One of those was Abū Bakr al-Ṣiddīq ؓ. Before he died he foresaw that the child his wife Ḥabība bint Khārija ibn Zayd al-Khazrajiyya bore in her womb was a girl and he told ʿĀ'isha she would have to share her inheritance with "two brothers and two sisters." She said, "Is it not just Asmā'? Who is the other one?"He said: "The one in the womb of Khārija's daughter. I was shown it is a girl." Later, his daughter Umm Kulthūm was born.[325]

narrations (*min ṣaḥīḥi ḥadīthih*)." Also narrated from Abū Saʿīd al-Khudrī by al-Tirmidhī (*gharīb*); al-Bukhārī in *Al-Tārīkh* (7:354); al-Ṭabarī and Ibn Kathīr in their *Tafsīrs* (14:31-32 and 2:556); Abū Nuʿaym, *Ḥilya* (10:281-282); al-ʿUqaylī, *al-Ḍuʿafā'* (4:129); Abū al-Shaykh, *al-Amthāl* (p. 78); al-Sulamī, *Ṭabaqāt al-Ṣūfiyya* (p. 156) and *al-Arbaʿīn*; al-Khaṭīb, *Tārīkh Baghdād* (3:191, 7:242); al-Quḍāʿī, *Musnad al-Shihāb* (1:387); al-Mālīnī, *al-Arbaʿīn fī Shuyūkh al-Ṣūfiyya* (p. 91), and Ibn al-Subkī, *Ṭabaqāt al-Shāfiʿiyya al-Kubrā* (2:268), all with weak chains because of ʿAṭiyya ibn Saʿd al-ʿAwfī who concealed his sources. Also with very weak chains from Thawbān, Ibn ʿUmar, and Abū Hurayra by al-Ṭabarī, Abū al-Shaykh, Abū Nuʿaym, Ibn Abī Ḥātim, and Ibn Kathīr in their commentaries of the verse {*Therein lie portents for those who read the signs*} (15:75); also from other Companions with very weak chains. Among the incorrect rulings on the grade of this ḥadīth are those by Ibn al-Jawzī and the philologist al-Ṣaghānī who included it among the forgeries in their *Mawḍūʿāt* (3:147 and p. 27). Al-Sakhāwī in *al-Maqāṣid al-Ḥasana* (§23) rejects Ibn al-Jawzī's grading of *mawḍūʿ* but considers its chains all weak as does al-Aḥdab in *Zawā'id Tārīkh Baghdād* (4:340-343 §687).

[324] Narrated from Anas by al-Bazzār in his *Musnad* as cited in *Zawā'id Musnad al-Bazzār* (4:243), al-Ṭabarānī in *al-Awsaṭ* (§2956), al-Ṭabarī, al-Qurṭubī, and Ibn Kathīr in their *Tafsīrs* (14:32, 10:43, and 2:556), al-Quḍāʿī, *Musnad al-Shihāb* (2:170), Abū Nuʿaym and Ibn al-Sunnī in their *Ṭibb al-Nabawī* as per al-ʿAjlūnī , *Kashf al-Khafā'* (1:42 §3632) and al-Ghumārī, *Fatḥ al-Wahhāb* (2:170), all with fair chains according to Ibn Ḥajar, *Mukhtaṣar al-Zawā'id* (2:506 §2302), al-Haythamī (10:268), and al-Sakhāwī, *al-Maqāṣid al-Ḥasana* (p. 20). Al-Dhahabī in his *Mīzān* (1:334) declares it "disclaimed" (*munkar*) not because the ḥadīth itself is weak but only due to the fact that no one narrates it other than Bakr ibn al-Ḥasan (Abū Bishr ibn al-Muzalliq) whose actual grading is "truthful" (*ṣadūq*) as stated by al-Dhahabī, while others declared him "trustworthy" (*thiqa*). Mamdūḥ in *Bishārat al-*

The Prophet ﷺ also said: "In the nations long before you were people who were communicated to although they were not prophets. If there is anyone of them in my Community, it is ʿUmar ibn al-Khaṭṭāb!"[326] This narration is further elucidated by two ḥadīths:

(a) "Allah has engraved truth on the tongue of ʿUmar and his heart."[327]

(b) "Had there been a Prophet after me, truly, it would have been ʿUmar!"[328]

Al-Tirmidhī said Ibn ʿUyayna said "communicated to" (*muḥaddathūn*) meant "made to understand" (*mufahhamūn*), while in his narration Muslim added: "Ibn Wahb explained 'communicated to'

Mu'min bi-Taṣḥīḥi Ḥadīth Ittaqū Firāsat al-Mu'min (p. 35-38) faulted as incorrect ʿAbd al-Raḥmān al-Muʿallimī al-Yamānī's grading of this ḥadīth as weak in his notes on al-Shawkānī's *Fawā'id* (p. 245).

325 Narrated from ʿĀ'isha by Mālik, *al-Muwaṭṭa'*, Ibn Saʿd (3:194-195), al-Bayhaqī, *al-Sunan al-Kubrā* (6:169-170 §11728, 6:178 §11784, 6:257 §12267), ʿAbd al-Razzāq (9:101), al-Ṭaḥāwī, *Maʿānī al-Āthār* (4:88), *Istīʿāb* (4:1807), *Naṣb* (4:122), Ibn al-Jawzī, *Ṣifat al-Ṣafwa* (1:265), al-Nawawī, *Tahdhīb al-Asmā'* (2:574, 2:630), al-Lālikā'ī, *Karāmāt al-Awliyā'* (p. 117), al-Mizzī, *Tahdhīb* (35:380), and Muḥibb al-Dīn al-Ṭabarī, *al-Riyāḍ al-Naḍira* (2:122-123 §576).

326 Narrated from Abū Hurayra and ʿĀ'isha by al-Bukhārī and Muslim, the latter without the words "although they were not Prophets."

327 Narrated from Ibn ʿUmar by al-Tirmidhī (*ḥasan ṣaḥīḥ gharīb*), Aḥmad, and Ibn Ḥibbān (15:318 §6895); from Abū Dharr by Aḥmad, Abū Dāwūd, and al-Ḥākim; from Abū Hurayra by Aḥmad, Ibn Ḥibbān (15:312-313 §6889), Abū Yaʿlā, al-Ḥākim, Ibn Abī Shayba (12:21), Ibn Abī ʿĀṣim in *al-Sunna* (§1250), and al-Bazzār (§2501) with a sound chain as indicated by al-Haythamī (9:66); and from Bilāl and Muʿāwiya by al-Ṭabarānī in *al-Kabīr*. See al-Baghawī, *Sharḥ al-Sunna* (14:85), Ibn Abī ʿĀṣim, *al-Sunna* (p. 567 §1247-1250), Ibn Saʿd (21:99), and Ibn al-Athīr, *Jāmiʿ al-Uṣūl* (9:444).

328 Narrated from ʿUqba ibn ʿĀmir by Aḥmad and al-Tirmidhī who graded it *ḥasan*, and by al-Ḥākim (3:85) who graded it *ṣaḥīḥ* as confirmed by al-Dhahabī. Also narrated from ʿIṣma ibn Mālik by al-Ṭabarānī with a weak chain in *al-Kabīr* (17:298), as stated by al-Haythamī (9:68) and al-Munāwī in the *Fayḍ*.

as 'inspired' (*mulham*)." This is the majority's opinion according to Ibn Ḥajar who said: "'Communicated to' means 'by the angels.'"[329]

Following are the definitions given by al-Ḥakīm al-Tirmidhī and al-Nawawī respectively in *Khatm al-Awliyā'* and *Sharḥ Ṣaḥīḥ Muslim*:

> "The difference between prophethood (*nubuwwa*) and sainthood (*wilāya*) is that the former consists in speech (*kalām*) proceeding (*yanfaṣil*) from Allah ﷻ by revelation (*waḥyan*) accompanied by a spirit (*rūḥ*) from Allah. Revelation comes to pass and is sealed with the spirit. Thus does revelation come. This phenomenon obligates its confirmation [by the recipient]. Whoever rejects it commits disbelief, since he rejected the Speech of Allah. But sainthood is for those upon whom Allah bestows His communication (*ḥadīth*) in a different way, connecting them with Him. The recipient thus receives communication which proceeds from Allah ﷻ in the authoritative language of truth (*'alā lisān al-ḥaqq*), accompanied by tranquillity (*al-sakīna*). It is received by the tranquillity that lies in the heart of the one communicated to (*al-muḥaddath*) who then accepts it and rests therein. Someone asks: What is the difference between 'communication' and 'speech'? Communication is what emerges from the recipient's knowledge manifesting itself at the time that Allah wills. This is the communication of the inmost self (*ḥadīth al-nafs*), such as the secret thought (*al-sirr*). Such communication only takcs place because of the love of Allah for that particular servant. It moves on to his heart with truth and the heart accepts it with tranquillity. Whoever rejects this does not commit disbelief but failure. It turns into a calamity for him and his heart becomes dulled (*yubhatu qalbuh*). This person has rejected, in the face of truth, what the

[329] In *Fatḥ al-Bārī* (7:62:§3689).

love of Allah brought him inside himself in the form of knowledge from Allah, using him as a recipient for truth and granting his heart support. Whereas the first has rejected, in the face of Allah, the very Speech of Allah, inspiration, and spirit. Furthermore, those being communicated to (*al-muḥaddathūn*) have levels. Some are given a third of prophethood, some half, and some more than that, all the way to the level of the one who receives the most – he who possesses the seal of Sainthood. Someone says: 'It shocks me to say that someone other than the Prophets may possess any part of prophethood!' Have you not heard the ḥadīth of the Messenger of Allah ﷺ: 'Following a middle course (*al-iqtiṣād*), taking the right way (*al-hadī*), and keeping good demeanor (*al-samt al-ṣāliḥ*) are one in twenty-four parts of Prophethood'?[330] If {*those who follow a middle course*} (35:32) possess the afore-mentioned portions of prophethood, then what about {*those foremost in good deeds*} (35:32)?"[331]

[330] Narrated with the wording "one in twenty-five parts" from Ibn 'Abbās by Abū Dāwūd, Aḥmad, al-Bukhārī in *al-Adab al-Mufrad* (p. 276), *al-Jāmi' li-Akhlāq al-Rāwī* (1991 ed. 1:230-231 §210=1983 ed. 1:155) and al-Ṭabarānī, *al-Awsaṭ*, all with a fair to weak chain because of Qābūs ibn Abī Ẓabyān as indicated by al-Haythamī (8:90). Also narrated from 'Abd Allah ibn Sarjis al-Muzanī with "gentleness" (*al-ta'uda*) instead of "taking the right way" and the wording "one in twenty-four parts" by al-Tirmidhī (*ḥasan gharīb*), al-Maqdisī, *al-Mukhtāra* (9:404-405), 'Abd ibn Ḥumayd, *Musnad* (p. 183), al-Khaṭīb, *Tārīkh Baghdād* (3:66) and *al-Jāmi' li-Akhlāq al-Rāwī* (1:619 §928=1:394), all with a weak chain because of 'Abd Allah ibn 'Imrān. The narration from ibn Sarjis corroborates and strengthens that from Ibn 'Abbās, the ḥadīth is therefore fair as stated by al-Tirmidhī and al-Khaṭīb's editor in *al-Jāmi' li-Akhlāq al-Rāwī* (1991 ed. 1:231), but not sound as claimed by al-Ḥākim and Aḥmad Shākir in Aḥmad's *Musnad* (3:205 §2698, 2:459 §1946), and Allah knows best. Also narrated with the wording "one in seventy parts" from Ibn 'Abbās by al-Bukhārī in *al-Adab al-Mufrad* (p. 276) with a chain containing Qābūs and with the wording "one in twenty-seven parts" from Ibn 'Abbās by al-Ṭabarānī with a weak chain as stated by al-Haythamī.

[331] Al-Ḥakīm al-Tirmidhī, *Khatm al-Awliyā'* (p. 346-347), chapter ten titled "Signs of the Saints" (*'alāmāt al-awliyā'*).

> "The Scholars have differed concerning 'communicated to.' Ibn Wahb said it meant 'inspired' (*mulham*). It was said also: 'Those who are right, and when they give an opinion it is as if they were communicated to, and then they give their opinion.' It was said also: 'The angels speak to them...' Al-Bukhārī said: 'Truth comes from their tongues.' This ḥadīth contains a confirmation of the miracles of the Saints (*karāmāt al-awliyā'*)."[332]

To the minimalist claim that since the ḥadīth states "If there is anyone in my *Umma*, it is ʿUmar," it must follow that the number of such inspired people is at most one – namely ʿUmar – Ibn Ḥajar replied with the reminder that it is wrong to think that other Communities had many but this Community only one![333]

Thus, what is meant by the ḥadīth is the perfection of the quality of *ilhām* – inspiration – in ʿUmar, not its lack in other Muslims. Another proof is that Abū Bakr was even more inspired than ʿUmar by the Consensus of *Ahl al-Sunna*. This is shown by Abū Bakr's unique leadership at the time of the Prophet's ﷺ death and, again, when he took up arms to exact the *zakāt* from the rebellious Arab tribes.

A miraculous illustration of the Prophet's ﷺ saying about ʿUmar took place in the latter's rule when, from his pulpit in Madīna as he was delivering the *Jumuʿa* sermon, he began to shout at the top of his lungs: "Sāriya, the mountain! Sāriya, the mountain!" in reference to Sāriya ibn Zunaym al-Du'alī, one of his expeditionary commanders who was besieging Nihāwand or Fasā and Dārābajird in Persia at the time and was about to fall into an ambush, whereupon Sāriya and his troops heard him and took to the mountain, saying: "This is the voice of the Commander of the Believers!" After this they fought with their back protected and were granted victory.[334]

[332] Al-Nawawī, *Sharḥ Ṣaḥīḥ Muslim* (*Kitāb* 44, *Bab* 2, §2398).

[333] Ibn Ḥajar, *Fatḥ al-Bārī* (7:62-63 §3689).

The Qāḍī Abū Bakr ibn al-ʿArabī al-Mālikī said of this miracle: "It constitutes a tremendous rank and an evident gift from Allah, and it is present in all of the righteous incessantly until the Day of Resurrection."[335] Ibn Qutayba related that al-Aḥnaf ibn Qays once exclaimed: "By Allah! ʿUmar knows what shall be better than the rest of us know what has been."

A group were visiting our liege-lord ʿUthmān ﷺ but one of them had gazed at a woman on the way. ʿUthmān said: "One of you comes in with fornicating eyes!" They said: "What! Is there revelation after the Prophet ﷺ?" He replied: "Not revelation but truthful insight" (*lā wa-lākin firāsatun ṣādiqa*).[336]

The Prophet ﷺ also said: "Seek your heart's answer even if all people answer you."

The Prophet ﷺ asked Ḥāritha ﷺ: "How are you this morning, Ḥāritha?" He replied: "This morning I am a real believer." The Prophet ﷺ said: "Take care of what you say: what is the reality of your belief?" He said: "I have turned myself away from this world until its rocks and its gold became the same for me, by keeping awake at night and by keeping myself thirsty by day; and I can almost see the Throne of my Lord in full sight; and I can almost

[334] Narrated by al-Wāqidī, *Futūḥ al-Shām* (2:42), Ibn ʿAsākir, *Tārīkh* (*Tahdhīb* 6:46), al-Khaṭīb, *Ruwāt Mālik* as cited by al-Suyūṭī in *Tārīkh al-Khulafā'* (p. 125= p. 134), al-Bayhaqī through the narrators of the *Ṣaḥīḥ* in *Dalā'il al-Nubuwwa* and *al-Iʿtiqād* (p. 314=p. 178), Abū Nuʿaym with four chains in *Dalā'il al-Nubuwwa* (p. 579 §525-528), and others cf. al-Ṭabarī, *Tārīkh* (4:178=2:553-554), Ibn al-Jawzī, *Manāqib 'Umar* (p. 172-173), al-Nawawī, *Tahdhīb al-Asmā'* (2:10), Ibn al-Athīr, *Usd al-Ghāba* (4:65), Ibn Kathīr, *Bidāya* (7:131-135 *isnād jayyid ḥasan*), Ibn al-Qayyim, *al-Rūḥ* (p. 239=p. 534 "Difference between insight and conjecture, *al-firāsatu wal-ẓann*"), Ibn Ḥajar, *Iṣāba* (2:3=3:6 *isnād ḥasan*), and al-Sakhāwī, *Maqāṣid* (p. 468 *isnād ḥasan*). Al-Suyūṭī in *Ziyādat al-Jāmiʿ al-Ṣaghīr*, the *Durar* (p. 288-289 §483), and the *La'āli' al-Maṣnūʿa* said the ḥadīth Master al-Quṭb al-Ḥalabī wrote a monograph demonstrating the soundness of this report.

[335] In *'Āriḍat al-Aḥwadhī* (13:150).

[336] Cited by al-Qurṭubī in his *Tafsīr* (10:44) and al-Qārī in *Sharḥ Musnad Abī Ḥanīfa*, ḥadīth *ittaqū firāsat al-mu'min*.

see the people of the Garden of Paradise visiting each other; and I can almost see the people of the Fire wailing to each other in it." The Prophet ﷺ said: "Ḥāritha! You do know: therefore cleave to it!" (*'arifta fa-ilzam*). Some versions add: "This is a believer, Allah has illumined his heart" (*mu'minun nawwara Allahu qalbah*).[337]

Among the most explicit texts on *kashf*-authentication is the narration of the Prophet ﷺ : "If you hear a ḥadīth reported from me which your hearts recognize, at which your hair and skin become tender, and you feel that it is near to you: know that I am nearer to it than you. And if you hear a ḥadīth being reported from me of which your hearts disapprove, from which your hair and skin recoil, and you feel that it is far from you: know that I am even farther from it than you."[338]

Echoing the above ḥadīth is al-Khaṭīb's narration from al-Rabī' ibn Khuthaym: "A ḥadīth bears a light like daylight by which you may recognize it or a darkness similar to that of night by which you may disown it." Al-Qārī mentions it in the introduction of the *Asrār*.

[337] Narrated from al-Ḥārith ibn Mālik al-Anṣārī (some chains have al-Ḥāritha ibn al-Na'mān al-Anṣārī) by al-Ṭabarānī in *al-Kabīr* (3:266 §3367), al-Quḍā'ī, *Musnad al-Shihāb* (2:127 §1028), 'Abd ibn Ḥumayd, *Musnad* (p. 165 §445); al-Bazzār, Abū Nu'aym, *Ḥilya* (1985 ed. 1:242), al-Haythamī (1:57 "Chapter on the Reality of Belief and its Perfection" *Bāb ḥaqīqat al-īmān*), al-'Askarī, *al-Amthāl*, Ibn al-Mubārak, *al-Zuhd*, 'Abd al-Razzāq through two chains, Ibn Mandah, al-'Uqaylī, *al-Ḍu'afā'* (2:290 §864, 4:455 §2085), al-Bayhaqī with three chains in *al-Shu'ab* (7:362-363) and *al-Zuhd* (p. 355), al-Dhahabī, *Mīzān* (4:469 *munkar*) from Ibn al-Najjār, Ibn Aṣram in *al-Istiqāma*, Ibn Sa'īd, and Ibn Abī Shayba (6:170 §30425 *mu'ḍal*). Abū Ḥanīfa mentions it in *al-Fiqh al-Akbar*, Ibn Kathīr, *Tafsīr* for verse (8:4). Ibn Ḥajar in *Iṣāba* (1:597 §1480) lists its many chains and says that this is a *ḥadīth mu'ḍal* (with a chain missing at least two sub-narrators) yet *mawṣūl* (identical with *muttaṣil*, i.e linked back to a Companion through a Successor). Ibn 'Aṭā' Allah explains this ḥadīth at length in *Laṭā'if al-Minan* (1:176-186).

[338] Narrated from Abū Ḥumayd al-Anṣārī and Abū Usayd al-Sā'idī by Aḥmad (al-Arna'ūṭ ed. 25:456 §16058 *isnād ṣaḥīḥ 'alā sharṭ Muslim*), al-Bazzār (*Mukhtaṣar al-Zawā'id* §187), Ibn Ḥibbān, *Ṣaḥīḥ* (1:263 §63) and others with a sound chain of *Ṣaḥīḥ* narrators cf. al-Haythamī (1:150) and Ibn Kathīr, *Tafsīr* (1:473, 2:264).

The author of one of the prominent "famous-ḥadīth" works, Muḥammad Darwīsh al-Ḥūt in his *Asnā al-Maṭālib fī Aḥādīth Mukhtalifat al-Marātib*, refers to the above rule when he discusses the forgery:

> "A son is a prince and chief for seven years; a slave and prisoner for seven years; and a minister and brother for seven years. Then, if you are not satisfied with him, strike his flanks; in such a case, you would be excused for your severity toward him."

Al-Ḥūt says: "Indeed, the light of Prophethood does not shine over this report!"[339] The ḥadīth Scholars often make such remarks.

Asked how he could tell the authentic ḥadīth from the inauthentic, Ibn Mahdī replied: "As the physician knows the madman." Challenged about his dismissal of a man's narration he replied: "Do you see the man who brings a coin to the jeweller, asking him to examine a certain coin? If the jeweller says to him, 'It is counterfeit' and he challenges his opinion the jeweller will reply: 'Stick to my job for twenty years as I have done so that you will know what I know.'" Another time he said: "The knowledge of ḥadīth is inspiration (*ilhām*)."

Seeing the Prophet ﷺ in Dream

The Prophet ﷺ said: "A true vision is one-fortysixth of prophecy."[340] The pious Predecessors understood this ḥadīth literally. When Imām Mālik was asked, "Can anyone interpret dreams?" he replied fiercely, "Are they toying with prophethood?"[341] Abū Muṣʿab recounts the following dream someone had about his teacher:

[339] In *Asnā al-Maṭālib fī Aḥādīth Mukhtalifat al-Marātib* (p. 33).
[340] Narrated in the *Ṣaḥīḥayn* from Anas, Abu Saʿīd, Abū Hurayra, and Ibn ʿUmar.
[341] Ibn ʿAbd al-Barr, *al-Tamhīd* (1:288) cf. Ibn Ḥajar, *Fatḥ al-Bārī* (12:363), ʿIyāḍ in his commentary on Muslim cf. al-Nawawī, *Sharḥ Ṣaḥīḥ Muslim* (15:30), al-Qurṭubī, *Tafsīr* (9:126) *Sūrat Yūsuf*, v. 5, and al-Zarqānī, *Sharḥ al-Muwaṭṭa'* (4:448).

> "I went in to see Mālik ibn Anas. He said to me: 'Look under my place of prayer or prayer-mat and see what is there.' I looked and found a certain writing. He said: 'Read it.' It contained the account of a dream which one of his brothers had seen and which concerned him. Mālik recited it [from memory]: 'I saw the Prophet ﷺ in my sleep. He was in his mosque and the people were gathered around him, and he said: 'I have hidden for you under my pulpit (*minbar*) something good – or: knowledge – and I have ordered Mālik to distribute it to the people.'' Then Mālik wept, so I got up and left."[342]

The background to our liege-lord ʿUmar's famous prayer for rain was an explicit *tawassul* through and dream-vision of the Prophet ﷺ by the Companion Bilāl ibn al-Ḥārith as narrated in two versions:

(a) Version 1 from the Companion Mālik al-Dār:

> The people suffered a drought in ʿUmar's *khilāfa*, whereupon a man came to the grave of the Prophet ﷺ and said: "Messenger of Allah! Ask for rain for your Community, for verily they have but perished." After this the Prophet ﷺ appeared to him in a dream and told him: "Go to ʿUmar and give him my greeting, then tell him that they will be watered. Tell him: Be clever!" The man went and told ʿUmar. The latter wept and said: "My Lord! I spare no effort except in what escapes my power."[343]

[342] Narrated by Ibn al-Jawzī, *Ṣifat al-Ṣafwa* (1/2:120), chapter titled "Layer 6 of the People of Madīna." The account is also in Abū Nuʿaym's *Ḥilya*, ʿIyāḍ's *Tartīb*, al-Dhahabī's *Siyar*, and al-Harawī al-Anṣārī's *Dhamm al-Kalām* (4:132).

[343] Narrated by Ibn Abī Shayba (6:356 §32002=12:31-32) and al-Bayhaqī, *Dalā'il al-Nubuwwa* (7:47) with a sound (*ṣaḥīḥ*) chain per Ibn Kathīr in *Jāmiʿ al-Masānīd* (1:223 *isnāduhu jayyidun qawī*), *Musnad 'Umar* and *al-Bidāya* (7:91-92=7:105 *isnāduhu ṣaḥīḥ*), Ibn Ḥajar, *Fatḥ al-Bārī, Istisqā'*, (1989 ed. 2:629-630=1959 ed. 2:495 *isnād ṣaḥīḥ*) and *al-Iṣāba* (6:164 §8350=3:484) where he says that Ibn Abī Khaythama cited it. It is also thus narrated by al-Khalīlī in *al-Irshād* (1:313- 314).

(b) Version 2 from al-Ṭabarī's *Tārīkh*:

> In the year of the drought called al-Ramāda during the successorship of ʿUmar the Companion Bilāl ibn al-Ḥārith, while slaughtering a sheep for his kin, noticed that the sheep's bones had turned red because the drying flesh was clinging to them. He cried out, "*Yā Muḥammadāh!*" Then he saw the Prophet ﷺ in a dream ordering him to go to ʿUmar with the tidings of coming rain on condition that ʿUmar show wisdom. Hearing this, ʿUmar assembled the people and came out to pray for rain with al-ʿAbbās the uncle of the Prophet ﷺ.[344]

Ibn ʿAbd al-Barr cites it in *al-Istīʿāb* (2:464=3:1149) and al-Dhahabī in *Siyar* (Fikr ed. 1/2:524). Ibn Ḥajar identifies Mālik as ʿUmar's treasurer and says that the man who visited and saw the Prophet ﷺ in his dream is identified as the Companion Bilāl ibn al-Ḥārith. Ibn Ḥajar counts this ḥadīth among the reasons for al-Bukhārī's naming of the chapter "The people's request to their leader for rain if they suffer drought" in the *Ṣaḥīḥ*, even if al-Bukhārī does not narrate it there. In his aspersions on *Fatḥ al-Bārī* the Wahhābī Ibn Bāz condemns the act of the Companion who came to the grave, calling it "abominable" (*munkar*) and "a means to associating partners to Allah" (*wasīla ilāl-shirk*) while Nāṣir Albānī even denies the authenticity of the ḥadīth in his booklet *al-Tawassul* (p. 120) on the claim that Mālik al-Dār is "unknown" (*majhūl*) on the sole basis of his brief mention by Ibn Abī Ḥātim in *al-Jarḥ wal-Taʿdīl* (8:213 §14252). This is contradicted by the notices of three authorities which Albānī ignores: Ibn Saʿd, al-Khalīlī, and Ibn Ḥajar! What is more, Ibn Abī Khaythama and al-Bukhārī narrated from him. "Mālik al-Dār [was] ʿUmar ibn al-Khaṭṭāb's freedman. He narrated from Abū Bakr and ʿUmar. He was known." Ibn Saʿd (5:12). "Mālik al-Dār is agreed upon and the Successors have approved highly of him," said Abū Yaʿlā al-Khalīl ibn ʿAbd Allah al-Khalīlī al-Qazwīnī in *Kitāb al-Irshād* (1:313) cf. ʿAbd Allah al-Ghumārī, *Irghām al-Mubtadiʿ* (p. 9). Ibn Ḥajar said in the *Iṣāba* (6:164 §8350): "Mālik ibn ʿIyāḍ [was] ʿUmar's freedman. He is the one named Mālik al-Dār. He saw the Prophet ﷺ and heard narrations from Abū Bakr al-Ṣiddīq. He narrated from Abū Bakr and ʿUmar, Muʿādh, and Abū ʿUbayda. From him narrated Abū Ṣāliḥ al-Samān and Mālik's two sons ʿAwn and ʿAbd Allah. Al-Bukhārī narrated from him in *al-Tārīkh al-Kabīr* (7:304 §10633)... as well as Ibn Abī Khaythama." Albānī is further refuted in the lengthy analysis given by Mamdūḥ in *Rafʿ al-Mināra* (p. 262-278), which refutes other similar attempts cf. Ibn Bāz's aspersions

Shaykh Muṣṭafa al-Shaṭṭī wrote: "The legal inference here is not from the dream, because although the dream [of seeing the Prophet ﷺ] is truthful, yet a dream cannot be used to establish a ruling due to the possibility that the person who saw it makes an error in its wording. Rather, the inference from this hadith is based on the action of the Companion Bilāl ibn al-Ḥārith." The praiseworthy action is the visitation to the Prophet ﷺ and the already-established ruling is the licitness and appropriateness of the prayer for rain of which the dream vividly reminded our liege-lord ʿUmar.

The poet Muḥammad ibn ʿAbd Allah ibn ʿAmr ibn Muʿāwiya al-ʿUtbī al-Umawī (d. 228) said: "As I was sitting by the grave of the Prophet ﷺ, a Bedouin Arab came and said: 'Peace be upon you, Messenger of Allah! I have heard Allah say: {*If they had only, when they wronged themselves, come unto you and asked the forgiveness of Allah and the Messenger had asked forgiveness for them, they would have found Allah indeed Oft-Returning, Most Merciful*} (4:64), so I have come to you asking forgiveness for my sin, seeking your intercession with my Lord.' Then he began to recite poetry:

O best of those whose bones are buried in the deep earth,
From whose fragrance the depth and height have become sweet
May I be the ransom for a grave in which you dwell,
Where one finds purity, bounty and munificence!

Then he left and I dozed off and saw the Prophet ﷺ in my sleep. He said to me: "ʿUtbī! Run after the Bedouin and give him glad tidings that Allah has forgiven him.'"[345]

on *Fatḥ al-Bārī*, Abū Bakr al-Jazā'irī's tract *Wa-Jā'ū Yarkuḍūn*, Ḥammād al-Anṣārī's all-too-typical articles "*al-Mafhūm al-Ṣaḥīḥ lil-Tawassul*" also titled "*Tuḥfat al-Qārī fil-Radd ʿalāl-Ghumārī*," and other such literature.

[344] Narrated by al-Ṭabarī, *Tārīkh* (2:509).

Even if according to some this report does not have a sound chain of transmission it is confirmed by two other closely similar incidents, one narrated from our liege-lord ʿAlī ﷺ through Sufyān ibn ʿUyayna and Abū Saʿīd al-Samʿānī, the other from Abū Ḥarb al-Hilālī.[346] The report is adduced by many of the Scholars of *tafsīr* and *fiqh* to point out the timeless meaning of the verse and the fact that it applies to all those who come after the time of the Prophet ﷺ.[347]

Wahb ibn Munabbih said:

> "I saw the Prophet ﷺ in my sleep and said: 'Messenger of Allah! Where are the *abdāl* of your Community?' He gestured with his hand towards Syro-Palestine. I said: 'Messenger of Allah! Are there not any in Iraq?' He said: 'Yes, Muḥammad ibn Wāsiʿ, Ḥassān ibn Abī Sinān, and Mālik ibn Dīnār, who walks among the people like Abū Dharr in his time.'"[348]

[345] Narrated by Ibn ʿAsākir in *Mukhtaṣar Tārīkh Dimashq* (2:408), Ibn al-Jawzī in *Muthīr al-Gharām al-Sākin ilā Ashraf al-Amākin* (p. 490), and Ibn al-Najjār in *Akhbār al-Madīna* (p. 147).

[346] Cf. al-Qurṭubī's *Tafsīr* (5:265-266) and al-Bayhaqī's *Shuʿab* (3:495-496 §4178).

[347] In al-Nawawī, *Adhkār* (Makka: al-Maktabat al-Tijāriyya, 1412/1992, p. 253-254), *Majmūʿ* (8:217), *al-Īḍāḥ fī Manāsik al-Ḥajj* (p. 144), chapter on visiting the grave of the Prophet ﷺ; Ibn Kathīr, *Tafsīr* (2:306) and *Bidāya* (Maʿārif ed. 1:180); Ibn Jamāʿa, *Hidāyat al-Sālik* (3:1384); Ibn ʿAqīl, *Tadhkira*; Ibn Qudāma, *Mughnī* (3:556-557= 3:298=5:465), Ibn Mufliḥ, *Mubdiʿ* (3:259), Shams al-Dīn Ibn Qudāma, *al-Sharḥ al-Kabīr* (3:494-495), al-Buhūtī, *Kashshāf al-Qināʿ* (2:515=5:30); al-Qurṭubī, *Tafsīr* (v. 4:64), cf. *Aḥkām al-Qur'ān* (5:265); al-Samhūdī, *Khulāṣat al-Wafā* (p. 121, from al-Nawawī); Taqī al-Dīn al-Subkī, *Shifā' al-Siqām* (p. 52); al-Haytamī, *al-Jawhar al-Munaẓẓam fī Ziyārat al-Qabr al-Mukarram*; Daḥlān, *Khulāṣat al-Kalām* (year 1204). The ḥadīth of al-ʿUtbī is among the passages suppressed from the late ʿAbd al-Qādir al-Arna'ūṭ's Ryaḍ edition at Dār al-Hudā (1409/1989) It took al-Arna'ūṭ three years to issue a disavowal of that edition and a facsimile of his handwritten letter of retraction (dated 1413/1992) was published by Shaykh Maḥmūd Mamdūḥ in his *Rafʿ al-Mināra* (p. 73-75 and 377-379)!

[348] Narrated from Julays by Aḥmad in *al-Zuhd*, Ibn Abī al-Dunyā, Abū Nuʿaym, al-Bayhaqī, and Ibn ʿAsākir (1:302).

The Qur'ān-copyist Yazīd al-Fārisī said:

> "I saw the Prophet ﷺ in my sleep in the time of Ibn ʿAbbās. I told the latter and he said: 'The Prophet ﷺ used to say: 'Truly, the devil cannot take my likeness, therefore whoever sees me in his sleep has seen me (truly).' Can you describe for us that man whom you saw?' I said: 'Yes, I saw a man of medium build, his complexion was tawny to fair (*laḥmuhu asmarun ilā al-bayāḍ*), his smile was beautiful, his eyes were jet-black, he had a handsome, round face which his beard filled from here to here, and it almost filled his upper chest.' Ibn ʿAbbās said: 'Had you seen him while awake you could not have described him better!'"[349]

A contemporary specialist of the *Shamā'il* said, "'From here to here' means 'from this ear to this ear'... indicating by this that his noble beard is wide and very large (*ʿarīḍatun ʿaẓīma*), and it is an indication of its length."[350]

Sulaymān ibn Suḥaym said: "I saw the Prophet ﷺ in my sleep and said, 'Messenger of Allah, those people that visit you and greet you, do you discern (*atafqahu*) their *salām*?' He said, 'Yes, and I reply to them.'"[351] Ibn Suḥaym is one of the narrators of the ḥadīth, "Nothing remains of the beginnings of Prophethood except the good vision a Muslim sees" in Muslim, al-Nasā'ī, and others.

Since Ibn Suḥaym, Yazīd al-Fārisī and Wahb ibn Munabbih were Successors who had never seen the Prophet ﷺ, their reports constitute a refutation of those who have claimed without basis other than their own speculation that the ḥadīth of the vision of

349 Narrated by Aḥmad in his *Musnad* with a chain of trustworthy narrators as per al-Haythamī in *Majmaʿ al-Zawā'id* although Yazīd al-Fārisī is only "passable" (*maqbūl*).
350 Al-Laḥjī (d. 1410), *Muntahā al-Sūl ʿalā Wasā'il al-Wuṣūl ilā Shamā'il al-Rasūl* ﷺ (4:339-340).
351 Narrated by al-Bayhaqī in the *Shuʿab* (3:491 §4165) and elsewhere cf. ʿIyāḍ, *Shifā'* (p. 576 §1444) and al-Sakhāwī in *al-Qawl al-Badīʿ* (p. 323).

the Prophet ﷺ in dream applies only to those Muslims who knew his appearance from having seen him while awake, namely, the Companions! Also among the non-Companion *Salaf* related to see the Prophet ﷺ in dream: Sulaymān ibn Nu'aym, Nāfi' al-Qāri' – one of the Seven canonical readers – 'Umar ibn 'Abd al-'Azīz, 'Āṣim ibn Kulayb's father, Abū al-Ḥasan al-Ash'arī, and others.[352]

Three Visions of Ibn 'Abbās رضي الله عنهما

[1] Ibn 'Abbās said: "I passed by the Messenger of Allah ﷺ as he was discussing in private with Diḥya. I was unaware that this was Gibrīl. I passed by without giving salām. On my way back, the Prophet ﷺ said to me: 'What prevented you from giving salām?' [I said:] 'I saw you discussing in private with Diḥyat al-Kalbī and loathed to interrupt you.' He said: 'You saw him?' I said yes. He said: 'It was Gibrīl and lo! your sight shall fade and return to you only at the time of your death.'"[353]
[2] "I saw the Prophet ﷺ in my mid-day sleep disheveled and dust-covered. He held a jar containing blood. I said: 'Messenger of Allah! What is this?' He replied: 'This is the blood of al-Ḥusayn and his companions which I have been collecting without cease today.' They recorded the day and later found that al-Ḥusayn had been killed the previous day."[354]
[3] Al-Suyūṭī mentions in *Tanwīr al-Ḥalak fī Imkān Ru'yat al-Nabī wal-Malak* that Ibn 'Abbās saw the Prophet ﷺ in his dream then visited one of the Mothers of the Believers who brought out the Prophet's mirror for him. When Ibn 'Abbās looked into it, he saw the image of the Prophet ﷺ.

[352] See Shaykh 'Īsā ibn Māni' al-Ḥimyarī's *Ru'yā al-Nabī* ﷺ *Ḥaqqun ilā Qiyāmi al-Sā'a* ("The Vision of the Prophet ﷺ is a Reality Until the Rising of the Hour").
[353] Narrated from Maymūn ibn Mahrān by Abū Nu'aym (1985 ed. 1:329) and al-Ṭabarānī in *al-Kabīr* (10:237 §10586) cf. al-Suyūṭī, *Khaṣā'iṣ* (2:202).
[354] Aḥmad (1:283), al-Ḥākim (4:439 *ṣaḥīḥ 'alā sharṭ Muslim*), and others.

Seeing the Prophet ﷺ and Authenticating Ḥadīth

Muslim narrates in his *Ṣaḥīḥ* from ʿAlī ibn Mus-hir that the latter had asked the Prophet ﷺ in a dream about one thousand ḥadīths he had heard from Abān ibn Abī ʿIyāsh – one of the discarded narrators due to his poor memory – whereupon the Prophet ﷺ did not recognize more than five or six of them

Al-Tirmidhī narrates in his *Sunan*:

> "Aḥmad ibn Muḥammad ibn Mūsā narrated to us: ʿAbd Allah ibn al-Mubārak told us: From Maʿmar [ibn Rāshid]: From Khuṣayf who said: 'I saw the Prophet ﷺ in my sleep and I said, 'Messenger of Allah! The people are differing over [the wording of] *tashahhud*!' He replied: 'Stick to Ibn Masʿūd's *tashahhud*.'"

Al-Bayhaqī narrates in the *Shuʿab* that when Muḥammad ibn Hārūn saw the Prophet ﷺ in his dream he asked him whether he did say the ḥadīth, "Whoever condoles with someone afflicted receives the same reward" (narrated by al-Tirmidhī with a weak chain) and the Prophet ﷺ replied yes. Ibn Hārūn wept every time he related it.[355]

Commenting on Imām Muslim's narration of ʿAlī ibn Mus-hir's dream, al-Nawawī said:

> "Al-Qāḍī ʿIyāḍ – Allah have mercy on him! – said: 'Such reports are taken into consideration to show what is already decided concerning the weakness of Abān. **Not that dreams are definitive, nor can an established sunna be abrogated because of them, nor a previously unestablished sunna be established**, by consensus of the scholars.' These are al-Qāḍī's words. Others of our [Shāfiʿī] companions said something similar and reported agreement to the effect that **nothing of what has been decided**

[355] Cf. al-Suyūṭī's *Taʿaqqubāt*, chapter of *Janāʾiz*.

> **by the Law can be changed because of what the sleeper saw.** What we mentioned here does not contradict the saying of the Prophet ﷺ: "Whoever sees me in vision or dream sees me truly."[356] For the meaning of this ḥadīth is that the dreamer's vision is true and not from the fantasies of dreams nor the delusions of the devil. However, **it is not permissible to establish a legal ruling on the basis of this dream,** because the state of sleep is not a state of accuracy and verification for whatever the dreamer is seeing. The scholars all agree that among the conditions necessary for accepting one's narration or legal testimony is that he be awake, not somnolent, nor poor in his memorization, nor prone to making many mistakes, nor lacking accuracy. A sleeper does not meet these criteria. Therefore his narration is not accepted because he lacks accuracy. This all pertains to a dream that contains a ruling that contravenes what those in authority ruly by. **As for seeing the Prophet ﷺ ordering him something which is recommended, or forbidding him something which is forbidden, or directing him to do something beneficial, there is no disagreement that it is desirable that he go ahead and act according to his dream.** For here the ruling does not depend on the dream but on what has been decided from the principles at hand, and Allah knows best."[357]

Al-Nawawī apparently viewed Muslim's narration of the dream-discreditation of Abān's reports as a vision of the Prophet ﷺ "directing someone to something beneficial" without there being any contradiciton of an established principle of the Law. Al-Suyūṭī similarly adduces 'Alī ibn Mus-hir's report and other reports in support of disauthentication through dreams in

[356] Narrated by al-Bukhārī. The remainder of the ḥadīth states: "for Satan cannot take on my form, and the believer's dream is one forty-sixth of prophecy."
[357] Al-Nawawī, *Sharḥ Ṣaḥīḥ Muslim* (1:115), as quoted by Abū Ghudda in his notes on Ibn 'Abd al-Barr's *al-Intiqā'* (77-78).

section 6 of *Taḥdhīr al-Khawāṣṣ*, in one of which the Prophet ﷺ says: "Tell Ibn Simʿān to fear Allah and not tell lies about me." (Yet Ibn Simʿān was an assiduous worshipper!)

Such dreams are beneficial but only confirm suspicions that were already in circulation with regard to certain narrators before the dreams took place. What is impermissible is, in al-Nawawī's words, to establish a wholly original legal ruling by means of a dream. For example, al-Sakhāwī in *al-Maqāṣid al-Ḥasana* said of the entry: "Whoever circumambulates this House seven times, prays two *rakʿas* behind the Station of Ibrāhīm, and drinks *Zamzam* water, all his sins shall be forgiven as many as they may be":

> "It is inauthentic although the populace go on and on about it, especially in Makka where it is written on some of the walls adjacent to *Zamzam*! They resorted to dreams to establish it and to other ways which can never be used to establish the Prophetic ḥadīths."

Al-Sakhāwī rejected *kashf*-based authentication here because its sole basis was the dream without any objective precedent.

Confirming al-Nawawī's rule acceptance-wise is al-Qārī's defense of *kashf*-authentication in *al-Asrār al-Marfūʿa* as in the following examples:

1. In the entry "O Shaykh! If you want your safety look for it in the safety of others from you," al-Qārī says:

> "Shaykh Abū Isḥāq al-Shīrāzī is narrated [by Ibn al-Samʿānī in *al-Dhayl*] to have said: 'I saw the Prophet ﷺ in dream and asked him if I could hear from him a ḥadīth and then narrate it from him, whereupon he said to me: 'O Shaykh…' Al-Shirāzī was happy for it and used to say, 'The Messenger of Allah called me a Shaykh!'"

Al-Qārī goes on to quote the words of al-Suyūṭī's student Abū al-Ḥasan ʿAlī ibn Muḥammad al-Minnawfī (857-939) who said in his abridgment of al-Sakhāwī's *Maqāṣid*:

> "There is nothing objectionable about reporting such as this from him ﷺ in dream nor in putting it into practice. For it is not a ruling over which there is a the kind of difference of opinion which our colleagues cite in specific instances."

Then al-Qārī quotes al-Nawawī:

> Al-Nawawī said in his commentary on *Ṣahīh Muslim*: "Nothing that is stipulated in the Law can be modified by something someone sees in his sleep." He went on to say: ... "If one only sees a dream that commands one to do something that is recommendable, or a dream that forbids him to do something that is prohibited, or directs one to something of benefit, then there is no disagreement that it is desirable to act in compliance with it. For this does not amount to a ruling-by-dream (*ḥukman bil-manām*) but rather by what was already stipulated originally with regard to that."

2. Al-Qārī says of the report, "I saw my Lord in the image of a long-haired youth":

> "If the ḥadīth is about a dream, there is no problem at all; but if it is understood that the vision took place in a wakeful state, then Ibn al-Humām replied that it refers to "the veil of image" (*ḥijāb al-ṣūra*)."

Shaykh Muḥyī al-Dīn Ibn ʿArabī in the *Futūḥāt al-Makkiyya* affirmed by way of *kashf* the ascription of the sayings "Whoever knows himself knows his Lord" and "I was a Treasure unknown" to the Prophet ﷺ:

> "It came in the ḥadīth that is *ṣaḥīḥ* per unveiling (*kashf*) but unestablished (*ghayr thābit*) per transmission from the Messenger of Allah ﷺ from his Lord ﷻ that Allah said something in the meaning of this: 'I was a Treasure unknown then I desired to be known so I created a creation to which I made Myself known; then they knew Me.'"[358]

Maḥmūd al-Alūsī cites the Hidden Treasure report in his *Tafsīr* while commenting the verse {*I created the jinn and humankind only that they might worship Me*} (51:56) but derides its *kashf*-based authentication as *shinshinatun lahum* – "typical of them [Sufis]!"[359]

The Mālikī Muḥammad ʿUlaysh excoriated *kashf*-authentication as invalid among the authorities of ḥadīth,[360] endearing himself to Jamāl al-Dīn al-Qāsimī and ʿAbd al-Fattāḥ Abū Ghudda who quote him in full[361] to inveigh against its endorsement by Imām al-Lacknawī, Shaykh Muḥyī al-Dīn Ibn ʿArabī, Imām al-Shaʿrānī, and the Akbarī Damascene ḥadīth Master al-ʿAjlūnī in his introduction to *Kashf al-Khafā'*. Nevertheless, greater than all of them, namely Imam Muslim and Imām al-Tirmidhī saw fit to mention it in the *Ṣaḥīḥ* and *Sunan* respectively!

Al-Lacknawī said of the *kashf*-authentication of the *Shuyūkh* that are knowledgeable in the branches of the Law as well as the spiritual realities: "If one of them declares it we will certainly accept his assertion on the strength of his truthfulness, his trustworthiness, and his high rank."[362] A fervent admirer of Ibn ʿArabī, Imām al-Lacknawī said of the "pattern-chained" ḥadīth, each of the narrating links of which hosts the next link with "the two

[358] *Futūḥāt* (3:399 *Bāb* 198).

[359] In *Rūḥ al-Maʿānī* (21:27) provided the text of *Rūḥ al-Maʿānī* to that effect is uncorrupted!

[360] In his *Fatḥ al-ʿAlī al-Mālik fil-Fatwā ʿalā Madhhab al-Imām Mālik* (1:45).

[361] Cf. al-Qāsimī, *Qawāʿid al-Taḥdīth* (p. 183-185), Abū Ghudda in his marginalia on al-Qārī's *Maṣnūʿ* (p. 216-217, cf. 142, 273) and other works of al-Lacknawī's.

[362] Al-Lacknawī, *al-Āthār al-Marfūʿa* (p.19).

black ones – dates and water" (*al-musalsal bil-aswadayn*) in his commentary on al-Jurjānī titled *Ẓafar al-Amānī*:

> "Whoever hosts a Believer, it is as if he hosted Ādam; whoever hosts two Believers, it is as if he hosted Ādam and Ḥawwā'; whoever hosts three, it is as if he hosted Gibrīl, Mīkā'īl, and Isrāfīl; whoever hosts four, it is as if he read the Torah, the Injīl, the Zābūr, and the Furqān; whoever hosts five, it is as if he prayed the five prayers in congregation from the first day Allah created creation until the day of Resurrection; whoever hosts six, it is as if he freed sixty slaves from the descendents of Ismā'īl; whoever hosts seven, the seven gates of hell shall be closed shut without him; whoever hosts eight, the eight gates of Paradise shall be thrown open for him; whoever hosts nine, Allah shall record for him good deeds to the number of all those that disobeyed him from the first day Allah created creation until the day of Resurrection; and whoever hosts ten, Allah shall record for him the reward of all those that prayed, fasted, and made *Ḥajj* and *'Umra* until the day of Resurrection."

"The Amīr al-Mālikī said, 'The Scholars mentioned that these exaggerations assuredly point to inauthenticity....' I say: of this ḥadīth – with the poverty of its phrasing and incoherent structure – my heart bears witness that it is forged, and Allah knows best."[363]

'Abd al-Fattāḥ Abū Ghudda comments petulantly on the above:

> "There is infraction and deception in the wording of the Shaykh, for we do not have ḥadīths which the heart declares sound so they are sound, nor ḥadīths which the heart declares false so they are false, but only ḥadīths which science declares sound or false on the basis of the Book and the Sunna... and I declare a million times that this ḥadīth is a fabricated lie forged

[363] Al-Lacknawī's *Ẓafar al-Amānī* (p. 279-280).

against the Messenger of Allah ﷺ and will oppose whoever disputes me over this verdict, for the Law and reason bear witness to its falsehood!"[364]

Rather, al-Lacknawī's words are entirely in keeping with the spirit and the letter of the above-cited ḥadīths of the Prophet ﷺ: "If you hear a ḥadīth reported from me which your hearts recognize"; "Allah has engraved truth on the tongue of ʿUmar and his heart"; "Seek your heart's answer even if all people answer you"; "This is a believer, Allah has illumined his heart"; as well as the expressions of the Imāms of ḥadīth among the *Salaf* such as al-Rabīʿ ibn Khuthaym, ʿAbd al-Raḥmān ibn Mahdī, and Sahl al-Tustarī (not to mention al-Ḥakīm al-Tirmidhī) while the rebuttal of Shaykh ʿAbd al-Fattāḥ Abū Ghudda smacks of modernism because of its artificial contrast between the heart on the one hand and, on the other, "science" (*al-ʿilm*) and "reason" (*al-ʿaql*).[365]

Canonization of *Ṣaḥīḥ al-Bukhārī* by *Kashf*

Al-Khaṭīb narrated with his chain that Imām Abū Zayd Muḥammad ibn Aḥmad ibn ʿAbd Allah al-Marwazī al-Fāshānī (d. 371) said: "I was sleeping between the *Rukn* and the *Maqām* when I saw the Prophet ﷺ in my sleep and he said to me, 'Abū Zayd! Until when will you teach the book of al-Shāfiʿī and not teach my book?' I said, 'Messenger of Allah! and what is your book?' He said, 'The *Jāmiʿ* of Muḥammad ibn Ismāʿīl.'"[366]

[364] Abū Ghudda, notes on his edition of al-Lacknawī's *Ẓafar al-Amānī* (p. 280).
[365] The founder of Niẓāmiyya University in Hyderābād, Muḥammad Anwar Allah al-Fārūqī, in his booklet *al-Kalām al-Marfūʿ* (p. 21) cites in support of *kashf* authentication a book by a contemporary Shādhilī Sufi, Ibn Mughayzil (ʿAbd al-Qādir ibn al-Ḥusayn ibn ʿAlī) titled *al-Kawākib al-Ẓāhira fī Ijtimāʿ al-Awliyā' Yaqaẓatan bi-Sayyid al-Dunyā wal-Ākhira* (Cairo: Dār Jawāmiʿ al-Kalim, 1999).
[366] In Ibn Ḥajar's *Hadī al-Sārī* (p. 489).

Kashf-Authentication of *Ijmāʿ*

Imām al-Shaʿrānī in *Ṭabaqāt al-Awliyā'* narrated from his Shaykh Abū al-Mawāhib al-Shādhilī that the latter said:

> "A dispute took place between me and a certain person in the Mosque of al-Azhar over the statement of the author of *al-Burda* [al-Būṣīrī]:
>
> *"Famablaghu al-ʿilmi fīhi annahu basharun*
> *wa-annahu khayru khalqillāhi kullihimi."*
>
> ("The sum of knowledge concerning him ﷺ is that he is a human being and that he is the best of all the creation of Allah.")
>
> Whereupon that person said: 'He [al-Būṣīrī] has no proof for this!' I said to him: 'Consensus (*ijmāʿ*) has formed over this!' But he did not change his view. Later I saw the Prophet ﷺ and with him were Abū Bakr and ʿUmar, Allah be well-pleased with them, sitting at the pulpit of the Azhar Mosque. He said to me: '*Marḥaban bi-ḥabībī* – Welcome to my dear beloved!' Then he said to his friends: 'Do you know what happened today? So-and-so the Wretch (*fulān al-taʿīs*) believes the angels are better than me! What is wrong with him, disbelieving in the *Ijmāʿ*?'"

Sayyid ʿAbd Allah al-Ghumārī mentioned the above story in his book *Dilālat al-Qur'ān al-Mubīn 'alā anna al-Nabiyya* ﷺ *Afḍalu al-'Ālamīn* ("The Proofs of the Manifest Qur'ān that the Prophet ﷺ is the Best of the Universes") in which he listed the verses to that effect Sūra by Sūra – Allah reward him and have mercy on him!

And Allah knows best, from Him comes all success. The blessings and peace of Allah upon our liege-lord Muḥammad, his Family, his Companions, his Wives, and his Descendants until the Day of Judgment. Praise belongs to Allah, the Lord of the worlds!

Here ends the first volume of *Sunna Notes* on ḥadīth history and principles by the slave and pauper in need of the Divine Mercy, Gibril ibn Fouad ibn Naṣrī ibn Iskandar ibn Ḥabīb Haddad – *ʿufiya ʿanh.*

CHOSEN THOUGHTS
on the Nomenclature of Ḥadīth Specialists

(*Nukhbat al-Fikar fī Musṭalaḥ Ahl al-Athar*)

by the Commander of the Believers in Ḥadīth, Shaykh al-Islam, Aḥmad ibn ʿAlī ibn Muḥammad ibn Aḥmad, known as

Ibn Ḥajar al-ʿAsqalānī
(773-852 AH)

Translation by Musa Furber
revised by Gibril Fouad Haddad
from the 3rd (2000) edition of the *Nukhba*'s text
established by Nūr al-Dīn ʿItr

CONTENTS

NUKHBAT AL-FIKAR

Introduction 173

Reports and Their Paths 174

- Dividing accepted Reports into sound and fair 176
- Fair Reports 176
- Additions from Trustworthy Narrators 177
- Contradiction and Objection 178

The Rejected and its Divisions 178

- Lacunas 179
- Aspersions 180

To Whom the Report is Attributed 183

How the Report is Attributed 184

Forms of Conveyance 186

Names of Narrators 188

Conclusion 188

Miscellaneous Topics 190

Index of Technical Terms in *Nukhbat al-Fikar* 193

Introduction

Praise to Allah who never ceases being knowing, able. May Allah bless our liegelord Muḥammad, whom He sent to mankind as a bearer of good tidings and a warner, and upon his folk, Companions, and many salutations.

To commence: The books of the nomenclature of ḥadith specialists are many and were expanded and condensed. One of my brothers asked that I summarize for them what is important. I responded to his request seeking to be counted among those who trod the [scholarly] paths. So I say:

Reports and Their Paths

The paths of a report (*khabar*) are either:

(1) without specific number

(2) more than two paths

(3) two paths

(4) one path

- The first is the mass-transmitted report (*mutawātir*), and conveys sure knowledge (*ʿilm yaqīnī*) when its conditions are met.
- The second is the well-known report (*mashhūr*) and it is also called the well-circulated report (*mustafīḍ*) according to one opinion.
- The third is the rare report (*ʿazīz*). It is not the [minimal] condition for authenticity, contrary to whoever claimed it.
- The fourth is the singular report (*gharīb*).

All of them except for the first are solitary reports (*āḥād*). They [=these reports] encompass the accepted and the rejected since using them as evidence hinges on investigating the status of the reporters, contrary to the first category. Yet they might contain what conveys inductive knowledge (*ʿilm naẓarī*) with external indicators, according to the preferred opinion.

Then the singularity (*gharāba*) is either:

(1) in the chain itself

(2) or not.

- The first is the absolutely-unique report (*fard muṭlaq*) [*e.g.* one-ḥadīth narrator, one-compiler narrator, one-narrator ḥadīth, one-locality narrations].
- The second is the relatively-unique report (*fard nisbī*), and it is rare that the term 'unique' (*fard*) is used for it without qualification.

Dividing Accepted Reports into Sound and Fair

The solitary report (*āḥād*) transmitted by:

(1) an upright (*ʿadl*)

(2) thoroughly accurate person (*tāmm al-ḍabṭ*)

(3) with a continuous chain (*sanad*)

(4) that is not defective (*muʿallal*)

(5) nor anomalous (*shādhdh*)

is the sound-in-itself report (*ṣaḥīḥ bi-dhātihi*). Its ranks are commensurate to variation in these conditions. Hence al-Bukhārī's *Ṣaḥīḥ* was put first, then Muslim's, and then what matches their criteria (*shurūṭ*).

Fair Reports

If the accuracy decreases then it is the fair-in-itself report (*ḥasan li-dhātihi*); with multiple paths it is considered sound (*ṣaḥīḥ*).

If the grading is composite [*e.g.* fair-sound (*ḥasan ṣaḥīḥ*)] it is [either] because of indecision regarding the reporter when it [=his report] is unique [either fair or sound]; otherwise it is from examining two chains [one fair and one sound].

Additions from Trustworthy Narrators

An addition from a narrator of each of these two types of chains [the sound and the fair] is accepted as long as his addition does not negate [the report of] someone who is more trustworthy.

- If the addition is contrary to something superior (*arjaḥ*), the stronger is the preserved report (*maḥfūẓ*), and its opposite is the anomalous report (*shādhdh*).
- If in addition to being contrary it is weak (*ḍaʿīf*), the stronger is the well-recognized (*maʿrūf*), and its opposite is the disclaimed report (*munkar*).

When a report agrees with a relatively-unique report (*fard nisbī*) it is called a corroborative chain (*mutābiʿ*).

If a report's content (*matn*) is found that resembles it, then it is a witness-report (*shāhid*).

Investigating the paths of transmission for the above is called evaluation (*iʿtibār*).

Contradiction and Objection

That which is accepted (*maqbūl*):

– if it is free from contradiction or objection (*muʿāraḍa*), then it is decisive (*muḥkam*).

If it is contradicted by something equal to it [in soundness]:

– if reconciliation (*jamʿ*) is possible, they are reconcilable reports (*mukhtalif al-ḥadīth*);

– if not and the later one is positively established (*thābit*), then one is the abrogating report (*nāsikh*) and the other is the abrogated report (*mansūkh*);

– if not, superiority is sought (*tarjīḥ*);

– and lastly, neither one is confirmed or denied (*tawaqquf*).

The Rejected and its Divisions

Reports are rejected because of:

(1) lacuna (*saqṭ*)

(2) or aspersion (*ṭaʿn*).

Lacunas

Lacunas are either:

(1) at the beginning of the chain (*sanad*) on the part of the compiler,

(2) at the end of the chain after the Successor ﷺ,

(3) or elsewhere.

- The first [case] is the suspended report (*muʿallaq*).

- The second is the expedient report (*mursal*).

- The third:

  If the lacuna consists in two or more narrators consecutively then it is the problematic report (*muʿḍal*),

  If not, then it is the broken-chained report (*munqaṭiʿ*).

The lacunas can be:

(1) obvious

(2) or hidden.

- The first is recognized by lack of meeting [between interconnected reporters]. Hence the need for [biographical] history.

- The second is the camouflaged report (*mudallas*), a report related with a phrase which implies possible meeting, such as "From so-and-so", "He said...", (*ʿan, qāla*). Likewise, the hidden expedient report (*mursal khafī*) from a contemporary he did not meet [or did not meet as a narrator, such as a baby Companion from the Prophet ﷺ , *e.g.* Mūsā ibn Ṭalḥa ﷺ].

Aspersion

Aspersion (*ṭaʿn*) is because of one of the following:

(1) the narrator lying
(2) being accused of lying
(3) making enormous mistakes
(4) being heedless (*ghafla*)
(5) being morally corrupt (*fāsiq*)
(6) being delusionary (*wahm*)
(7) contradicting others (*mukhālafa*)
(8) being unknown (*jahāla*)
(9) being an innovator
(10) being chronically forgetful

- The first is the forged report (*mawḍūʿ*).
- The second is the discarded report (*matrūk*).
- The third is the disclaimed report (*munkar*) according to one opinion, as are the fourth and fifth.
- When **delusion** (*wahm*) is discovered through external indications (*qarāʾin*) and gathering the paths of transmission, then it is the defective report (*muʿallal*).
- As for **contradicting others** (*mukhālafa*), if it results from:

  changing the wording of the chain, it is the chain-interpolated report (*mudraj al-isnād*) conflating a halted Companion-report (*mawqūf*) with a raised Prophetic-report (*marfūʿ*), then it is the content-interpolated report (*mudraj al-matn*)

or transposition, then the topsy-turvy report (*maqlūb*)

or inserting a narrator, then it is the insertion into an already-connected-chain report (*mazīd fī muttaṣil al-masānīd*)

or it is substituting one narrator for another [without preponderance of one chain over the other], then it is the inconsistent report (*muḍṭarib*). Substitution may occur intentionally for the sake of testing

or alternating dots or vowels while orthography remains the same, then it is the dot-distorted report (*muṣaḥḥaf*) and the vowel-distorted report (*muḥarraf*).

It is not permissible to intentionally alter a ḥadīth's content (*matn*) by omission or paraphrase, except for someone knowledgeable of what changes meanings.

If the meaning is obscure, explaining odd words and clarifying the problematic is needed.

– The causes for which a **narrator is unknown** (*jahāla*) are:

The narrator may have many names and he is mentioned with one that is not well-known, for a purpose. Concerning this they compiled the clarifier (*al-mūḍiḥ*).

The narrator has few [narrations] and is not frequently taken from. Concerning this they wrote single-report narrators (*al-wuḥdān*).

Or he may be left unnamed out of brevity. Concerning this [they compiled] the anonymous mentions (*mubhamāt*).

The anonymous narrator (*mubham*) is not accepted, even if he is mentioned anonymously with a grading of commendation (*ta'dīl*), according to the soundest opinion.

If the narrator is named:

If only one person related from him, then he is an unidentifiable reporter (*majhūl al-'ayn*).

If two or more related from him and he is not [explicitly] declared reliable, then he is a reporter of unknown status (*majhūl al-ḥāl*); and that is the veiled reporter (*mastūr*).

– **Innovation** is of two types:

(1) tantamount to apostasy

(2) or tantamount to moral corruption.

As for the first: The vast majority do not accept any narrator thus described.

As for the second: Someone who is not inviting people to it is accepted according to the soundest opinion, unless he related something supporting his innovation: in that case he is rejected according to the preferred opinion. This is what al-Nasā'ī's shaykh, al-Jūzajānī, explicitly said.

– Then **poor memory**:

If it is chronic, then it is the anomalous report (*shādhdh*) according to one opinion

or occasional, then the jumbled report (*mukhtalaṭ*).

Whenever a chronically-forgetful reporter is corroborated by a reporter worthy of consideration, the veiled reporter (*mastūr*), the expedient reporter (*mursil*), and likewise the camouflager-reporter (*mudallis*), the ḥadīth becomes the fair (*ḥasan*) report, not in itself, but on the whole (*lā li-dhātihi bal bil-majmūʿ*).

To Whom the Report is Attributed

The chain's ascription (*isnād*) explicitly or implicitly goes to

(1) the Prophet ﷺ: consisting in his statements, or his actions, or his tacit approval

(2) a Companion ؓ. He is whoever encountered the Prophet ﷺ believing in him and died as a Muslim, even if [his Islam] was interrupted by apostasy according to the strongest opinion

(3) or a Successor, namely anyone who met one of the Companions.

The first is the raised-chain (Prophetic) report (*marfūʿ*).

The second is the halted-chain (Companion) report (*mawqūf*).

The third is the severed-chain (sub-Companion) report (*maqṭūʿ*). It is the same for anyone subsequent to the Successor.

The last two are said to be non-Prophetic reports (*āthār*).

How the Report is Attributed

A grounded report (*musnad*) is a report that a Companion raised to the Prophet ﷺ with a chain that has the outward appearance of being connected. If the numbers [of narrators in the chain] are few, either it ends with:

(1) the Prophet ﷺ

(2) or an Imām with a distinguished description, like Shuʿba.

The first is absolute elevation (*ʿulūw muṭlaq*)

The second is relative elevation (*ʿulūw nisbī*). It includes:

> concurrent chain (*muwāfaqa*) which arrives at the shaykh of one of the compilers without using the compiler's path;
>
> convergent chain (*badal*) which arrives at the shaykh's shaykh in the same way;
>
> parity (*musāwāt*) which is the number of narrator-links in the chain from the narrator to the end equaling [the length of] the chains of one of the compilers;
>
> and handshaking (*muṣāfaḥa*) which equals the chain of that compiler's student.

Descent (*nuzūl*) corresponds to elevation (*ʿulūw*) in all of its categories.

If the narrator is the same age as someone who narrates from him and they met, then it is peer narration (*aqrān*).

If each of them related from each other then it is reciprocal narration (*mudabbaj*).

If he relates from someone inferior [in age, teachers or knowledge] to him, then it is seniors-from-juniors narration (*akābir ʿan aṣāghir*). It includes: fathers-from-sons narration (*al-ābāʾ ʿan al-abnāʾ*); its opposite is frequent. It includes son-from-father or grandfather narration (*ʿan abīhi ʿan jaddihi*).

If two share the same shaykh and one's death precedes, then it is predecessor-successor narration (*sābiq wa-lāḥiq*).

If he relates from two shaykhs whose names match and cannot be differentiated, then the fact that he specializes in narrations from one of them is a sign that the other one is irrelevant.

If he denies what is related from him

> categorically, the report is rejected
>
> or possibly, then it is accepted according to the soundest opinion.

Concerning this is the genre of those-who-narrated-and-forgot (*man ḥaddatha wa-nasiya*).

If the narrators conform in the phrasing used to convey or in some other manner, then it is pattern-chained narration (*musalsal*).

Forms of Conveyance

The forms of conveyance are:

(1) "*Sami'tu*" (I heard)

(2) and "*ḥaddathanī*" (he narrated to me)

(3) then "*akhbaranī*" (he reported to me)

(4) and "*qara'tu 'alayhi*" (I read to him)

(5) then "*quri'a 'alayhi wa-ana asma'u*" (it was read to him while I heard)

(6) then "*anba'anī*" (he informed me)

(7) then "*nāwalanī*" (he put into my hands)

(8) then "*shāfahanī*" (he told me verbally)

(9) then "*kataba ilayya*" (he wrote to me)

(10) then "*'an*" (from) and the like

- The first two are for someone who heard the shaykh verbatim one-on-one. If pluralized then [he heard] with someone else. The first is the most explicit and is the highest-ranked in ḥadīth dictation.
- The third and fourth are for someone who read [to the shaykh] while alone. If the plural is used it is like the fifth.
- Informing [the sixth] is synonymous with reporting [the third]. However, in the custom of the later generations it is for authorization (*ijāza*), like *'an* [from].

- The indecisive-transmission terminology [*ʿanʿana i.e.* "from so-and-so, from so-and-so"] of contemporaries is understood to be direct audition unless from a camouflaging reporter (*mudallis*). It is said that a condition is that the meeting of the said contemporaries be positively proven, even if only once; it is the preferred opinion (*mukhtār*).
- They used *mushāfaha* for an oral authorization and *mukātaba* for a written authorization [with the late scholars].
- For the authenticity of *munāwala,* they stipulated that it be accompanied by permission to relate; it is the highest type of authorization (*ijāza*).
- They also stipulated permission for a report found (*wijāda i.e.* "something found in a book"), likewise a book bequeathed (*waṣiyya bil-kitāb*), and in a shaykh's public announcement that he narrates something (*iʿlām*), otherwise it is of no consequence; as is an authorization that is universal or to someone unknown [to us], or to someone nonexistent – according to the soundest opinion concerning all of the above.

Names of Narrators

If the names of the narrators and the names of their fathers and on up match although they are different individuals, then it is same-name different-identity narrator (*muttafiq wa-muftariq*).

If the names match in writing but differ in pronunciation, then it is homographic-heterophonic (*mu'talif wa-mukhtalif*).

If the names match but differ in their fathers, or the opposite, it is same-name-different-father-or-son narrators (*mutashābih*), and likewise if the similarity occurred in the name and the name of the father while there is a difference in the affiliation (*nisba*).

This and the previous can form various combinations, including:

- similarity or difference occurring except in one or two letters

- or transposition

- or the like.

Conclusion

It is also important to know:

(1) the synchronous layers (*ṭabaqāt*) of narrators

(2) the dates of their birth and death

(3) their lands and regions

(4) and their conditions: commendation (*taʿdīl*), discreditation (*jarḥ*), and being unknown (*jahāla*).

The **categories of discreditation** (*jarḥ*) are [from worst to slight] :

(1) To be described with the superlative (*af'al*), *e.g.* "greatest of all liars" (*"akdhab al-nās"*)

(2) "Arch-imposter", "arch-fabricator", "arch-liar" (*"dajjāl"*, *"waḍḍā'"*, or *"kadhdhāb"*)

(3) The slightest is "malleable", "chronically forgetful", and "he leaves something to be desired" (*"layyin"*, *"sayyi' al-ḥifẓ"*, and *"fīhi maqāl"*).

And the **ranks of commendation** (*ta'dīl*) are [from highest to lowest]:

(1) To be described with the superlative (*af'al*), *e.g.* "most trustworthy of people" (*"awthaq al-nās"*)

(2) What is emphasized with one attribute or two, *e.g.* "trustworthy-trustworthy", "trustworthy and memorizer" (*"thiqa thiqa"* or *"thiqa ḥāfiẓ"*)

(3) Something that suggests proximity to the slightest levels of discreditation, *e.g.* "honest layman" (*"shaykh"*).

Attesting someone's good record (*tazkiya*) is accepted from someone knowledgeable in its criteria, even if from a single person according to the soundest opinion (*aṣaḥḥ*).

Discreditation (*jarḥ*) takes precedence over commendation (*ta'dīl*) if it comes in detail from someone knowledgeable in its criteria. When lacking commendation, discreditation is accepted without specifics, according to the preferred opinion (*mukhtār*).

Miscellaneous Topics

It is also important to know:

- agnomens (*kunā*, sing. *kunya*) of the people referred to by [first] name,
- the names of people referred to by agnomen,
- those whose agnomen and name are one and the same,
- those with multiple agnomens or multiple titles;
- the one whose agnomen matches his father's name,
- or vice-versa;
- or his agnomen [matches] his wife's agnomen;
- and whoever is affiliated to someone other than his father or is affiliated to his mother,
- or to something that does not immediately come to mind;
- and whose name matches the name of his father and his grandfather,
- or his shaykh's name and the shaykh's shaykh, and on up;
- and whose name matches the shaykh's name and the person narrating from him;
- and the basic names of narrators;
- and the names exclusive to one person (*mufrada*),
- and agnomens and nicknames.

[It is also important to know:]

- Affiliations, *i.e.* to tribes, homelands, countries, localities, roads and alleys, proximity, crafts and professions. It gives rise to similarities (*ittifāq*) and confusions (*ishtibāh*), as with names; and affiliations sometimes take place as nicknames
- and the reasons for these [because it may be contrary to the obvious].
- The *mawālī*: topwise [patrons and masters], and bottomwise [clients and freedmen],
- male and female siblings,
- and the etiquette of the shaykh and the student.
- Including it is the age of procurement and conveyance; the manner of writing ḥadīth, reading [the shaykh's own narrations] back to the shaykh, audition, recital, and traveling for ḥadīth;

One should also know how ḥadīth is compiled: according to chains of narrators (*masānīd*), subject matter (*abwāb*), defects (*ʿilal*), or keywords (*aṭrāf*); and knowing the historical context for the ḥadīth. One of the shaykhs of al-Qaḍī Abū Yaʿlā ibn al-Farrā' wrote about it.

They have written books in most of these genres. This is a basic list mentioning definitions without examples. It is difficult to be thorough, so consult the longer books.

Allah is the One Who grants success. He is the Guider. There is no god except He.

Index of Technical Terms in *Nukhbat al-Fikar*

al-ābāʾ ʿan al-abnāʾ 185
abwāb 191
ʿadl 176
afʿal 189
āḥād 174,176
akābir ʿan aṣāghir 185
akdhab al-nās 189
ʿan 179, 186
ʿan abīhi ʿan jaddihi 185
ʿanʿana 187
aqrān 184
arjaḥ 177
āthār 183
aṭrāf 191
awthaq al-nās 189
ʿazīz 174
badal 184
ḍaʿīf 177
dajjāl 189
fard 175
fard muṭlaq 175
fard nisbī 175, 177
fāsiq 180
fīhi maqāl 189
ghafla 180
gharāba 174
gharīb 174
ḥasan 183
— *lā li-dhātihi bal bil-majmūʿ* 183
ḥasan li-dhātihi 176
ḥasan ṣaḥīḥ 176
ijāza 186,187
ʿilal 191
iʿlām 187
ʿilm naẓarī 174
ʿilm yaqīnī 178
isnād 183
ishtibāh 191
iʿtibār 177
ittifāq 191
jahāla 180, 181, 188
jamʿ 178
jarḥ 188, 189
kadhdhāb 189
khabar 174
kunā 190
kunya 190
layyin 189
maḥfūẓ 177
majhūl al-ʿayn 182
majhūl al-ḥāl 182
man ḥaddatha wa-nasiya 185
mansūkh 178
maqbūl 178
maqlūb 181
maqṭūʿ 183
marfūʿ 181, 183
maʿrūf 177
masānid 191
mashhūr 174
mastūr 182,183
matn 177, 181
matrūk 180
mawālī 191
mawḍūʿ 180
mawqūf 181, 183

mazīd fī muttaṣil al-masānīd **181**
mu'allal **176**, 180
mu'allaq **179**
mu'āraḍa **178**
mubham **182**
mubhamāt **181**
mudabbaj **184**
mudallas **179**
mudallis **183**,187
mu'ḍal **179**
mūḍiḥ **181**
mudraj al-isnād **180**
mudraj al-matn **181**
muḍṭarib **181**
mufrada **190**
muḥarraf **181**
muḥkam **178**
mukātaba **187**
mukhālafa **180**,181
mukhtār **187**
mukhtalaṭ **182**
mukhtalif al-ḥadīth **178**
munāwala **187**
munkar **177**, 180
munqaṭi' **179**
mursal **179**
mursal khafī **179**
mursil **183**
muṣāfaḥa **184**
muṣaḥḥaf **181**
musalsal **185**
musāwāt **184**
mushāfaha **187**
musnad **184**
mustafīḍ **174**
mutābi' **177**
mu'talif wa-mukhtalif **188**
mutashābih **188**
mutawātir **174**
muttafiq wa-muftariq **188**
muwāfaqa **184**
nāsikh **178**
nisba **188**
nuzūl **184**
qāla **179**
qarā'in **180**
sābiq wa-lāḥiq **185**
sanad **176**, 179
ṣaḥīḥ 176
ṣaḥīḥ bi-dhātihi **176**
saqṭ **178**
sayyi' al-ḥifẓ **189**
shādhdh **176**, 177,182
shāhid **177**
shaykh **189**
shurūṭ **176**
ṭabaqāt **188**
ta'dīl **182**, 188, 189
tāmm al-ḍabṭ **176**
ṭa'n **178**, 180
tarjīḥ **178**
tawaqquf **178**
tazkiya **189**
thābit **178**
thiqa **189**
'ulūw **184**
waḍḍā' **189**
wahm **180**
waṣiyya bil-kitāb **187**
wijāda **187**
wuḥdān **181**

Index of Qur'ānic Verses

2:44 25
2:129 33
2:164 25
2:171 25
2:197 53
2:269 25, 36
3:7 25
3:48 33
3:110 129
3:190 25
4:64 155
4:65 15
4:110 128
5:103 26
6:32 25
6:37 26
6:112 78
9:100 19
9:128-129 134
10:22 79
10:43 26
12:76 9
13:4 25
13:19 26
15:9 12
15:75 144, 145
16:12 25
17:85 9
18:65 144
19:12 33
20:55 79
21:79 31
22:46 27
25:44 26
29:35 25
29:43 25
29:63 26
30:24 25
30:28 25
31:12 25
31:25 26
33:34 34
35:19-22 26
35:32 148
37:138 25
38:29 25
39:9 26
39:21 25
40:54 25
40:67 25
43:63 33
45:5 25
48:29 19
49:6 131
50:37 25, 27
51:56 163
57:17 25
62:2 9, 33
77:25-26 79
95:1 28
95:4-5 29

Index of Narrations (Including Forgeries)

‘Abd al-Raḥmān is an agreeable witness… (‘Uthmān), 127
Abū Bakr tells the truth… (‘Alī), 128; 130
‘Ā’isha gave a dīnār to al-Ḥasan and al-Ḥusayn… 94
Allah curse your killer [O al-Ḥusayn]… 93
Allah gave preference to the Messengers over the angels… 93
Allah greets you and sent me to you with this bunch of grapes… 90
Allah has engraved truth on the tongue of ‘Umar and his heart, 146, 165
Allah has servants who know through reading the signs, 145
Allah has three angels, one in charge of the *Ka‘ba*… 90, 92
Allah have mercy on someone who hears a ḥadīth from me… 37
Allah looks not at your bodies… but He looks at your hearts, 27
Allah revealed to Dāwūd… 123
Allah revealed to the world, ‘Serve whoever serves Me…’ 93
‘Alī is the best of human beings, who doubts it commits disbelief, 90, 92
Always look into the *muṣḥaf*… 90
Am I one of them?… (‘Umar), 126
Among you women are those that spend half their lives not praying, 78
Anyone whose patron (*mawlā*) I am, ‘Alī is his patron… 63
[The] Arabs are the leaders of the non-Arabs, 78
As long as one adduces the meaning, let him narrate… (Ibn Mas‘ūd), 138
As long as you do not make licit the illicit… 137
Avoid relating my words except what you know for sure… 23
[The] bearers of knowledge …are the caliphs of Prophets… 91, 93
Beware the insight (*firāsa*) of the believer… 144
Be wellsprings of the Science and beacons in the night… (‘Alī), 30
[The] believer is easy and lenient… 33
[The] believer is guileless and noble… 33
[The] believer is vulnerable and the disbeliever is covered, 78
[The] believers and their children are in the heaven… 94
[The] believer’s back is a *qibla*, 78
[The] believer’s dream is one forty-sixth of prophecy, 160
[The] believer’s heart is sweet, he loves sweetness, 75

[The] believer speaks truth and believes what he is told, 78
[The] best of you after the year 200 are the wifeless and childless, 88
[The] best worship is the hardest one, 78
Blessed is the servant that cries constantly to Allah... (ʿAlī), 29
Blood-money for the stillborn, 120
Bright does Allah make the face of his servant that records... 17
Bring me someone to witness with you (ʿUmar), 130
Cheese is a disease and walnuts a cure, 88, 92
[The] consecration-place of the people of Iraq is Dhātu ʿIrqin, 97
[The] dead person gets punished if his family weeps over him, 116
[The] devil cannot take my likeness... 157
Do not beat your children for their weeping... 90-91
Do not hasten to commend him... 26
Do you bear witness that there is no God except Allah... 120
Do you have qualms about denouncing the openly corrupt man?!, 92
Eat *balaḥ* with *tamr*, ...for the devil is angered... 81
Eat young dates with old dates, 81
Eggplant fulfills whatever [need] it is eaten for, 88
[The] energy of the Ulema is care and help... 42
Every Community has its Zoroastrians, its Jews, its Christians... 59
Every Jumuʿa night Allah delivers 100,000 people from the Fire... 93
[The] evil of those who call others...standing at the gates of the Fire, 57
Fear of Allah is right here... 27
Foetus blood-money Ḥadīth, 121
Following a middle course... parts of Prophethood, 148
Forbidden to the Fire is every gentle, lenient, easy-going one... 32
From every...generation its upright...shall carry this knowledge, 17, 60
Generosity is a tree in paradise, 91
Gibrīl brings Abū Bakr water for *wuḍū'*... 90
Go to ʿUmar and give him my greeting, then tell him... (dream), 154
Had I not heard it I would have ruled something else (ʿUmar), 121
Had there been a Prophet after me, truly, it would have been ʿUmar, 146
Had you seen him while awake... (Ibn ʿAbbās), 157

Ḥadīth of Jābir on the light of the Prophet ﷺ, 88
Has any of you recited anything from the Qur'ān?... (Wāthila), 138
He for whom Allah desires immense good, He grants him... 31, 36, 59
He gestured with his hand towards Syro-Palestine... (dream), 156
[The] Hour will not rise before... 94
How are you this morning, Ḥāritha?... 150
How intelligent is he?... 26
How much does the grandmother inherit? (Abū Bakr), 120
I adjure by Allah any man that heard the Messenger ﷺ... ('Umar), 123
I am the Seal of Prophets and you, 'Alī, are the Seal of Saints, 93
I asked Allah not to answer the supplication of... 92
I bid you to climb on my back... ('Umar), 127
I did not mean to prohibit that... (a Companion), 138
I fear lest I die with those [ḥadīths]...in your possession (Abū Bakr), 122
I feared lest people start attributing things... ('Umar), 122
I hated that the ḥadīth...not be exposed in full... ('Umar), 123
I have hidden for you under my *minbar* something good... (dream), 153
I have seen a remnant of the Companions of the Messenger... ('Alī), 29
I saw marjoram growing under the Throne, 93
I saw my Lord in the image of a long-haired youth, 162
I only distribute and it is Allah Who gives, 36, 59
I was a Prophet when Ādam was still between water and clay, 78
I was a Treasure unknown... 78, 163
I was given superiority to people in four things... 94
I was shown it is a girl... (Abū Bakr), 145
If one circumcised part penetrates the other... ('Ā'isha), 126
If one of you has doubts in his *ṣalāt*... 124
If you are a Prophet, tell me what I have in my possession... 91
If you are pleased to make your prayer pure... 92
If you hear a ḥadīth reported...which your hearts recognize... 151, 165
In the nations long before you... 146
In the two 'Eids the Prophet ﷺ used to recite Sūrat Qāf and... 124
Isolate yourself from those sects... 57

It may be that one carries understanding… 36, 38
Jizya from the Zoroastrians… (ʿUmar), 124
Al-Khaḍir and Ilyās meet… every year at ʿArafa… 94
Lā ilāha illa Allah is My Word…the Qur'ān My Speech… 90
Land is kindest to its own sons and daughters, 79
Lawful is manifest and the forbidden is manifest… 27
Learning Necessitates Deeds (Ibn Masʿūd *et al.*), 41
[To] look at a beautiful face is worship, 76
Looking at a beautiful woman and greenery… 76
[A] man came to the grave of the Prophet ﷺ and said… 153
[A] man will come after me named al-Nuʿmān… Abū Ḥanīfa… 93
May direct relatives embrace you… 94
Memorization of Qur'ān ḥadīth, 99
Mendacity is only when one… intends to lie (Companions), 135
[The] Messenger of Allah ﷺ allotted him such-and-such a land…, 127
[The] Messenger of Allah ﷺ gave her [the grandmother] one sixth, 120
[The] Messenger of Allah ﷺ gave me al-Baḥrayn… (al-ʿAbbās), 124
My Community is not taken to task for fleeting thoughts, 95
My Companions are like the stars, 55
My daughter Fāṭima is a human houri, she never got menses…. 93
My daughter Fāṭima is pure and purified… 87
My father gathered the ḥadīth from the Messenger ﷺ … (ʿĀ'isha), 122
Most of the people of Paradise are the naïve, 32
[The] names of twelve of the hypocrites… (Ḥudhayfa), 126
Narrate, for you are the well-agreed upright one… (ʿUmar), 125
[The] night I was taken up to heaven I saw on the gate of Paradise… 92
[The] night of my wedding to the Messenger of Allah… 93
No *ghusl* is required if there was mere penetration… (Zayd), 125
None may convey [this news] on my part except… 133
None sins but then rises, purifies himself and prays… 128
Nothing but truth issues from this [pointing to his noble mouth ﷺ], 17
Not revelation but truthful insight (ʿUthmān), 150
O ʿAlī, fear Allah regarding worldly promises… 92

O ʿAlī, the Qur'ān is the Speech of Allah uncreated, 89
O Allah! Do not make any loss of ours be in our Religion, 32
Of my Companions there will be those whom I shall never see... 126
One of you comes in with fornicating eyes (ʿUthmān), 150
On the Day of Resurrection the people will be made to stand.... 92
On the Day of Resurrection the scholars of ḥadīth will come... 93
O Shaykh! If you want your safety look for it in... (dream), 161
Paradise says: None enters me except the weak and wretched, 32
Paying due rights and keeping trusts is our Religion... 92
People gave *bayʿa* to Abū Bakr although I am worthier...(ʿAlī), 94
People of our complexion... 57
[The] people suffered a drought in ʿUmar's *khilāfa*..., 153
[A] pious son makes the best husband, 79
Plague in Syro-Palestine... (ʿUmar), 124
[The] Prophet ﷺ bled his sacrificial animal as a pre-slaughter marking, 97
[The] Prophet ﷺ had sent al-Walīd ibn ʿUqba... 131
[The] Prophet ﷺ joining prayers during the campaign of Tabūk, 91
[The] Prophet's ﷺ order to have gold teeth made, 83
[The] Prophet's ﷺ parents brought back to life, 85
[The] Prophet ﷺ prayed over an adultress and her daughter, 92
[The] Prophet ﷺ sent Khālid ibn Walīd to verify... 132
[The] Prophet ﷺ showed the names of all the people of Paradise... 83
[The] Prophet ﷺ used to clip his nails... on the day of Jumuʿa, 98
[As the] Prophet ﷺ was praying he replied to someone's greeting... 94
Pursuing *ʿilm* is an obligation upon every Muslim, 93
[The] Qur'ān is the Speech of Allah neither creator nor created, 89
[The] Qur'ān was revealed in seven dialects, 138
Rajab, reports emphasizing the month of, 88
Removing his ring upon entering the privy... 81
Righteousness is whatever your chest becomes dilated in doing, 27
Salām comes before [all other] talk... 97
Satan cannot take on my form... 160
Sāriya, the mountain! (ʿUmar), 149

[The] seat of the intellect is the heart (ʿAlī), 27-28
Seek your heart's answer even if all people answer you, 151, 165
Send the question to the wives of the Prophet ﷺ (ʿAlī), 126
Sharīʿa is my words, *Ṭarīqa* is my actions, *Ḥaqīqa* is my state… 88
[A] son is a prince and chief for seven years… 152
Son of Ādam, I am your indispensable need… 92
Stick to the Congregation of the Muslims, 57
Stick to Ibn Masʿūd's *tashahhud* (dream), 159
Suffice yourself… with the general meaning (Wāthila), 140
Tafsīr of Sūrat al-Naṣr (Ibn ʿAbbās), 127
Take care of what you say: what is the reality of your belief?… 150
Tell Ibn Simʿān to fear Allah and not tell lies about me! (dream), 161
Tell us, for you are in our view the well-agreed upright one (ʿUmar), 130
That group shall remain in charge of the Command of Allah… 59
There is in the body a small piece of flesh…it is the heart, 26-27
There is no Mahdī but ʿĪsā ibn Maryam, 94
There is no marriage without guardian, 92
There is no harm in it as long as he adduces the meaning, 138
There shall not cease to be a group … 59
There will be in my Community a man named al-Nuʿmān… 93
There will be no rider besides us on the Day of Resurrection… 92
There will be, towards the end of time, Anti-Christs and arch-liars… 57
This is a believer, Allah has illumined his heart, 151, 165
This knowledge is Religion, so watch from whom you take it… 17
This morning I am a real believer (Ḥāritha), 150
Three things of the world pleased the Messenger of Allah… 74
[The] Throne shook at the death of Saʿd, 93
Thus did I see the Messenger ﷺ make his ablution (ʿUthmān), 127
Thus does Knowledge die: when those who possess it die (ʿAlī), 30
Time shall grow short, knowledge decrease, dissensions appear… 35
[The] traveller and his money are at risk, 76
[The] true…*faqīh* is he who does not push people to despair… (ʿAlī), 30
[A] true vision is one-fortysixth of prophecy, 152

Treat people according to their ranks, 103
Two types of my Community have no part in Islam… 92
Ukaydar's gift of a jar of ginger to Madīna, 83
ʿUmar asked al-ʿAbbās to sell or donate his house… 123
ʿUmar assembled the people…to pray for rain with al-ʿAbbās, 154
Until when will you teach the book of al-Shāfiʿī…? (dream), 165
ʿUtbī! Run after the Bedouin and give him glad tidings… (dream), 155
We are Bedouin Arabs, we may cite a saying… (Ḥudhayfa), 139
We [Prophets] do not bequeath inheritance… 121
We seven of Banū al-Muṭṭalib… 91
Welcome to my dear beloved!… (dream), 166
What is this camel? O ʿAlī, fear Allah… 92
What is wrong with him, disbelieving in the *Ijmāʿ*? (dream), 166
Whatever you give the womenfolk it is a *ṣadaqa*, 121
When Allah desires good for a nation… 99
When an innovator dies, Islam gains a new victory, 92
When I heard something from the Messenger of Allah… (ʿAlī), 114, 128
When I was taken up to the heaven…an apple fell into my lap… 92
When I was taken up to the heaven Gibrīl brought me to… 92
When one of you asks permission to enter thrice… 122
When the orphan weeps his tears fall… 91
When Saʿd narrates something to you, do not reject it! (ʿUmar), 127
When you see the new moon of Muḥarram… (Ibn ʿAbbās), 128
Whenever someone narrated something to me … (ʿAlī), 130
[The] white rooster is my friend and the friend of my friend… 77
Who will witness [to this] with you? (ʿUmar), 121
Whoever associates in partnership with a covenantee (*dhimmī*)… 92
Whoever attributes a lie to me or rejects something I have ordered… 53
Whoever circumambulates this House seven times… 66, 161
Whoever condoles with someone afflicted receives the same reward, 159
Whoever falls passionately in love but remains chaste… 86
Whoever feeds his brother a mouthful of sweet… 91
Whoever finds a book containing knowledge… (ʿUmar), 56, 130

Whoever harms a covenanted citizen… 92
Whoever hopes that prices will rise in my Community… 91
Whoever hosts a Believer, it is as if… 164
Whoever knows himself knows his Lord, 78, 162
Whoever learns the Qur'ān and memorizes it… 92
Whoever lies about me willfully, let him take…his seat in the Fire, 23
Whoever loves me, let him love 'Alī… 93
Whoever makes his ablution just as he was commanded… 127
Whoever plays chess is cursed, 76
Whoever receives a present while he has company… 76
Whoever says that I said something which I did not say… 138
Whoever sees me in his sleep has seen me (truly), 157
Whoever sees me in vision or dream sees me truly, 160
Whoever takes the hand of someone afflicted, Allah takes his… 91, 93
Whoever wears a helmet for *jihād*… 91
Why do you all ask me about something… ('Umar), 125
[The] widow's home waiting-period ('*idda*) (al-Furay'a bint Mālik), 127
Wildcat and the dog, prohibition of the sale of, 97
Wisdom is the lost property of the believer, wherever he finds it… 77
[A] woman who visited the House then entered menses… (Thaqafī), 125
[The] world is the prison of the believer… 78
[The] worst of you are those who teach young pupils, 88
Yā Muḥammadāh!… (Bilāl ibn al-Ḥārith), 154
[I swear by Allah that] you are going to have to prove this…('Umar), 122
You do know: therefore cleave to it!, 151
You do not know what they did after you… 40
You little foe of himself! Is this what you are telling people? ('Umar), 125
Your friend does not reach the level that you think, 26
Your Lord built a house and prepared a banquet… 92
Your menses are not in your hand, 44

Bibliography

'Abd ibn Ḥumayd. *Al-Muntakhab min Musnad 'Abd ibn Ḥumayd*. Eds. Subḥī al-Sāmirā'ī, Maḥmūd al-Sa'īdī. Cairo: Maktabat al-Sunna, 1988.

'Abd al-Qāhir al-Baghdādī. *Uṣūl al-Dīn*. Istanbul: Dār al-Funūn fī Madrasat al-Ilāhiyyāt, 1928.

'Abd al-Razzāq. *Al-Muṣannaf*. 11 vols. Ed. Ḥabīb al-Raḥmān al-A'ẓamī. Beirut: al-Maktab al-Islāmī, 1983. With Ma'mar ibn Rāshid al-Azdī's *Kitāb al-Jāmi'* as the last two volumes.

Abū Dāwūd al-Sijistānī. *Al-Marāsīl*. Ed. Shu'ayb al-Arna'ūṭ. Beirut: Mu'assasat al-Risāla, 1988.

———. *Sunan*. 3 vols. Ed. Muḥammad Fu'ād 'Abd al-Bāqī. Beirut: Dār al-Kutub al-'Ilmiyya, 1996. See also al-'Aẓīm Ābādī, *'Awn al-Ma'būd*.

Abū Dāwūd al-Ṭayālisī, see al-Ṭayālisī.

Abū Ghudda, 'Abd al-Fattāḥ. *Al-Isnād min al-Dīn*. With *Safḥatun Mushriqatun min Tārīkh Samā' al-Ḥadīth 'ind al-Muḥaddithīn*. Aleppo: Maktab al-Maṭbū'āt al-Islāmiyya, 1992.

———. *Jawāb al-Ḥāfiẓ Abī Muḥammad 'Abd al-'Aẓīm al-Mundhirī al-Miṣrī 'alā As'ilatin fil-Jarḥ wal-Ta'dīl*. With *Umarā' al-Mu'minīn fil-Ḥadīth* and *Kalimāt fī Kashf Abāṭīl wa-Iftirā'āt*. Aleppo: Maktab al-Maṭbū'āt al-Islāmiyya, 1991.

———, ed. *Al-Maṣnū'*. See al-Qārī.

———. *Al-Rasūl al-Mu'allim wa-Asālībuhu fīl-Ta'līm*. 2nd ed. Aleppo: Maktab al-Maṭbū'āt al-Islāmiyya, 1996.

Abū Nu'aym al-Aṣfahānī. [*Al-Muntakhab min*] *Dalā'il al-Nubuwwa*. 4th ed. Eds. Muḥammad Rawwās Qal'ajī and 'Abd al-Barr 'Abbās. Beirut: Dār al-Nafā'is, 1999.

———. *Ḥilyat al-Awliyā' wa-Ṭabaqāt al-Asfiya'*. 12 vols. Ed. Muṣṭafā 'Abd al-Qādir 'Aṭā. Beirut: Dār al-Kutub al-'Ilmiyya, 1997.

Abū al-Shaykh [Ibn Ḥayyān al-Aṣbahānī]. *Al-Amthāl fīl-Ḥadīth al-Nabawī*. 2nd ed. Ed. 'Abd al-'Alī 'Abd al-Majīd Ḥāmid. Bombay: al-Dār al-Salafiyya, 1988.

Abū Shuhba, Muḥammad. *Al-Sīrat al-Nabawiyya fī Ḍaw' al-Qur'ān wal-Sunna*. 2 vols. 5th ed. Damascus: Dār al-Qalam, 1999.

Abū Ya'lā al-Mawṣilī. *Musnad*. 13 vols. Ed. Ḥusayn Salīm Asad. Damascus: Dār al-Ma'mūn līl-Turāth, 1984.

Al-Aḥdab, Khaldūn. *Zawā'id Tārīkh Baghdād 'alā al-Kutub al-Sitta.* 10 vols. Damascus: Dār al-Qalam, 1996.

Aḥmad ibn Ḥanbal. *Faḍā'il al-Ṣaḥāba.* 2 vols. Ed. Waṣī Allah Muḥammad 'Abbās. Beirut: Mu'assasat al-Risāla, 1983.

———. *Al-'Ilal wa-Ma'rifat al-Rijāl.* 4 vols. Ed. Waṣī Allah ibn Muḥammad 'Abbās. Beirut and Riyadh: al-Maktab al-Islāmī, 1988.

———. *Al-Musnad.* 20 vols. Ed. Aḥmad Shākir and Ḥamza Aḥmad al-Zayn. Cairo: Dār al-Ḥadīth, 1995.

———. *Al-Musnad.* 50 vols. Ed. Shu'ayb al-Arna'ūṭ *et al.* Beirut: Mu'assasat al-Risāla, 1999-2001.

———. *Al-Zuhd.* Beirut: Dar al-Kutub al-'Ilmiyya, 1978.

Al-'Ajlūnī. *Kashf al-Khafā.* 2nd ed. 2 vols. Beirut: Dār Iḥyā' al-Turāth al-'Arabī, 1932.

Al-Ājurrī. *Al-Sharī'a.* Ed. 'Abd al-Razzāq al-Mahdī. Beirut: Dār al-Kitāb al-'Arabī, 1996.

Al-Āmidī. *Al-Iḥkām fī Uṣūl al-Aḥkām.* 4 vols. Ed. Sayyid al-Jumaylī. Beirut: Dār al-Kitāb al-'Arabī, 1984.

Al-Anṣārī, Zakariyyā. See Zakariyyā al-Anṣārī.

'Awwāma, Muḥammad. *Adab al-Ikhtilāf.* 2nd ed. Beirut: Dār al-Bashā'ir, 1997.

———. *Athar al-Ḥadīth al-Sharīf fī Ikhtilāf al-A'immat al-Fuqahā' RaḍyAllahu 'Anhum.* 4th ed. Beirut: Dār al-Bashā'ir al-Islāmiyya, 1997.

A'ẓamī, Muḥammad Muṣṭafā. *Manhaj al-Naqd 'ind al-Muḥaddithīn.* Followed by Muslim's *Kitāb al-Tamyīz.* 3rd ed. Al-Marba' (Saudi Arabia): Maktabat al-Kawthar, 1990.

———. *Studies in Early Ḥadīth Literature: with a critical edition of some early texts.* 2nd ed. Indianapolis: American Trust Publications, 1978.

Al-Azdī. *Al-Jāmi'.* See 'Abd al-Razzāq, *Muṣannaf.*

Al-Baghawī. *Sharḥ al-Sunna.* 8 vols. Eds. Shu'ayb al-Arna'ūṭ and Zuhayr al-Shāwīsh. Beirut: al-Maktab al-Islāmī, 1971.

Al-Bayhaqī. *Al-Asmā' wal-Ṣifāt.* Ed. Muḥammad Zāhid al-Kawtharī. Beirut: Dār Iḥyā' al-Turāth al-'Arabī, n.d. Reprint of the 1358/1939 Cairo edition.

———. *Al-Asmā' wal-Ṣifāt.* 2 vols. Ed. 'Abd Allah al-Ḥāshidī. Riyad: Maktabat al-Sawādī, 1993.

———. *Dalā'il al-Nubuwwa wa-Ma'rifat Aḥwāl Ṣāḥib al-Sharī'a*. 7 vols. Ed. 'Abd al-Mu'ṭī Amīn Qal'ajī. Beirut: Dār al-Kutub al-'Ilmiyya, 1985.

———. *Al-I'tiqād 'alā Madhhabi al-Salaf Ahl al-Sunnati wal-Jamā'a*. Beirut: Dār al-Afāq al-Jadīda, 1981; Dār al-Kutub al-'Ilmiyya, 1986.

———. *Manāqib al-Shāfi'ī*. 2 vols. Ed. Aḥmad Saqr. Cairo: Dār al-Turāth, n. d.

———. *Ma'rifat al-Sunan wal-Āthār*. 15 vols. Ed. 'Abd al-Mu'ṭī Amīn Qal'ajī. Aleppo and Cairo: Dār al-Wa'ī, 1991.207

———. *Shu'ab al-Īmān*. 8 vols. Ed. Muḥammad Zaghlūl. Beirut: Dār al-Kutub al-'Ilmiyya, 1990.

———. *Al-Sunan al-Kubrā*. 10 vols. Ed. Muḥammad 'Abd al-Qādir 'Aṭa. Makka: Maktabat Dār al-Baz, 1994.

———. *Al-Zuhd al-Kabīr*. 3rd Ed. 'Āmir Aḥmad Ḥaydar. Beirut: Mu'assasat al-Kutub al-Thaqāfiyya, 1996.

Al-Bazzār. *Al-Musnad*. [*Al-Baḥr al-Zakhkhār*.] 9 vols. Ed. Maḥfūẓ al-Raḥmān Zayn Allah. Beirut and Madīna: Mu'assasat 'Ulūm al-Qur'ān & Maktabat al-'Ulūm wal-Ḥikam, 1989.

———. See also Ibn Ḥajar, *Mukhtaṣar Zawā'id Musnad al-Bazzār*.

Al-Bukhārī, Muḥammad ibn Ismā'īl. *Al-Adab al-Mufrad*. 3rd ed. Ed. Muḥammad Fu'ād 'Abd al-Bāqī. Beirut: Dār al-Bashā'ir, 1989.

———. *Ṣaḥīḥ*. 6 vols. 3rd ed. Ed. Muṣṭafā Dīb al-Bughā. Beirut: Dār Ibn Kathīr, 1987.

———. *Ṣaḥīḥ*. See Ibn Ḥajar, *Fatḥ al-Bārī*.

———. *Al-Tārīkh al-Kabīr*. 8 vols. Ed. al-Sayyid Hāshim al-Nadwī. Beirut: Dār al-Fikr, n.d.

Daḥlān, Aḥmad Zaynī. *Khulāṣat al-Kalām fī Bayān Umarā' al-Balad al-Ḥarām*. Cairo: al-Maṭba'at al-Khayriyya, 1888. Repr. Cairo: Maktabat al-Kulliyyāt al-Azhariyya, 1977.

Al-Dārimī. [*Al-Musnad al-Jāmi'*.] *Fatḥ al-Mannān Sharḥ wa-Taḥqīq Kitāb al-Dārimī al-Musammā bil-Musnad al-Jāmi'*. 10 vols. Ed. Abū 'Āṣim Nabīl Hāshim al-Ghamrī. Makka and Beirut: al-Maktbat al-Makkiyya and Dār al-Bashā'ir al-Islāmiyya, 1999.

Al-Daylamī, Shīrūyah ibn Shahradār. *Firdaws al-Akhbār bi-Ma'thūr al-Khiṭāb 'alā Kitāb al-Shihāb*. Ed. Fawwāz Aḥmad al-Zayralī and Muḥammad al-Mu'taṣim Billāh al-Baghdādī. Beirut: Dār al-Kitāb al-'Arabī, 1987.

Al-Dhahabī, Muḥammad Shams al-Dīn. *Mīzān al-I'tidāl*. 4 vols. Ed. 'Alī Muḥammad al-Bajawī. Beirut: Dār al-Ma'rifa, 1963.

———. *Mīzān al-I'tidāl*. 8 vols. Eds. 'Alī Muḥammad Mu'awwaḍ and 'Ādil Aḥmad 'Abd al-Mawjūd. Beirut: Dār al-Kutub al-'Ilmiyya, 1995.

———. *Al-Mughnī fil-Ḍu'afā'*. 2 vols. Ed. Nūr al-Dīn 'Itr. Qatar: Idārat Iḥyā' al-Turāth al-Islāmī, 1987.

———. *Al-Mūqiẓa fī 'Ilm Muṣṭalaḥ al-Ḥadīth*. 3rd ed.Ed. 'Abd al-Fattāḥ Abū Ghudda. Aleppo: Maktab al-Maṭbū'āt al-Islāmiyya, 1998.

———. *Siyar A'lām al-Nubalā'*. 19 vols. Ed. Muḥibb al-Dīn al-'Amrāwī. Beirut: Dār al-Fikr, 1996.

———. *Siyar A'lām al-Nubalā'*. 23 vols. Ed. Shu'ayb al-Arna'ūṭ and Muḥammad Na'īm al-'Araqsūsī. Beirut: Mu'assasat al-Risāla,1992-93.

———. *Tadhkirat al-Ḥuffāẓ*. 4 vols. in 2. Ed. 'Abd al-Raḥmān ibn Yaḥyā al-Mu'allimī. A fifth volume, titled *Dhayl Tadhkirat al-Ḥuffāẓ*, consists in al-Ḥusaynī's *Dhayl Tadhkirat al-Ḥuffāẓ*, Muḥammad ibn Fahd al-Makkī's *Lahẓ al-Alḥāẓ bi-Dhayl Tadhkirat al-Ḥuffāẓ*, and al-Suyūṭī's *Dhayl Ṭabaqāt al-Ḥuffāẓ*. Ed. Muḥammad Zāhid al-Kawtharī. Beirut: Dār Iḥyā' al-Turāth al-'Arabī and Dār al-Kutub al-'Ilmiyya, n.d. Reprint of the 1968 Hyderabad edition.

———. *Tārīkh al-Islām wa-Wafayāt al-Mashāhīr wal-A'lām*. 52 vols. Ed. 'Umar 'Abd al-Salām Tadmurī. Beirut: Dār al-Kitāb al-'Arabī, 1989-2000.

———. *Tartīb al-Mawḍū'āt li-Ibn al-Jawzī*. Ed. Kamāl ibn Basyūnī Zaghlūl. Beirut: Dār al-Kutub al-'Ilmiyya, 1994.

Al-Fattanī. *Tadhkirat al-Mawḍū'āt*. Cairo: al-Maṭba'at al-Munīriyya, 1343/1924-1925.

Al-Ghazzālī. *Iḥyā' 'Ulūm al-Dīn*. 4 vols. 1374/1929. Repr. Beirut: 'Ālam al-Kutub, n.d.

———. *Al-Mustaṣfā fī 'Ilm al-Uṣūl*. Ed. Muḥammad 'Abd al-Salām 'Abd al-Shāfī. Beirut: Dār al-Kutub al-'Ilmiyya, 1993.

Al-Ghumārī, 'Abd Allah ibn Muḥammad ibn al-Ṣiddīq. *Irghām al-Mubtadi' al-Ghabī bi-Jawāz al-Tawassul bil-Nabī*. Ed. Ḥasan 'Alī al-Saqqāf. 2nd ed. Amman: Dār al-Imām al-Nawawī, 1992.

Al-Ghumārī, Aḥmad ibn Muḥammad ibn al-Ṣiddīq. *Dar' al-Ḍa'f 'an Ḥadīth Man 'Ashiqa fa-'Aff*. Ed. Aḥmad al-Ghawj. Cairo: Dār al-Imām al-Tirmidhī, 1996.

———. *Fatḥ al-Wahhāb bi-Takhrīj Aḥādīth al-Shihāb*. 2 vols. Ed. Ḥamdī ʿAbd al-Majīd al-Salafī. Beirut: ʿĀlam al-Kutub, 1988.

———. *Al-Mughīr 'alā al-Aḥādīth al-Mawḍūʿa fīl-Jāmiʿ al-Ṣaghīr*. Cairo: Maktabat al-Qāhira, 1998. Reprint.

Ḥajjī Khalīfa. *Kashf al-Ẓunūn 'an Asāmī al-Kutub wal-Funūn*. 2 vols. Beirut: Dār al-Kutub al-ʿIlmiyya, 1992.

Al-Ḥākim. *Al-Madkhal ilā Maʿrifati Kitāb al-Iklīl*. Ed. Muʿtazz ʿAbd al-Laṭīf al-Khaṭīb. Damascus: Dār al-Fayḥā', 2000.

———. *Maʿrifat 'Ulūm al-Ḥadīth*, ed. Sayyid Muʿaẓẓam Ḥusayn. Dacca: n.p. 1935. Reprint Beirut: Dār al-Kutub al-ʿIlmiyya, 1977.

———. *Al-Mustadrak 'alā al-Ṣaḥīḥayn*. With al-Dhahabī's *Talkhīṣ al-Mustadrak*. 5 vols. Indexes by Yūsuf ʿAbd al-Raḥmān al-Marʿashlī. Beirut: Dār al-Maʿrifa, 1986. Reprint of the 1916 Hyderabad edition.

———. *Al-Mustadrak 'alā al-Ṣaḥīḥayn*. With al-Dhahabī's *Talkhīṣ al-Mustadrak*. 4 vols. Annotations by Muṣṭafā ʿAbd al-Qādir ʿAṭā'. Beirut: Dār al-Kutub al-ʿIlmiyya, 1990.

Al-Ḥakīm al-Tirmidhī. *Khatm al-Awliyā'*. Ed. ʿUthmān Ismāʿīl Yaḥyā. Institut de lettres orientales de Beyrouth. Beirut: Imprimerie Catholique, n.d.

———. *Nawādir al-Uṣūl*. Beirut: Dār Sadir, n.d. Repr. of Istanbul ed.

Al-Harawī al-Anṣārī. *Dhamm al-Kalām wa-Ahlih*. 5 vols. Ed. ʿAbd Allah ibn Muḥammad al-Anṣārī. Madīna: Maktabat al-Ghuraba', 1998.

Al-Haytamī, Aḥmad. *Al-Fatāwā al-Ḥadīthiyya*. Cairo: Muṣṭafā al-Bābā al-Ḥalabī, Repr. 1970, 1989.

Al-Haythamī, Nūr al-Dīn. *Majmaʿ al-Zawā'id wa-Manbaʿ al-Fawā'id*. 10 vols. in 5. Cairo: Maktabat al-Qudsī, 1932-1934. Repr. Beirut: Dār al-Kitāb al-ʿArabī, 1967, 1982, and 1987.

Al-Ḥāzimī. *Shurūṭ al-A'immat al-Khamsa*. With Ibn Ṭāhir al-Maqdisī's *Shurūṭ al-A'immat al-Sitta*. Ed. Muḥammad Zāhid al-Kawtharī. Cairo: Maktabat ʿĀṭif, n.d.

Al-Muʿallimī al-Yamānī, ʿAbd al-Raḥmān. *Al-Anwār al-Kāshifa limā fī kitāb "Aḍwā' 'alā al-Sunna" min al-Zalal wal-Taḍlīl wal-Mujāzafa*. Cairo: al-Maṭbaʿat al-Salafiyya, 1959.

Ibn ʿAbd al-Barr. *Al-Intiqā' fī Faḍā'il al-A'immati al-Thalāthati al-Fuqahā': Mālik wal-Shāfiʿī wa-Abī Ḥanīfa*. Ed. ʿAbd al-Fattāḥ Abū Ghudda. Beirut: Dār al-Bashā'ir al-Islāmiyya, 1997.

———. *Al-Istī'ab fī Ma'rifat al-Aṣḥāb*. 8 vols. in 4. Ed. 'Alī Muḥammad al-Bajawī. Beirut: Dār al-Jil, 1992.

———. *Jāmi' Bayān al-'Ilm wa-Faḍlih*. 2 vols. Ed. Abū al-Ashbal al-Zuhayrī. Dammam: Dār Ibn al-Jawzī, 1994.

———. *Al-Tamhīd limā fīl-Muwaṭṭa' min al-Ma'ānī wal-Asānīd*. 22 vols. Eds. Muṣṭafā ibn Aḥmad al-'Alawī and Muḥammad 'Abd al-Kabīr al-Bakrī. Morocco: Wizārat 'Umūm al-Awqāf wal-Shu'ūn al-Islāmiyya, 1967-1968.

Ibn 'Abd al-Salām. *Al-Fatāwā al-Mawṣiliyya*. Ed. Iyād Khālid al-Ṭabbā'. Beirut and Damascus: Dār al-Fikr, 1999.

Ibn Abī 'Āṣim. *Al-Sunna*. Ed. Muḥammad Nāṣir al-Albānī. Beirut and Damascus: Al-Maktab al-Islāmī, 1993.

Ibn Abī Dāwūd. *Al-Maṣāḥif*. 2 vols. 2nd ed. Ed. Muḥibb al-Dīn 'Abd al-Sabḥān Wā'iz,. Beirut: Dār al-Bashā'ir al-Islāmiyya, 2003.

Ibn Abī Ḥātim. *Ādāb al-Shāfi'ī wa-Manāqibuh*. Ed. 'Abd al-Ghanī 'Abd al-Khāliq. Cairo: *s.n.*, 1953.

Ibn Abī Shayba. *Al-Muṣannaf*. 7 vols. Ed. Kamāl al-Ḥūt. Riyadh: Maktabat al-Rushd, 1989.

Ibn Abī Ya'lā. *Ṭabaqāt al-Ḥanābila*. 2 vols. Ed. Muḥammad Ḥāmid al-Fiqqī. Cairo: Dār Iḥyā' al-Kutub al-'Arabiyya, n.d.

Ibn Abī Zayd al-Qayrawānī. *Al-Jāmi' fīl-Sunan wal-Adab wal-Maghāzī wal-Tārīkh*. Ed. M. Abū al-Ajfān and 'Uthmān Baṭṭīkh. Beirut: Mu'assasat al-Risāla; Tunis: al-Maktabat al-'Atīqa, 1982.

Ibn 'Adī. *Al-Kāmil fī Ḍu'afā' al-Rijāl*. 7 vols. Ed. Yaḥyā Mukhtār Ghazawī. Beirut: Dār al-Fikr, 1988.

Ibn al-'Arabī, Abū Bakr. *'Āriḍat al-Aḥwadhī Sharḥ Sunan al-Tirmidhī*. 13 vols. Beirut, Dār al-Kutub al-'Ilmiyya, n.d.

———. *Al-Maḥṣūl fī Uṣūl al-Fiqh*. Ed. Ḥusayn 'Alī al-Yadarī and Sa'īd 'Abd al-Laṭīf Fawda. Amman and Beirut: Dār al-Bayāriq, 1999.

Ibn 'Arabī, Muḥyī al-Dīn. *Al-Futūḥāt al-Makkiyya*. 4 vols. Eds. 'Uthmān Yaḥyā and Ibrāhīm Madkūr. Cairo: al-Hay'at al-Miṣriyya al-'Āmma līl-Kitāb, 1972-1992 .

Ibn 'Arrāq. *Tanzīh al-Sharī'at al-Marfū'a*. 2 vols. 2nd ed. Ed. 'Abd Allah al-Ghumārī. Beirut: Dār al-Kutub al-'Ilmiyya, 1981.

Ibn 'Asākir, Abū al-Qāsim. *Tārīkh Madīnat Dimashq*. 70 vols. Ed. 'Alī Shayrī. Damascus: Dār al-Fikr, 1995.

Ibn ʿAṭāʾ Allah. *Al-Ḥikam*. 2nd ed. Ed. and trans. Paul Nwiya. In *Ibn 'Aṭā' Allah et la naissance de la confrérie Shādhilite*. Beirut: Dār al-Machreq, 1990.

———. *Laṭā'if al-Minan fī Manāqib Abī al-'Abbās al-Mursī wa-Shaykhihi Abī al-Ḥasan*. 2 vols. Cairo: al-Maktabat al-Maymuniyya, 1321/1903.

Ibn al-Athīr al-Jazarī. *Jāmiʿ al-Uṣūl fī Aḥādīth al-Rasūl*. 12 vols. 2nd ed. Ed. Muḥammad Ḥāmid al-Fiqqī. Beirut: Dār Iḥyā' al-Turāth al-ʿArabī, 1980.

———. *Jāmiʿ al-Uṣūl fī Aḥādīth al-Rasūl*. 11 vols. Ed. ʿAbd al-Qādir al-Arna'ūṭ. Damascus: Ḥalwānī, 1973.

———. *Al-Kāmil fīl-Tārīkh*. 20 vols. Beirut: Dār Ṣādir, 1979.

———. *Al-Kāmil fīl-Tārīkh*. 10 vols. Ed. Abu al-Fidā' 'Abd Allāh al-Qāḍī. Beirut: Dār al-Kutub all-'Ilmiyya, 1995.

———. *Usd al-Ghāba fī Maʿrifat al-Ṣaḥāba*. 7 vols. Ed. Muḥammad ʿĀshūr, Muḥammad al-Bannā, and Aḥmad Fāyid. Beirut: Maktabat al-Shaʿb, 1970.

Ibn Faraḥ. *Gharāmī Ṣaḥīḥ fī Anwāʿ al-Ḥadīth*. With its commentary by Badr al-Dīn al-Ḥasanī. Ed. ʿAbd al-Ḥamīd Muḥammad al-Darwīsh. Damascus: Dār al-ʿIlm al-Ḥadīth, 1998.

Ibn Ḥajar. *Fatḥ al-Bārī Sharḥ Ṣaḥīḥ al-Bukhārī*. 13 vols. Ed. Muḥammad Fu'ād ʿAbd al-Bāqī and Muḥibb al-Dīn al-Khaṭīb. Beirut: Dār al-Maʿrifa, 1959-1960.

———. *Fatḥ al-Bārī Sharḥ Ṣaḥīḥ al-Bukhārī*. 14 vols. Notes by ʿAbd al-ʿAzīz ibn Bāz. Beirut: Dār al-Kutub al-ʿIlmiyya, 1989. Includes al-Bukhārī's *Ṣaḥīḥ*.

———. *Hadī al-Sāri Muqaddimat Fatḥ al-Bārī*. Ed. Muḥammad Fu'ād 'Abd al-Bāqī and Muḥibb al-Dīn al-Khaṭīb. Beirut: Dār al-Ma'rifa, 1959-1960. [1st vol. of *Fatḥ al-Bārī*].

———. *Al-Iṣāba fī Tamyīz al-Ṣaḥāba*. 8 vols in 4. Ed. ʿAlī Muḥammad al-Bijāwī. Beirut: Dār al-Jīl, 1992.

———. *Lisān al-Mīzān*. 7 vols. Hyderabad: Dā'irat al-Maʿārif al-Niẓāmiyya, 1329/1911. Repr. Beirut: Mu'assassat al-Aʿlamī, 1986.

———. *Mukhtaṣar Zawā'id Musnad al-Bazzār*. 2 vols. Ed. Ṣabrī ʿAbd al-Khāliq Abū Dharr. Beirut: Mu'assasat al-Kutub al-Thaqāfiyya, 1993.

———. *Al-Nukat 'alā Kitāb Ibn al-Ṣalāḥ*. 2 vols. Ed. Rabī' ibn Hādī 'Umayr. Riyadh: Dār al-Rāya, 1997.

———. *Al-Qawl al-Musaddad fil-Dhabb 'an Musnad al-Imām Aḥmad*. In the 1st volume of Shākir's edition of the *Musnad*.

———. *Sharḥ Nukhbat al-Fikar*. With 'Alī al-Qārī's commentary, *Sharḥ Sharḥ Nukhbat al-Fikar*. Ed. Muḥammad and Haytham Nizār Tamīm. Beirut: Dār al-Arqam, n.d.

———. *Sharḥ al-Nukhba Nuzhat al-Naẓar fī Tawḍīḥ Nukhbat al-Fikar*. Ed. Nūr al-Dīn 'Itr. Beirut and Damascus: Dār al-Khayr, 1993[2].

———. *Tahdhīb al-Tahdhīb*. 14 vols. Hyderabad: Dā'irat al-Ma'ārif al-Niẓāmiyya, 1327/1909. Repr. Beirut: Dār al-Fikr, 1984.

———. *Ta'jīl al-Manfa'a bi-Zawā'id Rijāl al-A'immat al-Arba'a*. Ed. Ikrām Allah Imdād al-Ḥaqq. Beirut: Dār al-Kitāb al-'Arabī, n.d.

———. *Taqrīb al-Tahdhīb*. Ed. Muḥammad 'Awwāma. Aleppo: Dār al-Rashīd, 1997.

Ibn al-Ḥanbalī. *Qafwu al-Athar fī Safwat 'Ulūm al-Athar*. With al-Zabīdī's *Bulghat al-Arīb fī Muṣṭalaḥ Āthār al-Ḥadīth*. Ed. 'Abd al-Fattāḥ Abū Ghudda. 2nd ed. Beirut: Dār al-Bashā'ir al-Islāmiyya; Aleppo: Maktab al-Maṭbū'āt al-Islāmiyya, 1988.

Ibn Ḥazm. *Al-Fiṣal fil-Milal*. 5 vols. Cairo: Maktabat al-Khānjī, repr. of the 1271 ed.

———. *Al-Iḥkām fī Uṣūl al-Aḥkām*. 8 vols. Cairo: Dār al-Ḥadīth, 1984.

Ibn Ḥibbān. *Ṣaḥīḥ Ibn Ḥibbān bi-Tartīb Ibn Balbān*. 18 vols. Ed. Shu'ayb al-Arna'ūṭ. Beirut: Mu'assasat al-Risāla, 1993.

Ibn Jamā'a. *Hidāyat al-Sālik ilā Ma'rifat al-Manāsik*. 4 vols. Ed. Nūr al-Dīn 'Itr. Beirut: Dār al-Bashā'ir al-Islāmiyya, 1994.

Ibn al-Jawzī. *Al-'Ilal al-Mutanāhiya fil-Aḥādīth al-Wāhiya*. 2 vols. Ed. Khalīl al-Mays. Beirut: Dār al-Kutub al-'Ilmiyya, 1983.

———. *Manāqib al-Imām Aḥmad*. 2nd ed. Ed. Muḥammad Amīn al-Khanjī al-Kutbi. Beirut: Khanjī wa-Ḥamdān, 1349/1930-1931.

———. *Al-Mawḍū'āt*. 3 vols. Ed. 'Abd al-Raḥmān Muḥammad 'Uthmān. Madīna: al-Maktabat al-Salafiyya, 1967. See also al-Dhahabī's *Tartīb al-Mawdū'āt*.

———. *Muthīr al-Gharām al-Sākin ilā Ashraf al-Amākin*. Cairo: Dār al-Ḥadīth, 1995.

———. *Al-Quṣṣāṣ wal-Mudhakkirīn*. Ed. Muḥammad Basyūnī Zaghlūl. Beirut: Dār al-Kutub al-ʿIlmiyya, 1986.

———. *Ṣayd al-Khāṭir*. Ed. "Board of Editors." Beirut: Dār al-Arqam, <1993?>.

———. *Ṣifat al-Ṣafwa*. 4 vols. 2nd ed. Eds. Maḥmūd Fākhūrī and Muḥammad Rawwās Qalʿajī. Beirut: Dār al-Maʿrifa, 1979.

Ibn Kathīr. *Al-Bidāya wal-Nihāya*. 15 vols. Ed. Editing Board of al-Turāth. Beirut: Dār Iḥyā' al-Turāth al-ʿArabī, 1993.

———. *Ibid*. 14 vols. Beirut: Maktabat al-Maʿārif, n.d.

———. *Ikhtiṣār ʿUlūm al-Ḥadīth*. In Aḥmad Shākir, *al-Bāʿith al-Ḥathīth Sharḥ Ikhtiṣār ʿUlūm al-Ḥadīth*. Ed. Badīʿ al-Sayyid Laḥḥām. Damascus. Dār al-Fayḥ.ā', 1994.

———. *Tafsīr al-Qur'ān al-ʿAẓīm*. 4 vols. Beirut: Dār al-Fikr, 1981.

Ibn Mājah. *Sunan*. Ed. Muḥammad Fu'ād ʿAbd al-Bāqī. Beirut: Dār al-Fikr, n.d. See also al-Suyūṭī *et al.*, *Sharḥ Sunan Ibn Mājah*.

Ibn al-Mubārak. *Al-Zuhd*. Ed. Ḥabīb al-Raḥmān al-Aʿẓamī. Beirut: Dār al-Kutub al-ʿIlmiyya, n.d.

Ibn Mufliḥ, Ibrāhīm. *Al-Mubdiʿ fī Sharḥ al-Muqniʿ*. 10 vols. Beirut: al-Maktab al-Islāmī, 1980

Ibn Mufliḥ, Muḥammad. *Al-Ādāb al-Sharʿiyya wal-Minaḥ al-Marʿiyya*. 3 vols. Ed. Muḥammad Rashīd Riḍā. Cairo. Maṭbaʿt al-Manār, 1929-1931

Ibn al-Mulaqqin. *Al-Muqniʿ fī ʿUlūm al-Ḥadīth*. 2 vols. Ed. ʿAbd Allah al-Judayʿ. Riyad: Dār Fawwāz, 1993.

Ibn al-Qābisī's abridgment of Ibn al-Qāsim's *Muwaṭṭa'*. See Ibn al-Qāsim.

Ibn Qāniʿ. *Muʿjam al-Ṣaḥāba*. 3 vols. Ed. Ṣalāḥ ibn Sālim al-Miṣrātī. Madīna: Maktabat al-Ghurabā' al-Athariyya, 1998.

Ibn al-Qāsim. *Muwaṭṭa'* abridged by Ibn al-Qābisī. Ed. Muḥammad ibn ʿAlawī al-Mālikī. 2nd ed. N.p.: s.n., 2003.

Ibn Qayyim al Jawziyya. *Iʿlām al-Muwaqqiʿīn ʿan Rabb al-ʿAlamīn*. 3 vols. Eds. Yūsuf Aḥmad al-Bakrī, Shākir Tawfīq al-ʿArūrī. Beirut: Dār Ibn Ḥazm, 1997.

———. *Iʿlām al-Muwaqqiʿīn ʿan Rabb al-ʿAlamīn*. 4 vols. Ed. Ṭaha ʿAbd al-Ra'ūf Saʿd. Beirut: Dār al-Jīl, 1973.

———. *Al-Manār al-Munīf fil-Ṣaḥīḥ wal-Ḍaʿīf*. 6th ed. Ed. ʿAbd al-Fattāḥ Abū Ghudda. Beirut: Dār al-Bashā'ir al-Islāmiyya; Aleppo: Maktab al-Maṭbūʿāt al-Islāmiyya, 1994.

———. *Al-Rūḥ*. 3rd ed. Ed. Yūsuf ʿAlī Badyawī. Damascus and Beirut: Dār Ibn Kathīr, 1998.

Ibn Qudāma, Muwaffaq al-Dīn. *Al-Mughnī fī Fiqh al-Imām Aḥmad ibn Ḥanbal al-Shaybānī*. 10 vols. Beirut: Dār al-Fikr, 1985; Dār al-Kitāb al-ʿArabī, 1994.

———. *Rawḍat al-Nāẓir wa-Jannat al-Munāẓir*. With its commentary by ʿAbd al-Qādir Badrān, *Nuzhat al-Khāṭir*. 2 vols. Cairo: Maktabat al-Kulliyyāt al-Azhariyya, 1991.

Ibn Qutayba. *Ta'wīl Mukhtalif al-Ḥadīth*. Ed. Muḥammad Zuhrī al-Najjār. Beirut: Dār al-Jil, 1972.

———. *Ta'wīl Mukhtalif al-Ḥadīth*. Ed. Muḥammad ʿAbd al-Raḥīm. Beirut: Dār al-Fikr, 1995.

Ibn Rajab. *Dhayl Ṭabaqāt al-Ḥanābila*. 2 vols. Ed. Muḥammad Ḥāmid al-Fiqqī. Cairo: Dār Iḥyā' al-Kutub al-ʿArabiyya, n.d.

———. *Sharḥ ʿIlal al-Tirmidhī*. 2 vols. Ed. Nūr al-Dīn ʿItr. Damascus: Dār al-Mallāḥ, 1978.

Ibn Saʿd. *Al-Ṭabaqāt al-Kubrā*. 8 vols. Beirut: Dār Sadir, n.d.

Ibn al-Ṣalāḥ. *ʿUlūm al-Ḥadīth*. Ed. Nūr al-Dīn ʿItr. 3rd ed. Damascus: Dār al-Fikr, 1984.

Ibn al-Subkī. *Ṭabaqāt al-Shāfiʿiyya al-Kubrā*. 10 vols. Ed. Maḥmūd al-Ṭannāhī and ʿAbd al-Fattāḥ al-Ḥilw. 2nd. ed. Jiza: Dār Hijr, 1992.

Ibn Taymiyya, ʿAbd al-Salām, ʿAbd al-Ḥalīm, and Aḥmad. *Miswaddat Āl Taymiyya*. Ed. Muḥammad Muḥyī al-Dīn ʿAbd al-Ḥamīd. Cairo: al-Madanī, n.d.

Ibn Taymiyya, Aḥmad. *Majmūʿ al-Fatāwā*. 36 vols. Cairo, 1984.

Al-ʿIrāqī, Zayn al-Dīn. *Al-Bāʿith ʿalā al-Khalāṣ min Ḥawādith al-Quṣṣāṣ*. Ed. Muḥammad Luṭfī al-Ṣabbāgh. Damascus: Dār al-Warrāq, 2001.

———. *Fatḥ al-Mughīth bi-Sharḥ Alfiyyat al-Ḥadīth*. Ed. Maḥmūd Rabīʿ. Beirut: Dār al-Fikr, 1995.

———. *Al-Taqyīd wal-Īḍāḥ limā Uṭliqa wa-Ughliqa min Muqaddimat Ibn al-Ṣalāḥ*. 5th ed. Beirut: Mu'assasat al-Kutub al-Thaqāfiyya, 1997.

———. *Ṭarḥ al-Tathrīb fī Sharḥ al-Taqrīb*. 8 vols. in 4. Ed. Maḥmūd Ḥasan Rabīʿ. Beirut: Dār Iḥyāʾ al-Turāth al-ʿArabī, 1992. Repr. of the Cairo edition.

Islambūlī, Sāmer. *Al-Āḥād, al-Naskh, al-Ijmāʿ*. Damascus: al-Ḥikma, 1995.

ʿItr, Nūr al-Dīn. *Hadī al-Nabī ﷺ fīl-Ṣalawāt al-Khāṣṣa*. 3rd ed. Damascus, Dār al-Fikr, 2001

———. *Al-Imām al-Tirmidhī wal-Muwāzana bayna Jāmiʿihi wa-bayn al-Ṣaḥīḥayn*. Beirut: Mu'assasat al-Risāla, 1988.

———. *Inaugural lecture to the Preparatory Class of Abū al-Nūr Institute*, Damascus. October 1997. Unpublished.

———. *Manhaj al-Naqd fī ʿUlūm al-Ḥadīth*. 3rd ed. Beirut: Dār al-Fikr, 1981, repr.1996.

———. *Muʿjam al-Muṣṭalahāt al-Ḥadīthiyya = Lexique des Termes Techniques de la Science du Hadith*. Ed. & Trans. ʿAbd al-Laṭīf al-Shīrāzī and Dāwūd Gril. Damascus: Maṭbūʿāt Majmaʿ al-Lughat al-ʿArabiyya, 1976.

ʿIyāḍ ibn Mūsā. *Al-Ilmāʿ ilā Maʿrifati Uṣūl al-Riwāyati wa-Taqyīd al-Samāʿ*. Ed. Sayyid Aḥmad Saqr. Cairo and Tunis: Dār al-Turāth and al-Maktabat al-ʿAtīqa, 1970.

———. *Al-Shifā bi-Taʿrīf Ḥuqūq al-Muṣṭafā*. Ed. ʿAbduh ʿAlī Kawshak. Damascus and Beirut: Maktabat al-Ghazālī and Dār al-Fayḥā', 2000.

———. *Tartīb al-Madārik li-Maʿrifati Aʿlāmi Madhhabi Mālik*. 8 vols. Ed. Saʿīd Aḥmad Aʿrab. Al-Muḥammadiyya (Morocco): Ministry of Awqāf and Religious Affairs of the Kingdom of Maghreb, 1981-1983.

Al-Jawraqānī. *Al-Abāṭīl wal-Manākīr wal-Ṣiḥāḥ wal-Mashāhīr*. 2 vols. Ed. ʿAbd al-Raḥmān al-Faryawāʾī. Naris, India: al-Jāmiʿa al-Salafiyya, 1983.

Al-Jazā'irī, Ṭāhir. *Tawjīh al-Naẓar ilā Uṣūl al-Athar*. 2 vols. Ed. 'Abd al-Fattāḥ Abū Ghudda. Aleppo: Maktab al-Maṭbūʿāt al-Islāmiyya, 1995.

Al-Kattānī, Muḥammad ibn Jaʿfar. *Naẓm al-Mutanāthir fīl-Ḥadīth al-Mutawātir*. Ed. Sharaf Ḥijāzī. Cairo: Dār al-Kutub al-Salafiyya, n.d. and Beirut: Dār al-Kutub al-ʿIlmiyya, 1980.

Al-Kawtharī, Muḥammad Zāhid. *Maqālāt*. Riyad and Beirut: Dār al-Aḥnāf, 1993.

———. *Maqālāt*. 2nd ed. Cairo: al-Maktabat al-Azhariyya līl-Turāth, 1994.

Al-Khalīlī. *Al-Irshād fī Maʿrifati ʿUlamāʾ al-Ḥadīth*. 3 vols. Ed. Muḥammad Saʿīd ʿUmar Idrīs. Riyad: Maktabat al-Rushd, 1989.

Al-Khaṭīb, Muḥammad ʿAjāj. *Al-Sunnatu Qabl al-Tadwīn*. 5th ed. Reprint Beirut: Dār al-Fikr, 1993.

Al-Khaṭīb al-Baghdādī. *Al-Faqīh wal-Mutafaqqih*. 2 vols. Ed. ʿĀdil Y. al-ʿAzāzī. Dammām: Dār Ibn al-Jawzī, 1997.

———. *Al-Faqīh wal-Mutafaqqih*. Ed. Ismāʿīl al-Anṣārī. Beirut: Dār al-Kutub al-ʿIlmiyya, 1980.

———. *Iqtiḍāʾ al-ʿIlm al-ʿAmal*. Ed. Muḥammad Nāṣir al-Albānī. Beirut: al-Maktab al-Islāmī, 1984.

———. *Al-Jāmiʿ li-Akhlāq al-Rāwī wa-Adab al-Sāmiʿ*. 2 vols. Ed. Muḥammad ʿAjāj al-Khaṭīb. Beirut: Muʾassasat al-Risāla, 1991.

———. *Al-Jāmiʿ li-Akhlāq al-Rāwī wa-Adab al-Sāmiʿ*. 2 vols. Ed. Maḥmūd al-Ṭaḥḥān. Riyad: Maktabat al-Maʿārif, 1983.

———. *Al-Kifāya fī ʿIlm al-Riwāya*. 2nd ed. Ed. Aḥmad ʿUmar Hāshim. Beirut: Dār al-Kitāb al-ʿArabī, 1986.

———. *Al-Kifāya fī ʿIlm al-Riwāya*. Eds. Abū ʿAbd Allah al-Ṣawraqī and Ibrāhīm Ḥamdī al-Madanī. Madīna: al-Maktabat al-ʿIlmiyya, n.d.

———. *Naṣīḥat Ahl al-Ḥadīth*. Ed. ʿAbd al-Karīm Aḥmad al-Wiraykat. Al-Zarqāʾ: Maktabat al-Manār, 1988.

———. *Sharaf Aṣḥab al-Ḥadīth*. Ed. Muḥammad Saʿīd Hatiboglu. Ankara: University Publications, 1972. Repr. Dār Iḥyāʾ al-Sunna al-Nabawiyya.

———. *Tārīkh Baghdād*. 14 vols. Madīna: al-Maktabat al-Salafiyya, n.d. See also al-Aḥdab, *Zawāʾid Tārīkh Baghdād*.

Al-Lacknawī. *Al-Ajwibat al-Fāḍila lil-Asʾilat al-ʿAshrat al-Kāmila*. Ed. ʿAbd al-Fattāḥ Abū Ghudda. Followed by *al-Taʿlīqāt al-Ḥāfila ʿalā al-Ajwibat al-ʿAshra* by Abū Ghudda. 3rd ed. Aleppo: Maktab al-Maṭbūʿāt al-Islāmiyya, 1994.

———. *Al-Āthār al-Marfūʿa fil-Akhbār al-Mawḍūʿa*. Ed. Muḥammad ibn Basyūnī Zaghlūl. Beirut: Dār al-Kutub al-ʿIlmiyya, 1984.

———. *Al-Rafʿ wal-Takmīl fil-Jarḥ wal-Taʿdīl*. Ed. ʿAbd al-Fattāḥ Abū Ghudda. 3rd ed. Beirut: Dār al-Bashāʾir al-Islāmiyya, 1987.

———. *Ẓafar al-Amānī Sharḥ Mukhtaṣar al-Jurjānī fī Muṣṭalaḥ al-Ḥadīth*. Ed. ʿAbd al-Fattāḥ Abū Ghudda. Aleppo and Beirut: Maktab al-Maṭbūʿāt al-Islāmiyya, 3rd ed. 1995.

Al-Lahjī, ʿAbd Allah ibn Saʿīd. *Muntahā al-Sūl ʿalā Wasāʾil al-Wuṣūl ilā Shamāʾil al-Rasūl* ﷺ. 4 vols. N.p. Dār al-Ḥāwī, 1998.

Laḥmar, Ḥāmid. *Al-Imām Mālik Mufassiran*. Beirut: Dār al-Fikr, 1995.

Al-Lālikāʾī. *Karāmāt al-Awliyāʾ*. Ed. Aḥmad Saʿd al-Ḥammān. Riyadh: Dār Ṭayba, 1992.

Mālik ibn Anas. *Al-Muwaṭṭaʾ*. 2 vols. Ed. Muḥammad Fuʾād ʿAbd al-Bāqī. Beirut: Dār al-Kutub al-ʿIlmiyya, n.d.

Al-Mālikī, ʿAlawī ibn ʿAbbās. *Al-Manhal al-Laṭīf fī Aḥkām al-Ḥadīth al-Laṭīf*. In *Majmūʿ Fatāwā wa-Rasāʾil*. Ed. Muḥammad ibn ʿAlawī al-Mālikī. N.p.: s.n., 1413.

Al-Malīnī. *Al-Arbaʿīn fī Shuyūkh al-Ṣūfiyya*. Ed. ʿĀmir Ḥasan Ṣabrī. Beirut: Dār al-Bashāʾir al-Islāmiyya, 1997.

Mamdūḥ, Maḥmūd Saʿīd. *Bishārat al-Muʾmin bi-Taṣḥīḥ Ḥadīth Ittaqū Firāsat al-Muʾmin*. N. p.: 1995.

———. *Rafʿ al-Mināra li-Takhrīj Aḥādīth al-Tawassul wal-Ziyāra*. 3rd ed. Cairo: Dār al-Imām al-Tirmidhī, 1997.

Al-Maqdisī. *Al-Aḥādīth al-Mukhtāra*. 10 vols. Ed. ʿAbd al-Mālik ibn ʿAbd Allah ibn Duhaysh. Makka: Maktabat al-Nahḍat, 1990.

Al-Mirṣafī, Saʿd. *Ḥadīth Badʾ al-Waḥī fil-Mīzān*. Beirut: Muʾassasat al-Rayyān, 1997.

Al-Mizzī. *Tahdhīb al-Kamāl*. 35 vols. Ed. Bashshār ʿAwwād Maʿrūf. Beirut: Muʾassasat al-Risāla, 1980.

Al-Munāwī. *Fayḍ al-Qadīr Sharḥ al-Jāmiʿ al-Ṣaghīr*. 6 vols. Cairo: al-Maktabat al-Tijāriyya, 1937. Repr. Beirut: Dār al Maʿrifa, 1972.

Muslim. *Ṣaḥīḥ*. 5 vols. Ed. Muḥammad Fuʾād ʿAbd al-Bāqī. Beirut: Dār Iḥyāʾ al-Turāth al-ʿArabī, 1954.

Al-Nasāʾī. *Khaṣāʾiṣ ʿAlī*. Ed. Aḥmad Mīrīn al-Balūshī. Kuwait: Maktabat al-Maʿlā, 1406.

———. *Sunan*. See al-Suyūṭī, *Sharḥ Sunan al-Nasāʾī*.

———. *Al-Sunan al-Kubrā*. 6 vols. Eds. ʿAbd al-Ghaffār al-Bandarī and Sayyid Kusrawī Ḥasan. Beirut: Dār al-Kutub al-ʿIlmiyya, 1991.

Al-Nawawī. *Al-Adhkār al-Muntakhaba min Kalām Sayyid al-Abrār*. Cairo: al-Ḥalabī 1348/1929.

———. *Irshād Ṭullāb al-Ḥaqāʾiq ilā Maʿrifati Sunan Khayri al-Khalāʾiq* ﷺ. 3rd ed. Ed. Nūr al-Dīn ʿItr. Beirut: Dār al-Bashāʾir al-Islāmiyya, 1992.

———. *Al-Majmūʿ Sharḥ al-Muhadhdhab*. 18 vols. Ed. Zakariyyā ʿAlī Yūsuf. Cairo: Maṭbaʿat al-ʿĀṣima, 1963-1970.

———. *Matn al-Arbaʿīn al-Nawawiyya*. Eds. ʿAbd al-Qādir and Maḥmūd al-Arnaʾūṭ. Kuwait: Dār al-ʿUrūba, 1989.

———. *Sharḥ Ṣaḥīḥ Muslim*. 18 vols. Ed. Khalīl al-Mays. Beirut: Dār al-Kutub al-ʿIlmiyya, n.d. Includes Muslim's *Ṣaḥīḥ*.

———. *Sharḥ Ṣaḥīḥ Muslim*. 18 vols. Beirut: Dār Iḥyāʾ al-Turāth al-ʿArabī, 1972.

———. *Tahdhīb al-Asmāʾ wal-Lughāt*. 3 vols. Cairo: Idārat al-Ṭibāʿat al-Munīriyya, [1927?].

———. *Al-Taqrīb wal-Taysīr li-Maʿrifat Sunan al-Bashīr al-Nadhīr*. Beirut: Dār al-Kutub al-ʿIlmiyya, 1987. Also in al-Suyūṭī's *Tadrīb*.

Al-Qārī. *Al-Asrār al-Marfūʿa fīl-Akhbār al-Mawḍūʿa*. (*Al-Mawḍūʿāt al-Kubrā*). 2nd ed. Ed. Muḥammad ibn Luṭfi al-Ṣabbāgh. Beirut and Damascus: al-Maktab al-Islāmī, 1986.

———. *Adillat Muʿtaqad Abī Ḥanīfat al-Imām al-Aʿẓam fī Abaway al-Rasūl Ṣalla Allahu ʿalyahi wa-Sallam*. Ed. Mashhūr ibn Ḥasan ibn Salmān. Madīna: Maktabat al-Ghurabāʾ al-Athariyya, 1993.

———. *Al-Maṣnūʿ fī Maʿrifat al-Ḥadīth al-Mawḍūʿ*. 5th ed. Ed. ʿAbd al-Fattāḥ Abū Ghudda. Beirut: Dār al-Bashāʾir al-Islāmiyya, 1994.

———. *Mirqāt al-Mafātīḥ Sharḥ Mishkāt al-Maṣābīḥ*. With Ibn Ḥajar's *Ajwiba ʿalā Risālat al-Qazwīnī Ḥawla Baʿḍ Aḥādīth al-Maṣābīḥ*. 11 vols. Ed. Ṣidqī Muḥammad al-ʿAṭṭār. Damascus: Dār al-Fikr, 1994.

———. *Sharḥ Musnad Abī Ḥanīfa*. Beirut: Dār al-Kutub al-ʿIlmiyya, 1985.

———. *Sharḥ al-Shifāʾ*. 2 vols. Bulāq: 1275/1858. Repr. Maṭbaʿat al-Ḥajj al-Busnawī, 1285/ 1868. Repr. Āsitāna [Istanbul]: 1290/1873. Repr. Āsitāna: al-Maṭbaʿat al-ʿUthmāniyya, 1316/1898. Repr. Cairo: 1312/1894. Repr. Beirut: Dār al-Kutub al-ʿIlmiyya, n.d.

———. *Sharḥ Sharḥ Nukhbat al-Fikar*. A supercommentary on Ibn Ḥajar's *Sharḥ Nukhbat al-Fikar*. Ed. Muḥammad and Haytham Nizār Tamīm. Beirut: Dār al-Arqam, n.d.

Al-Qāsimī. *Qawāʿid al-Taḥdīth*. Beirut: Dār al-Kutub al-ʿIlmiyya and Dār Iḥyāʾ al-Sunna al-Nabawiyya, n.d.

Al-Quḍāʿī. *Musnad al-Shihāb*. 2 vols. Ed. Ḥamdī ibn ʿAbd al-Majīd al-Salafī. Beirut: Muʾassasat al-Risāla, 1986.

Al-Qurṭubī. [*Tafsīr.*] *Al-Jāmi' li Aḥkām al-Qur'ān.* 2nd ed. 20 vols. Ed. Aḥmad 'Abd al-'Alīm al-Bardūnī. Cairo: Dār al-Sha'b and Beirut: Dār Iḥyā' al-Turāth al-'Arabī, 1952-1953. Reprint.

Al-Rāmahurmuzī. *Al-Muḥaddith al-Fāṣil.* Ed. Muḥammad al-Khaṭīb. Beirut: Dār al-Fikr, 1984.

Al-Rāzī, Muḥammad ibn Abī Bakr. *Mukhtār al-Ṣiḥāḥ.* Ed. Maḥmūd Khāṭir. Beirut: Maktabat Lubnan, 1995.

Al-Rāzī, Tammām. *Al-Fawā'id.* 2 vols. Ed. Ḥamdī 'Abd al-Majīd al-Salafī. Riyadh: Maktabat al-Rushd, 1992.

Al-Sakhāwī, Muḥammad ibn 'Abd al-Raḥmān. *Fatḥ al-Mughīth bi-Sharḥ Alfiyyat al-Ḥadīth lil-'Irāqī.* 5 vols. Ed. 'Alī Ḥusayn 'Alī. Cairo: Maktabat al-Sunna, 1995.

———. *Al-Jawāhir wal-Durar fī Manāqib Shaykh al-Islām Ibn Ḥajar.* Ed. Ḥāmid 'Abd al-Majīd and Ṭaha al-Zaynī. Cairo: Lajnat Iḥyā' al-Turāth al-Islāmī, 1986.

———. *Al-Maqāṣid al-Ḥasana.* Ed. Muḥammad 'Uthmān al-Khisht. Beirut: Dār al-Kitāb al-'Arabī, 1985.

———. *Al-Maqāṣid al-Ḥasana.* Ed. 'Abd Allāh Muḥammad al-Ṣiddīq [al-Ghumārī]. Beirut: Dār al-Kutub al-'Ilmiyya, 1987.

———. *Al-Qawl al-Badī' fīl-Ṣalāt 'alā al-Ḥabīb al-Shafī'.* Ed. Muḥammad 'Awwāma. Beirut: Mu'assasat al-Rayyān, 2002. Unedited: Beirut: Dār al-Kutub al-'Ilmiyya, 1987.

Al-Ṣan'ānī, Muḥammad ibn Ismā'īl. *Tawḍīḥ al-Afkār li-Ma'ānī Tanqīḥ al-Anẓār.* 2 vols. Ed. Muḥammad Muḥyī al-Dīn 'Abd al-Ḥamīd. Madīna: al-Maktabat al-Salafiyya, n.d.

Al-Shāfi'ī. [*Musnad.*] *Tartīb Musnad al-Imām al-A'ẓam wal-Mujtahid al-Muqaddam Abī 'Abd Allah Muḥammad ibn Idrīs al-Shāfi'ī.* 2 vols. Eds. Yūsuf 'Alī al-Zawlawī al-Ḥasanī and 'Izzat 'Aṭṭār al-Ḥusaynī. Cairo: n.p., 1951. Repr. Beirut: Dār al-Kutub al-'Ilmiyya, n.d.

———. *Al-Risāla.* Ed. Aḥmad Muḥammad Shākir. Cairo: n.p., 1939.

Al-Shawkānī. *Al-Fuwā'id al-Majmū'a fīl-Aḥādīth al-Mawḍū'a.* Ed. Muḥammad 'Abd al-Raḥmān 'Awad. Beirut: Dār al-Kitāb al-'Arabī, 1986.

———. *Al-Fawā'id al-Majmū'a fīl-Aḥādīth al-Mawḍū'a.* 3rd ed. Ed. 'Abd al-Raḥmān al-Mu'allimī al-Yamānī. Beirut: al-Maktab al-Islāmī, 1987.

―――. *Irshād al-Fuḥūl ilā Taḥqīq al-Ḥaqqi min ʿIlmi al-Uṣūl*. Beirut: Dār al-Maʿrifa, 1979 and Beirut: Dār al-Fikr, 1992.

Sirāj al-Dīn, ʿAbd Allah. *Sharḥ al-Bayqūniyya*. Aleppo: Maktabat Dār al-Falāḥ, n.d.

Al-Subkī, Tāj al-Dīn. See Ibn al-Subkī.

Al-Subkī, Taqī al-Dīn. *Al-Sayf al-Ṣaqīl fīl-Radd ʿalā Ibn Zafīl*. Ed. al-Kawtharī. Cairo: Maṭbaʿat al-Saʿāda, 1937.

―――. *Shifāʾ al-Siqām bi-Ziyārati Khayri al-Anām*. Beirut: Lajnat al-Turāth al-ʿArabī, 1971.

Al-Sulamī. *Ṭabaqāt al-Ṣūfiyya*. Ed. Nūr al-Dīn Shurayba. Aleppo: Dār al-Kitāb al-Nafīs, 1986. Reprint of the 1953 edition.

Al-Suyūṭī, Jalāl al-Dīn. *Asrār Tartīb al-Qurʾān*. Ed. ʿAbd al-Qādir Aḥmad ʿAṭā. Cairo: Dār al-Iʿtiṣām, n.d.

―――. *Al-Dībāj ʿalā Ṣaḥīḥ Muslim ibn al-Ḥajjāj*. 6 vols. Ed. Abū Isḥāq al-Juwaynī al-Atharī. Al-Khubar: Dār Ibn ʿAffān, 1996.

―――. *Al-Durar al-Muntathira fīl-Aḥādīth al-Mushtahara*. Ed. Muḥammad ʿAbd al-Raḥīm. Beirut: Dār al-Fikr, 1995.

―――. *Al-Durr al-Manthūr fīl-Tafsīr al-Maʾthūr*. 8 vols. Beirut: Dār al-Fikr, 1994.

―――. *Al-Ḥāwī lil-Fatāwī*. 2 vols. 3rd ed. Ed. Muḥammad Muḥyī al-Dīn ʿAbd al-Ḥamīd. Cairo: al-Maktabat al-Tijāriyya al-Kubrā, 1959.

―――. *Al-Itqān fī ʿUlūm al-Qurʾān*. 2 vols. Ed. Muṣṭafā Dīb al-Bugha. Damascus: Dār Ibn Kathīr, 1993.

―――. *Al-Khaṣāʾiṣ al-Kubrā aw Kifāyat al-Ṭālib al-Labīb fī Khaṣāʾiṣ al-Ḥabīb* ﷺ. 2 vols. Hyderabad al-Dakn: Dāʾirat al-Maʿārif al-Niẓāmiyya, 1901-1903. Beirut: Dār al-Kutub al-ʿIlmiyya, 1985.

―――. *Al-Laʾāliʾ al-Maṣnūʿa fīl-Aḥādīth al-Mawḍūʿa*. 2 vols. Beirut: Dār al-Maʿrifa, 1983.

―――. *Sharḥ Sunan al-Nasāʾī*. 9 vols. Ed. ʿAbd al-Fattāḥ Abū Ghudda. Aleppo & Beirut: Maktab al-Maṭbūʿāt al-Islāmiyya, 1986. Includes al-Nasāʾīs' *Sunan*.

―――. *Al-Taʿaqqubāt ʿalā al-Mawḍūʿāt*. Ed. Sayyid Muḥammad Maqshawqaʿlī. India: al-Maṭbaʿ al-ʿAlawī, 1303/1886.

―――. *Tadrīb al-Rāwī fī Sharḥ Taqrīb al-Nawāwī*. 2 vols. Ed. Abū Qutayba al-Firyābī. 3rd ed. Damascus and Beirut: Dār al-Kalim al-Ṭayyib, 1996.

———. *Tadrīb al-Rāwī fī Sharḥ Taqrīb al-Nawāwī*. 2 vols. Ed. ʿAbd al-Wahhāb ʿAbd al-Laṭīf. Riyad: Maktabat al-Riyaḍ al-Ḥadītha, n.d.

———. *Taḥdhīr al-Khawāṣṣ min Akādhīb al-Quṣṣāṣ*. 2nd ed. Ed. Muḥammad Luṭfī al-Ṣabbāgh, Beirut: al-Maktab al-Islāmī, 1984.

———. *Tārīkh al-Khulafā'*. Ed. Raḥāb Khiḍr ʿAkkāwī. Beirut: Mu'assasat ʿIzz al-Dīn, 1992.

———, ʿAbd al-Ghanī al-Dihlawī, and Fakhr al-Ḥasan al-Gangohi. *Sharḥ Sunan Ibn Mājah*. Karachi: Qadimi Kutub Khana, n.d. Includes Ibn Mājah's *Sunan*.

Al-Ṭabarānī. *Al-Muʿjam al-Awsaṭ*. 10 vols. Eds. Ṭāriq ibn ʿAwaḍ Allah and ʿAbd al-Muḥsin ibn Ibrāhīm al-Ḥusaynī. Cairo: Dār al-Ḥaramayn, 1995.

———. *Al-Muʿjam al-Kabīr*. 20 vols. Ed. Ḥamdī ibn ʿAbd al-Majīd al-Salafī. Mosul: Maktabat al-ʿUlūm wal-Ḥikam, 1983.

———. *Al-Muʿjam al-Saghīr*. 2 vols. Ed. Muḥammad Shakūr Maḥmūd. Beirut and Amman: Al-Maktab al-Islāmī, Dār ʿAmmār, 1985.

———. *Musnad al-Shāmiyyīn*. 2 vols. Ed. Ḥamdī ibn ʿAbd al-Majīd al-Salafī. Beirut: Mu'assasat al-Risāla, 1984.

Al-Ṭabarī, Muḥammad ibn Jarīr. *Jāmiʿ al-Bayān fī Tafsīr al-Qur'ān*. 30 vols. Beirut: Dār al-Maʿārif, 1980; Dār al-Fikr, 1985.

Al-Ṭabarī, Muḥibb al-Dīn. *Al-Riyāḍ al-Naḍira*. 2 vols. Ed. ʿĪsā al-Ḥimyarī. Beirut: Dār al-Gharb al-Islāmī, 1996.

Al-Taftazānī, Abū al-Wafā. *Madkhal ilā al-Taṣawwuf al-Islāmī*. Cairo: Dār al-Thaqāfa lil-Ṭibāʿati wal-Nashr, 1974.

Al-Tahānawī. *Qawāʿid fī ʿUlūm al-Ḥadīth*. Ed. ʿAbd al-Fattāḥ Abū Ghudda. Karachi: Idārat al-Qur'ān wal-ʿUlūm al-Islamiyya, 1995.

Al-Ṭaḥāwī. *Sharḥ Maʿānī al-Āthār*. 4 vols. Ed. Muḥammad Zuhrī al-Najjār. Beirut: Dār al-Kutub al-ʿIlmiyya, 1979.

———. *Sharḥ Mushkil al-Āthār*. 16 vols. Ed. Shuʿayb al-Arna'ūṭ. Beirut: Mu'assasat al-Risāla, 1994.

Al-Ṭayālisī, Abū Dāwūd. *Musnad*. Beirut: Dār al-Kitāb al-Lubnānī; Dār al-Maʿrifa; Dār al-Tawfīq, n.d. All three are offset reprints of the 1903 edition of Dā'irat al-Maʿārif al-ʿUthmāniyya, Hyderabad.

Al-Tirmidhī. *Al-ʿIlal*. See Ibn Rajab's *Sharḥ ʿIlal al-Tirmidhī*.

———. *Sunan*. 5 vols. Ed. Aḥmad Shākir and Muḥammad Fu'ād ʿAbd al-Bāqī. Beirut: Dār Iḥyā' al-Turāth al-ʿArabī, n.d.

Al-ʿUqaylī, *al-Ḍuʿafā' min al-Ruwāt*. 4 vols. Ed. ʿAbd al-Muʿṭī Amīn Qalʿajī. Beirut: Dār al-Kutub al-ʿIlmiyya, 1984.

Al-Wāqidī. *Futūḥ al-Shām*. 2 vols. Beirut: al-Maktabat al-Ahliyya, 1966.

———. *Al-Maghāzī*. 3 vols. Ed. Marsden Jones. London: Oxford University Press, 1966. Repr. Beirut: Mu'assasat al-Aʿlamī, n.d.

Al-Zabīdī, *Itḥāf al-Sādat al-Muttaqīn bi-Sharḥ Asrār Iḥyā' ʿUlūm al-Dīn*. With the text of the *Iḥyā'* in the margins, ʿAbd al-Qādir ibn ʿAbd Allah al-ʿAydarūs Bā ʿAlawī's *Taʿrif al-Aḥyā' bi Faḍā'il al-Iḥyā'*, and al-Ghazzālī's *al-Imlā 'an Ishkālāt al-Iḥyā*. 10 vols. Cairo: al-Maṭbaʿat al-Maymuniyya, 1311/1893.

Zakariyyā al-Anṣārī. *Al-Ḥudūd al-Anīqa wal-Taʿrīfāt al-Daqīqa*. Beirut: Dār al-Fikr al-Muʿāṣir, 1991.

Al-Zarkashī. *Al-Tadhkira fil-Aḥādīth al-Mushtahara*. Ed. Muṣṭafā ʿAbd al-Qādir ʿAṭā. Beirut: Dār al-Kutub al-ʿIlmiyya, 1986.

Al-Zarqānī. *Sharḥ al-Mawāhib al-Lāduniyya lil-Qasṭallānī*. 8 vols. Eds. Ibrāhīm ʿAbd al-Ghaffār al-Dusūqī, Ḥusayn Bayk Ḥisnī, Muḥammad Effendī Ḥisnī, Abū al-ʿAynayn Effendī Aḥmad. Published by the Khedive of Egypt Ismāʿīl ibn Ibrāhīm ibn Muḥammad. Cairo, 1291.

———. *Sharḥ al-Muwaṭṭa'*. 4 vols. Beirut: Dār al-Kutub al-ʿIlmiyya, 1981.

www.ingramcontent.com/pod-product-compliance
Lightning Source LLC
Chambersburg PA
CBHW030518080526
44586CB00011B/243
9781938058783